Optimizing™ the
Windows® Registry

Optimizing™ the Windows® Registry

Kathy Ivens

IDG Books Worldwide, Inc.
An International Data Group Company

Foster City, CA ◆ Chicago, IL ◆ Indianapolis, IN ◆ Southlake, TX

Optimizing™ the Windows® Registry

Published by
IDG Books Worldwide, Inc.
An International Data Group Company
919 E. Hillsdale Blvd., Suite 400
Foster City, CA 94404
www.idgbooks.com (IDG Books Worldwide Web site)

Library of Congress Catalog Card No.: 97-077544

ISBN: 0-7645-3159-X

Printed in the United States of America

10 9 8 7 6 5 4 3 2

1DD/RW/QR/ZY/FC

Distributed in the United States by IDG Books Worldwide, Inc.

Distributed by Macmillan Canada for Canada; by Transworld Publishers Limited in the United Kingdom; by IDG Norge Books for Norway; by IDG Sweden Books for Sweden; by Woodslane Pty. Ltd. for Australia; by Woodslane Enterprises Ltd. for New Zealand; by Longman Singapore Publishers Ltd. for Singapore, Malaysia, Thailand, and Indonesia; by Simron Pty. Ltd. for South Africa; by Toppan Company Ltd. for Japan; by Distribuidora Cuspide for Argentina; by Livraria Cultura for Brazil; by Ediciencia S.A. for Ecuador; by Addison-Wesley Publishing Company for Korea; by Ediciones ZETA S.C.R. Ltda. for Peru; by WS Computer Publishing Corporation, Inc., for the Philippines; by Unalis Corporation for Taiwan; by Contemporanea de Ediciones for Venezuela; by Computer Book & Magazine Store for Puerto Rico; by Express Computer Distributors for the Caribbean and West Indies. Authorized Sales Agent: Anthony Rudkin Associates for the Middle East and North Africa.

For general information on IDG Books Worldwide's books in the U.S., please call our Consumer Customer Service department at 800-762-2974. For reseller information, including discounts and premium sales, please call our Reseller Customer Service department at 800-434-3422.

For information on where to purchase IDG Books Worldwide's books outside the U.S., please contact our International Sales department at 415-655-3200 or fax 415-655-3295.

For information on foreign language translations, please contact our Foreign & Subsidiary Rights department at 415-655-3021 or fax 415-655-3281.

For sales inquiries and special prices for bulk quantities, please contact our Sales department at 415-655-3200 or write to the address above.

For information on using IDG Books Worldwide's books in the classroom or for ordering examination copies, please contact our Educational Sales department at 800-434-2086 or fax 817-251-8174.

For press review copies, author interviews, or other publicity information, please contact our Public Relations department at 415-655-3000 or fax 415-655-3299.

For authorization to photocopy items for corporate, personal, or educational use, please contact Copyright Clearance Center, 222 Rosewood Drive, Danvers, MA 01923, or fax 508-750-4470.

The IDG Books Worldwide logo is a trademark under exclusive license to IDG Books Worldwide, Inc., from International Data Group, Inc.

ABOUT IDG BOOKS WORLDWIDE

Welcome to the world of IDG Books Worldwide.

IDG Books Worldwide, Inc., is a subsidiary of International Data Group, the world's largest publisher of computer-related information and the leading global provider of information services on information technology. IDG was founded more than 25 years ago and now employs more than 8,500 people worldwide. IDG publishes more than 275 computer publications in over 75 countries (see listing below). More than 60 million people read one or more IDG publications each month.

Launched in 1990, IDG Books Worldwide is today the #1 publisher of best-selling computer books in the United States. We are proud to have received eight awards from the Computer Press Association in recognition of editorial excellence and three from *Computer Currents'* First Annual Readers' Choice Awards. Our best-selling *...For Dummies®* series has more than 30 million copies in print with translations in 30 languages. IDG Books Worldwide, through a joint venture with IDG's Hi-Tech Beijing, became the first U.S. publisher to publish a computer book in the People's Republic of China. In record time, IDG Books Worldwide has become the first choice for millions of readers around the world who want to learn how to better manage their businesses.

Our mission is simple: Every one of our books is designed to bring extra value and skill-building instructions to the reader. Our books are written by experts who understand and care about our readers. The knowledge base of our editorial staff comes from years of experience in publishing, education, and journalism — experience we use to produce books for the '90s. In short, we care about books, so we attract the best people. We devote special attention to details such as audience, interior design, use of icons, and illustrations. And because we use an efficient process of authoring, editing, and desktop publishing our books electronically, we can spend more time ensuring superior content and spend less time on the technicalities of making books.

You can count on our commitment to deliver high-quality books at competitive prices on topics you want to read about. At IDG Books Worldwide, we continue in the IDG tradition of delivering quality for more than 25 years. You'll find no better book on a subject than one from IDG Books Worldwide.

John Kilcullen
CEO
IDG Books Worldwide, Inc.

Steven Berkowitz
President and Publisher
IDG Books Worldwide, Inc.

*Eighth Annual
Computer Press
Awards ≥1992*

*Ninth Annual
Computer Press
Awards ≥1993*

*Tenth Annual
Computer Press
Awards ≥1994*

*Eleventh Annual
Computer Press
Awards ≥1995*

Credits

ACQUISITIONS EDITOR
Anne Hamilton

DEVELOPMENT EDITOR
Susannah Pfalzer

TECHNICAL EDITOR
Sally Neuman

COPY EDITOR
Larisa North

PRODUCTION COORDINATOR
Ritchie Durdin

BOOK DESIGNERS
Jim Donohue
Kurt Krames

GRAPHICS AND PRODUCTION
SPECIALISTS
Doris Figgemeier
E. A. Pauw
Trevor Wilson

QUALITY CONTROL SPECIALISTS
Mick Arellano
Mark Schumann

PROOFREADER
Arielle Carole Mennelle

INDEXER
Liz Cunningham

About the Author

Kathy Ivens has been a computer consultant for over a decade, specializing in the planning and installation of high-end accounting applications on large networks. She has taught diverse computer courses at a variety of institutions and has authored, coauthored, contributed to, and ghost written more than two dozen books on computer subjects.

To David Chernicoff, for years of sharing knowledge, providing opportunities, and for having faith in my skills . . . and for other reasons connected to this book that only he would understand.

Preface

Writing a book about the registry isn't just difficult, it's almost foolhardy. No two registries are the same, and no two users have the same machine environment and work habits. But we all have one thing in common: we believe that the best use of a computer is to get work done. Understanding the registry can help you get your work done better and faster.

Who Should Read This Book

This book is written for system administrators and advanced users. No one else should even think about hacking the registry. This is one of those approaches where the expression "do more harm than good" is a serious warning — take it literally.

What's in This Book

I put this book together in a way that reflects my own experiences with the registry. The chapters are organized by the subject matters that drove me to learn more about the registry. Because there's no logical "do this first, and then do that" format, as there is in writing and learning about applications, that seemed as good a plan as any. That doesn't mean you'll use this book in the order in which I wrote it (your computer problems may be different and your thinking process may also differ), but I think the book has a logic that will make it easy to use when you need to learn about a specific area of the registry.

Throughout the book, I've provided some registry dumps. This isn't just so you can look at how one of my computers is configured — the registry dumps are there so you have a reference for a particular section of the registry. I found that the more I looked at registry dumps, the more I understood about the way the registry database is arranged. After a while, I even saw the logic. Then I reached a point where, if I wanted to check the configuration to explain a slowdown, bottleneck, or error message, I knew exactly where to head.

As a result, I've covered the registry items I found helpful. You'll see information about desktop settings, hardware settings, software settings, and a great deal about controlling users. The last item is important to many administrators (it certainly is to me): you'll find discussions on how to limit user access to other computers, system settings, and so on, throughout many of the chapters.

I've made some assumptions while putting this book together. I assumed the presence of a network, so I mention connected computers and servers frequently (although most of the specific settings I discuss work just fine for stand-alone computers). I also assumed it's okay to use jargon, so you'll see a lot of terminology that experienced users employ. I do explain most of the jargon, however, the first time I use it.

The Windows 98 Registry

While writing this book, I began using Windows 98 (beta) on one of my computers; as I worked with the operating system, I viewed and manipulated the registry in the same way I work with the Windows 95 and Windows NT 4 registries.

The Windows 98 registry is essentially identical to the Windows 95 registry. I have to say "essentially" because a couple of things differ. The Windows 98 registry has two registry keys that don't exist in Windows 95: one for power management functions, the other for multiple monitors. Both of these keys are used mainly for laptop computers (if you've ever used a laptop that is hooked up to a projection unit, you appreciate the ability to configure and use the laptop's screen and the projection screen at the same time).

Conventions Used in this Book

As you move through these pages, you'll note a few special elements. First, the registry keys are printed in a monospace typeface to make them easier to see at a glance. Also, the tips, notes, and cautions are specially treated paragraphs that appear when there's urgent or helpful information you should know.

Tips are additional tidbits of information you may find useful, and they're usually related to implementing the topic under discussion.

Notes are informative paragraphs providing knowledge that is unnecessary to the task at hand, but nonetheless useful to know.

Cautions are exactly what you would expect: notes from me that tell you which functions, features, or actions may cause problems.

Move slowly and carefully when you use what you learn here — the registry is dangerous. Back it up before you make any changes, even if the changes seem innocuous.

Acknowledgments

The folks at IDG Books Worldwide have been terrific to work with, providing support as I struggled with the decisions and complications that accompanied the writing of this book. Anne Hamilton is an acquisitions editor par excellence. Her support, encouragement, and patience are almost entirely responsible for the fact that this book exists. Susannah Pfalzer exhibited a wonderfully reassuring level of fortitude and cheerfulness throughout the editorial process — she made sure the writing made sense when I rushed through explanations too fast or skipped an explanation that was needed. Sally Neuman had to try to emulate my steps to ensure their accuracy (using, of course, a computer with a totally different environment and therefore different registry data), and I'm grateful for the time and energy invested. Larisa North made me look literate and able to spell, and I offer my thanks.

Contents at a Glance

Contents

Chapter 1

Understanding the Registry

WITH THE INTRODUCTION OF WINDOWS 95, Microsoft created a single repository for system and application information called the registry. This cryptic and convoluted database is involved in every part of the operation of the Windows 95, Windows 98, and Windows NT 4 OSs. A good understanding of what the registry is, what it does, and how to manipulate it, can give users of either operating system (OS) a leg up in the management and control of their computing environments.

An Overview of the Registry

The registry contains information about your computer, computer users, the peripherals attached to the computer, and the system that makes your computer run. This database is essential to running your system. It's important to understand what the registry is, and how it works. This knowledge enables you to maintain your system, and also modify the registry safely if the need arises.

History of the Registry

The first successful and widely used version of the Windows OS, Microsoft Windows 3.1, used three different types of files to inform the OS of the computer's hardware and installed application software.

The first two types were .INI files. These initialization files were broken down into the system initialization files and private initialization files. In its normal installation pattern, Windows 3.1*x* used six .INI files to load and control the Windows environment (CONTROL.INI, PROGMAN.INI, PROTOCOL.INI, SYSTEM.INI, WIN.INI, and WINFILE.INI).

WIN.INI and SYSTEM.INI were the primary system initialization files used by Windows 3.1*x*. WINI.INI was the primary location for information pertaining to the software configuration of the OS and specific system-wide information, added by application software. With every newly installed application making changes to WIN.INI (and often operating as if it was the only application installed), this INI file got very large, very fast. This often caused problems for users when the file reached its size limit of 64K. The OS didn't bother to inform the user that the limit had been reached, and the file grew beyond 64K. It then ignored any entry beyond that 64K boundary. When applications added entries to the top sections in the WIN.INI file, information at the bottom of the file got pushed beyond the initialization boundary, and was not implemented. This could cause problems for an application expecting these (now lost) entries to be initialized. In an attempt to prevent this, Microsoft recommended that application developers store application-specific information in private INI files that pertained only to their application. While this helped, it didn't stop application developers from continuing to place large amounts of information in the WIN.INI file.

SYSTEM.INI served as the primary repository for system information pertaining to the computer's hardware. While WIN.INI contained the information for the system's behavior, SYSTEM.INI pointed the OS at hardware and software components (device drivers, shells, etc.). Both WIN.INI and SYSTEM.INI still exist in Windows 95 and 98 and continue to play a role in the function of that OS.

PROGMAN.INI contained the initialization settings for the Windows Program Manager, while WINFILE.INI contained the settings for the Windows File Manager. The absence of these files didn't prevent Windows from running (as it did with SYSTEM.INI or WIN.INI), but you'd get the default configuration for these applications, rather than any customizations you may have performed.

PROTOCOL.INI, added in the Windows for Workgroups version of Windows 3.1*x*, was the location for initialization information for Windows networking.

Private initialization files were the .INI files added to the Windows directory by third-party applications installed on the system. These files contained specific information about the state of the application, including such items as screen position and the most recently used file list.

The last file that Windows 3.1 used for system configuration was REG.DAT. This was the Windows 3.*x* Registration Database and is the direct predecessor of the Windows 95, Windows 98, and Windows NT 4 registries. This database, which held nested structures off of a single HKEY_CLASSES_ROOT root, contained the information needed to maintain file-extension associations and OLE drag and drop support. Unlike the .INI files, which were simple ASCII text files (editable in any word processor or text editor), the REG.DAT file was binary in format and came with its own editing application, the Registration Information Editor (REGEDIT.EXE). This application enabled users to edit and search the Registration Database. The Windows 3.*x* REG.DAT, however, didn't have anywhere near the complexity found in the Windows 95, Windows 98 or Windows NT 4 registries.

The Purpose of the Registry

The registry in Windows 95, Windows 98, and Windows NT 4 takes over most of the responsibilities of the system initialization files and REG.DAT files from Windows 3.*x*. A quick search of a Windows 95/98/NT 4 system, however, will show you a large number of .INI files still used by the OSs.

If the registry concept has one sterling quality, it's the centralized location for storing all critical system information. While there isn't anything explicitly wrong with the concept of INI files, trying to keep track of files related to a specific application is almost impossible. An application's INI files don't have to be tied to a specific directory or system folder but can be found anywhere on your computer's hard drives. This lack of rules regarding INI files is one of the reasons the centralized registry simplifies system management.

The centralized registry can also make applications interact more smoothly. When a new application is installed, it can check the registry for current file associations, .DLL links and versions, and so on, before reinstalling something that another application may have added to the system. This works both ways; in order for an application to gain the "Designed for Windows 95 and Windows NT" logo, the application contains an uninstall routine. The information about applications, stored in the registry, enables an application to uninstall itself without removing components (.DLLs, .OCX's, and so on). These may be used by other applications, even if installed later than the application being removed.

The OS also provides for the creation of multiple user profiles in Windows 95, Windows 98, and Windows NT. This means that information pertaining to an individual user name, and that user's rights, can be contained in the registry. The methodology for defining the security permissions differs considerably between Windows 95/98 and Windows NT, due to the lack of security in Windows 95 and 98. Some of those security issues can be addressed on networked Windows 95 or 98 systems; however, as a standalone system, the Windows 95 and 98 boxes provide little (or no) system security.

This lack of security doesn't prevent the storage of individual user preferences in the Windows 95 and 98 registry, however. Users have their own, customized interface tied to their login username.

The registry also lets the user store multiple hardware configurations. For instance, enabling a notebook user to create profiles for Docked and Undocked configurations, or to create profiles for switchable devices (see Figure 1-1). The configuration process is quite simple, and is covered in more detail in Chapters 3 and 4.

In summary, the registry provides a centralized location to store information relating to the hardware and software configuration of the local system. The configuration of the registry, itself, differs between Windows 95/98 and Windows NT, and is covered in the next section.

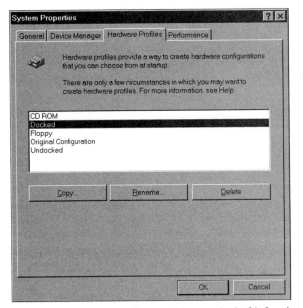

Figure 1-1: Hardware profiles provide a method of informing the operating system what hardware to expect during the current boot process.

Understanding the Differences Between the Windows 95/98 and Windows NT 4 Registries

The first version of Windows NT (Windows NT 3.1) introduced the registry concept, and the Windows 95 and 98 registries have their roots in this earlier version. There are, however, significant differences between the registry implementations in Windows 95/98 and Windows NT.

If you run REGEDIT.EXE side-by-side on a Windows 95/98 and a Windows NT 4 system, you'd be hard pressed to tell the systems apart. The most obvious difference is that the Windows 95 or 98 machine would have six top-level keys:

- ◆ HKEY_CLASSES_ROOT

- ◆ HKEY_CURRENT_USER

- ◆ HKEY_LOCAL_MACHINE

- ◆ HKEY_USERS

- ◆ HKEY_CURRENT_CONFIG

- ◆ HKEY_DYN_DATA

While the Windows NT 4 system, in contrast, would have only five top-level keys:

♦ HKEY_CLASSES_ROOT

♦ HKEY_CURRENT_USER

♦ HKEY_LOCAL_MACHINE

♦ HKEY_USERS

♦ HKEY_CURRENT_CONFIG

The HKEY_DYN_DATA key contains information about the system that Windows 95 and 98 need to keep handy, as it might need quick updating. This is registry information that the OS loads into memory instead of leaving on the hard disk. The data includes the hardware tree for the currently loaded configuration, performance information about any network connections and the Plug and Play status as reported by the Windows 95 or Windows 98 Configuration Manager (which doesn't exist in Windows NT 4).

Windows NT 4 doesn't use this key to store performance data. It tracks performance information via hooks to, and APIs for, the Windows NT Performance Monitor application. HKEY_DYN_DATA, in Windows 95 and 98, only contains dynamic data information which is memory resident. The Windows NT registry contains only static data.

The top-level keys common to both OSs behave in a comparable manner in both OSs. There are differences between the two, however.

HKEY_CLASSES_ROOT

HKEY_CLASSES_ROOT actually links to HKEY_LOCAL_ MACHINE\Software\Classes in NT, 95, and 98. The structure of this key differs slightly between OSs. Figure 1-2 exhibits the NT 4 structure, and Figure 1-3 displays the Windows 95 composition.

Figure 1-2: HKEY_CLASSES_ROOT in NT 4

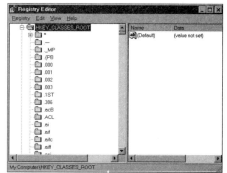

Figure 1-3: HKEY_CLASSES_ROOT for Windows 95

The Windows NT registry also requires that added shell extensions be registered in the key HKEY_LOCAL_MACHINE\Software\Microsoft\Windows\CurrentVersion\ ShellExtensions\Approved.

HKEY_CURRENT_USER

This key aliases the HKEY_USER key and contains information for the current user.

In Windows NT 4 (Figure 1-4), this key is created by default as a function of the security requirement. It requires an established user account in order to access the system, regardless of system status (standalone, networked, and so on).

In Windows 95 and 98 (see Figure 1-5) this key is filled when a user account is specifically created. In a standalone Windows 95 or 98 system there is no Create User program, but setting up profiles and logging on to the machine with any name creates a new current user.

Figure 1-4: NT 4 HKEY_CURRENT_USER

Figure 1-5: Windows 95 HKEY_CURRENT_ USER

HKEY_LOCAL_MACHINE

This is where the machine-specific information resides. Notice that the Windows NT registry (see Figure 1-6) contains the security-related subkeys for the SAM (the Security Account Manager, a critical piece of logon and access control). The key cannot be edited via REGEDIT, but must be accessed via the appropriate account management tools (for example, the Windows NT User Manager).

Windows 95 and 98 machines vary in the display of subkeys, depending upon the configuration of the particular computer. Figure 1-7 shows a typical system configuration in Windows 95.

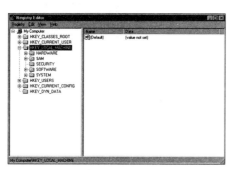

Figure 1-6: The Security Account Manager (SAM) is unique to NT.

Figure 1-7: The Windows 95 and 98 key reflects the way you've configured your system.

HKEY_USERS

In Windows NT, this subkey contains the user Security ID string. It is only editable by users with Administrator-equivalent permissions on the local machine (see Figure 1-8).

In Windows 95 and 98, the User subkey contains the user account names (see Figure 1-9).

Figure 1-8: The current NT 4 user is represented by the SID

Figure 1-9: The current Windows 95 user is named ACCNT

HKEY_CURRENT_CONFIG

HKEY_CURRENT_CONFIG contains information about the current configuration. For Windows NT 4 (see Figure 1-10), it contains information for the minimal Plug and Play support available in the OS. For Windows 95 and 98 (see Figure 1-11), hardware configuration information displays.

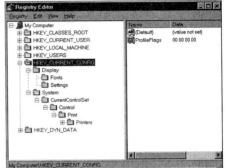

Figure 1-10: The Windows NT current configuration

Figure 1-11: The Windows 95 current configuration

Registry Data Storage

There is also a major difference in the way that Windows 95/98 and Windows NT store the registry data. In Windows 95 and 98, the registry information is stored mainly in two files; SYSTEM.DAT and USER.DAT. In Windows NT 4 the registry information is stored in a series of hive files (see the "Hive Files" section later in this chapter). You can find the names of these files in HKEY_LOCAL_MACHINE\ System\CurrentControlSet\Control\hivelist. Each hive has a single entry, which contains the name of the hive file. The hive files, themselves, are located in the \%systemroot%\SYSTEM32\CONFIG folder.

The Registry Structure

As mentioned in the preceding text, the registry starts with a series of top-level keys (also known as root keys or subtrees). Each of the top-level keys expands into keys, subkeys, and value entries.

Within each root key you'll find multiple keys and subkeys. At each level, as you drill down through the root key, you'll find that the key names are unique to that level. Key names may be reused throughout the registry, in multiple root keys and at different levels, but uniqueness is required at the same key level.

When a user or an application creates a key, the key can combine both upper-case and lowercase characters — and the case will be preserved when the key is displayed. The registry itself, however, is case-insensitive and often inconsistent in its application of case sensitivity. Normally, you cannot create two keys with the same name, at the same level, even if the keys are different combinations of uppercase and lowercase.

Keys may contain other keys or values. From a technical perspective, you might consider keys as container objects that contain either subkeys or values associated with the container. A number of data types are found in the registry, and are listed as follows:

- REG_MULTI_SZ — This can contain multiple values, delimited by the ASCII 0 null character. It is a string of text data, and the null character makes it more readable. The information and revision of your system BIOS is an example of this data type.

- REG_SZ — This data type contains a single string, which is usually in easily readable form. Program names are of this data type.

- REG_EXPAND_SZ — This contains variable data that is replaced when the key is written to by an application. Anyone who has ever used a % variable in a DOS batch file is comfortable with this concept. An example, in your registry, is any notation for the directory that holds your Windows files (%systemroot%).

- REG_BINARY — This is the standard data type for binary value entries, such as entries relating to your hardware.

- REG_DWORD — This includes 32-bit data (4 bytes long) and can be binary, decimal, or hexadecimal data. Most often the data is displayed in hexadecimal form, with a prefix of 0x. For instance, you'll see this data type in entries that refer to IRQ's.

INI files

While .INI files haven't gone away (a quick scan of the system I'm writing this on shows more than 150 of them), they are primarily of the private INI file variety. That is, they're installed by, and related to, specific applications. You'll also find the WIN.INI and SYSTEM.INI still exist, and, as a point of fact, are necessary for compatibility with older, 16-bit, applications.

Hive Files

The Windows NT hive files (mentioned in preceding text) are accompanied by a series of log files, which are transaction logs that record the changes made to critical sections of the registry. The HKEY_LOCAL_MACHINE subtree gets three log files, one for the Security, Software, and SAM subkeys; the System subkey, which can't be restored from a transaction log, gets the SYSTEM.ALT file (a mirror of the current System subkey).

The HKEY_CURRENT_USER subtree gets files named USER.xxx, USER.xxx.LOG in Windows 95 and 98 or ADMIN.xxx or ADMIN.xxx.LOG in Windows NT.

The HKEY_USERS\.DEFAULT subtree creates the files DEFAULT and DEFAULT.LOG.

Key Relationships

Now that you've learned something about the six (or five) top-level keys, and what can be contained in each entry, you're ready for the confusing part.

There are actually only two keys. They are HKEY_LOCAL_MACHINE and HKEY_USERS. The other keys are either aliases for subsections of these two keys, or dynamically created keys that are built when the system is booted.

HKEY_LOCAL_MACHINE

This key contains the global information about the system that pertains to system hardware and application software settings. The information contained therein applies to all users who log into the system in Windows 95/98 and Windows NT. This key has three aliases at the top level:

◆ HKEY_CLASSES_ROOT — This is the alias for HKEY_LOCAL_MACHINE\Software\Classes, and contains information that deals with file associations, drag-and-drop, shortcuts, and OLE/COM. This applies to Windows NT 4 and Windows 95/98.

◆ HKEY_CURRENT_CONFIG — This differs by OS. In Windows 95 and 98, this key is the alias for HKEY_LOCAL_MACHINE\Config\000n, where n is the specific configuration that is currently loaded (only pertinent if there are multiple hardware profiles). In Windows NT 4 two subkeys are directly below the root; \Software (which is an alias for HKEY_LOCAL_MACHINE\SYSTEM\ControlSet00n\Hardware Profiles\000n\Software), and \System (which is an alias for part of HKEY_LOCAL_MACHINE\SYSTEM\CurrentControlSet).

◆ HKEY_DYN_DATA — This also differs by OS. In Windows 95 and 98 this key derives its data from a number of different locations in the HKEY_LOCAL_MACHINE tree for the subkey \Config Manager. Its PerfStats subkey is derived from performance information reported by the local system. Both are dynamically created at boot time. While this key exists on Windows NT systems, it's related to the minimal Plug and Play support offered by NT 4's capability to support multiple hardware configurations.

The first-level subkeys of HKEY_LOCAL_MACHINE for Windows 95 and 98 are:

◆ Config — This subkey stores the configuration information for the system hardware profiles.

◆ Enum — This subkey enumerates the information found in the Windows 95 and 98 Device Manager. There is a separate entry for each class of hardware, as well as entries for each, specific piece of hardware.

- `hardware` – This subkey contains serial port and floating point hardware information.

- `Network` – This contains the network logon configuration information; the type of network and the default username.

- `Security` – This contains information about network security and configured Remote Access devices.

- `SOFTWARE` – This subkey contains information about applications installed on the system. It ranges from default window locations to file associations – to the keystrokes that fire your guns in Windows 95 shoot 'em-up games.

- `System` – This contains the Current Control Set configuration information.

The first-level subkeys of `HKEY_LOCAL_MACHINE` for Windows NT are:

- `HARDWARE` – This contains detailed information about the system's hardware configuration and locally attached devices, such as SCSI peripherals.

- `SAM` – This subkey is a placeholder for the security accounts manager.

- `SECURITY` – This is a placeholder for application security information.

- `SOFTWARE` – This subkey contains a complete range of information about installed applications.

- `SYSTEM` – This contains detailed information about the CurrentControlSet, as well as the previously configured Control Sets.

HKEY_USERS

This key contains information specific to each user configured on the system. Windows NT 4 requires user accounts, and will have a `\.Default` subkey along with a subkey identified by a Security ID code (SID) for each user. (Note that the period following `\` is required.) Windows 95 and 98 can contain only a `\.Default` subkey or specific user keys, which are not encrypted like the Security ID keys in Windows NT 4.

`HKEY_CURRENT_USER` is an alias for the `HKEY_USERS\`*Whatever user you logged in as.* This applies to Windows 95/98 and Windows NT 4. In Windows 95 and 98, if the system logon screen is canceled or nonexistent, the key will use the `\.Default` key.

The first two subkeys of `HKEY_USERS` for Windows 95 and 98 (there may be more depending on your system configuration) are:

- .Default — This contains the default user configuration information.

- USERNAME (substitute the user name) — This subkey contains the configuration for that specific user.

Both keys contain the following subkeys:

- AppEvents — This contains pointers to the sounds made by Windows 95 and 98 when an event occurs as well as configuration information for the desktop themes.

- Control Panel — This subkey contains the settings for some of the Control Panel applets. The settings stored here were previously stored in the Windows 3.x WIN.INI file, and some of them have been moved to the registry. Other settings remain in .INI files and are used by legacy applications.

- InstallLocationsMRU — The Most Recently Used list for application installation is stored here in this subkey.

- Keyboard layout — This subkey identifies the keyboard layout as specified in the Current Control Set.

- Network — This contains a list of subkeys that identify the current network connections (those defined as persistent), and a most recently used list.

- RemoteAccess — This subkey contains the addresses and profiles for the installed Dial-Up Networking configurations.

- Software — This subkey contains the individual settings for each users software configuration.

The second-level subkeys of HKEY_USERS for Windows NT are:

- Default — This subkey contains the default user configuration information.

- SID — This subkey contains the configuration for that specific user.

Both keys contain the following subkeys:

- AppEvents — This contains pointers to the sounds made by Windows NT when an event occurs, as well as configuration information for the desktop themes.

- Console — This subkey contains the current configuration of the MS-DOS Command Prompt window.

- `Control Panel` — This contains configuration information for some of the Control Panel applets, as well as screen savers and sounds.

- `Environment` — This subkey contains some of the system environment variables.

- `Keyboard Layout` — This contains the current information about the keyboard layout and any other stored keyboard layouts.

- `Software` — This contains information about the current users software configuration. It does not contain information about applications installed as Common.

- `UNICODE Program Groups` — This subkey stores any current user UNICODE information.

Backing Up and Restoring The Registry

Before you do anything that involves editing the registry, the first thing you must do is make a backup copy of the registry files. This cannot be stressed enough. DO NOT DO ANYTHING TO THE REGISTRY WITHOUT A BACKUP!

Consider this little snippet from a Microsoft KnowledgeBase article about an official Microsoft utility:

"Warning: Using Registry Editor incorrectly can cause serious, system-wide problems that may require you to reinstall Windows NT to correct them. Microsoft cannot guarantee that any problems resulting from the use of Registry Editor can be solved. Use this tool at your own risk."

Backing Up and Restoring the Windows NT 4 Registry

The only "official" method for backing up the Windows NT 4 registry requires the use of the Backup utility found in the Windows NT 4 Administrative Tools (Common) folder. Using this utility requires that a compatible (for NT 4) tape backup device be installed on the local system (this utility cannot backup the registry on a remote system, even if you have access permissions to that system). There are, however, other "unofficial" methods, which are discussed in this section.

USING THE NT 4 BACKUP SOFTWARE
If you have that tape backup system, first select the local drive where the registry resides (see Figure 1-12), then from the Operations menu, select Backup.

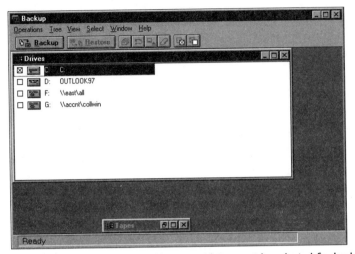

Figure 1-12: The drive that holds your registry must be selected for backup.

In the Backup Information dialog box, select the Backup Local Registry option so the backup process includes the system registry files.

To restore the registry files, you need to run the Backup utility and select the registry files to be restored from the tape. Just insert the appropriate tape into your tape drive, open the Tapes window, and drill down to the `\%systemroot%\system32\config folder`. Then select the registry hives or logs you wish to restore.

BACKING UP AND RESTORING MANUALLY

If you formatted your NT boot drive with NTFS, you cannot use this method. If, however, your NT boot drive is formatted using the FAT file system, you can back up the registry by booting another OS (such as MS-DOS) from a boot floppy or Windows 95 or 98 in a dual boot system. Then it's a simple matter of copying files. In MS-DOS you'll need to use the command line, in Windows 95 you can use Explorer.

Copy the contents of the `\%systemroot%\system32\config` folder to another device (ZIP drive, writeable CDR, or another storage device). It is unlikely you'll be able to fit the folder contents on a floppy disk, as the total size of the files will be larger than a single floppy's capacity.

The files you need to back up from the `\%systemroot%\system32\config` folder are:

AppEvent.Evt

default

default.LOG

default.sav

SAM

SAM.LOG

SecEvent.Evt

SECURITY

SECURITY.LOG

software

software.LOG

software.sav

SysEvent.Evt

system

SYSTEM.ALT

system.LOG

system.sav

userdiff

Restoring the registry after it has been backed up in this fashion requires booting the alternate OS. Then, the files must be copied from their saved location back to the `\%systemroot%\system32\config` folder.

EXPORTING THE REGISTRY HIVE FILES

Within Regedit, you can use the Export Registry command on the Registry menu to export the entire registry or individual registry keys. You can export the files to any device accessible to the local system.

TIP

I find it most convenient to export to a local directory I created for that purpose. That directory can then be moved to a floppy disk, or a network drive that is backed up to tape every night. It's a good idea to create a specific directory for your export files on the network. Or, if other users are doing the same thing, create a directory for exported registry files with subdirectories for each computer sending these files.

To export the registry:

1. In Regedit, select My Computer (for the entire registry) or the specific key you want to export.

2. Choose Export Registry from the Registry menu.

3. In the Export Registry File dialog box (see Figure 1-13), select a folder and name the file.

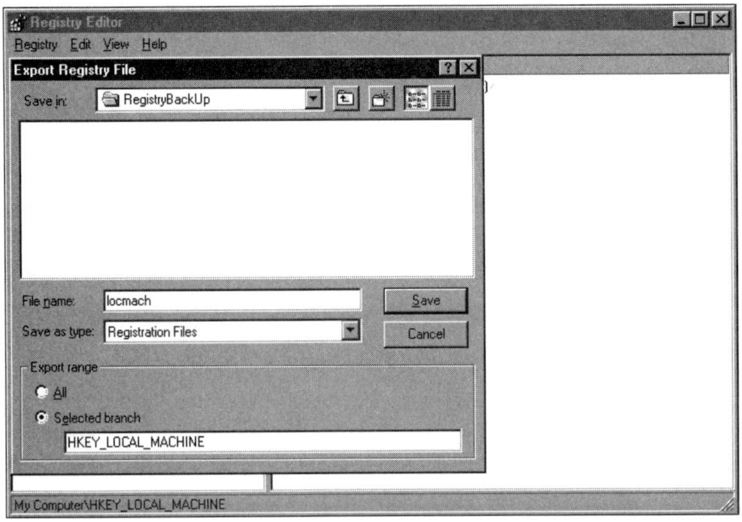

Figure 1-13: Save the exported registry or key the same way you save a file.

Following are some things to think about when you use this feature:

◆ Saving only one copy of this file to the local hard drive won't help much if a serious problem results with the registry – copy the file to removable media or a network drive.

◆ If you want to export more than one key (but not the entire registry), be sure to name the file as a reminder of the key it represents.

◆ Before you complete the process, check the bottom of the dialog box to note whether the export range is what you intended. The dialog box indicates All (for the entire registry) or Selected Branch (and names the key).

The exported file will be readable in any editor that can read ASCII text. Following is an example of what the file for an export of HKEY_LOCAL_MACHINE looks like:

```
[HKEY_LOCAL_MACHINE\HARDWARE]
[HKEY_LOCAL_MACHINE\HARDWARE\DESCRIPTION]
[HKEY_LOCAL_MACHINE\HARDWARE\DESCRIPTION\System]
"Component
 Information"=hex:00,00,00,00,00,00,00,00,00,00,00,00,00,00,00,00
"Identifier"="AT/AT COMPATIBLE"
"Configuration
 Data"=hex(9):ff,ff,ff,ff,ff,ff,ff,ff,00,00,00,00,02,00,00,00,05,\00
 ,00,00,30,00,00,00,00,00,00,00,00,00,00,00,80,00,f5,03,00,00,3e,00,
 20,00,\04,00,81,00,fc,03,00,00,3d,00,21,00,04,00,82,00,fc,03,00,00,
 3d,00,21,00,04,\00,83,00,0a,02,00,00,3f,00,fe,00,04,00,05,00,00,00,
 20,00,00,00,00,00,00,00,\00,00,00,00,00,00,00,0c,00,00,80,00,00,00,00,
 0d,00,00,40,00,00,00,0e,00,00,\00,01,00,00,00,0f,00,00,00,01,00
"SystemBiosDate"="12/15/93"
"VideoBiosDate"="03/01/94"
"VideoBiosVersion"=hex(7):43,4c,2d,47,44,35,34,33,78,20,50,43,49,20,
 56,47,41,\20,42,49,4f,53,20,56,65,72,73,69,6f,6e,20,31,2e,30,30,61,
 20,20,20,20,00,00
[HKEY_LOCAL_MACHINE\HARDWARE\DESCRIPTION\System\CentralProcessor]
[HKEY_LOCAL_MACHINE\HARDWARE\DESCRIPTION\System\CentralProcessor\0]
"Component
 Information"=hex:00,00,00,00,00,00,00,00,00,00,00,00,01,00,00,00
"Identifier"="x86 Family 5 Model 2 Stepping 1"
"Configuration
 Data"=hex(9):ff,ff,ff,ff,ff,ff,ff,ff,00,00,00,00,00,00,00,00
"VendorIdentifier"="GenuineIntel"
"~MHz"=dword:0000005a
[HKEY_LOCAL_MACHINE\HARDWARE\DESCRIPTION\System\CentralProcessor\1]
"Component
 Information"=hex:00,00,00,00,00,00,00,00,01,00,00,00,02,00,00,00
"Identifier"="x86 Family 5 Model 2 Stepping 1"
"Configuration
 Data"=hex(9):ff,ff,ff,ff,ff,ff,ff,ff,00,00,00,00,00,00,00,00
"VendorIdentifier"="GenuineIntel"
"~MHz"=dword:0000005a
```

Exporting the registry or specific registry keys is the easiest way to back up your registry before manipulating it. If you make unnecessary changes, you need only import the exported file to undo the changes.

To restore registry keys in Regedit, select the Import Registry Files command from the Registry menu. Then select the appropriate file, or files.

Once you are extremely comfortable (and expert) with the registry, you can tweak your system or solve minor problems by making changes in the file before importing it back to the registry. Make a copy of the file first, however, in case you make a mistake.

BACKING UP WITH THE WINDOWS NT RESOURCE KIT UTILITIES

The Windows NT 4 Resource Kit includes a pair of command-line utilities for backing up and restoring the registry, REGBACK.EXE and REGREST.EXE. To run this application, you need Administrator or Backup Operator access to the local system. The NT 4 Resource Kit must be purchased separately.

Regback.exe only backs up registry hives that are open and in use. Use the syntax:

Regback <directory>

to back up all the registry hives whose files reside in the config directory (usually all hives) to the named directory.

For hives, use the syntax: **Regback <filename> <hivetype> <hivename>** where hivetype is either "machine" or "users" and hivename is the name of an immediate subtree of HKEY_LOCAL_MACHINE or HKEY_LOCAL_USERS.

If the target media cannot hold the entire output file, the program fails (there's no polite request to put Disk #2 in the drive). It is a good idea to back up to your local drive and then copy the files to removable media.

Since Regback does not copy hives that aren't open, you can use Copy or Xcopy to make a safety backup of those hives. Regback reports that those hives need manual backup.

To restore hives, use Regrest.exe, which works by making RegReplaceKey calls. In effect, the old hive is stored into a .sav file and then the file created with Regback is renamed. There is no effect until you reboot the machine. You must have enough disk space for duplicate files (because of the .sav files) and all files must be on the same volume.

To use Regrest, use the syntax: **regrest <newfilename> <savefilename> <hivetype> <hivename>**.

The hivetype is either "machine" or "users" and hivename is the name of an immediate subtree of HKEY_LOCAL_MACHINE or HKEY_LOCAL_USERS.

The application renames the specified hive's file to <savefilename> and then moves the file specified by <newfilename> to be the backing for the specified hive. Regrest will indicate if there are any hives that must be backed up manually.

Backing Up and Restoring the Windows 95 and 98 Registries

Did I mention that you shouldn't make any changes to the registry without backing it up, first? WELL DON'T FORGET IT!

It is easier to back up and restore the Windows 95 and 98 registries than is the Windows NT 4 registry for several reasons:

◆ There are only two files to be backed up, SYSTEM.DAT and USER.DAT.

◆ There is no need to worry about restoring an NTFS formatted partition. With NT, if you are using NTFS, you can't just copy the registry hives back to the system after booting with a DOS floppy.

BACKING UP THE REGISTRY WITH CFGBACK

If you go to the Start menu, click Run, and type cfgback, you'll probably get an error message. In its infinite wisdom, Microsoft decided that the application isn't installed during the Windows 95 installation routine. You can find it on the Windows 95 distribution CD.

Copy the \Other\Misc\Cfgback folder to your local hard drive, and make yourself a shortcut to the Cfgback.exe file in a convenient place.

Cfgback will prompt you for the storage location of the proprietary *.rbk files it creates. You can place these files in any location, and Cfgback is capable of creating nine generations of .rbk files in any one directory. If you need more than nine generations, you can move the existing .rbk files to another location and let Cfgback start creating from scratch.

When you launch Cfgback a series of windows displays (like a wizard). Answer the queries and enter the appropriate information (see Figure 1-14).

The process takes a few moments, the files are copied and compressed. You can copy the .rbk file to a floppy disk for safety.

To restore any of these iterations of .rbk files as the registry, you need to move them to the \Windows folder. This is the only location the files can be restored from. Simply select an existing backup file and choose Restore.

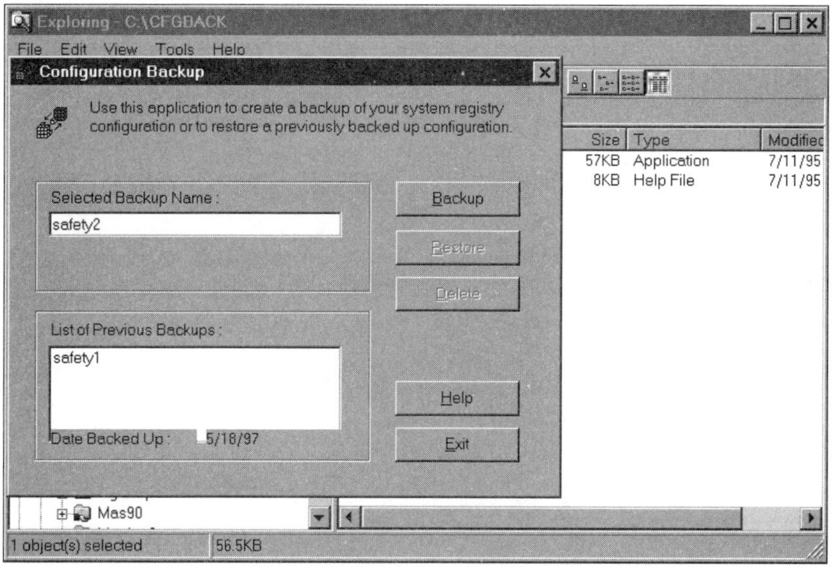

Figure 1-14: Enter a filename to launch the registry backup process.

BACKING UP THE REGISTRY WITH MICROSOFT BACKUP

You may choose to use the Windows 95 or 98 Backup software. If you didn't select to install it when Windows 95 or 98 was installed (it's not installed by default), you can use the Add/Remove Programs Control Panel applet to add it to your system. Once installed, you can launch it from the Accessories menu.

The software supports backing up to tape, floppy disk, or another computer on the network. Most of the time, tape is the efficient media (unless you like sitting around putting floppy disks into a drive, one after another).

The biggest problem with this software is that the backup application, itself, has only minimal support for tape drives – and many tape devices are not supported. If you happen to have a supported tape drive laying around, go ahead and use it. If you plan to buy one, just purchase one that comes with its own Windows 95 or 98 tape backup software.

The biggest problem with the Microsoft tape backup utility (besides getting it to work properly), is that the only way to restore the registry is to use the Full System Backup restore set. No other option will correctly restore the registry. Also, when you do any type of restore to the \Windows folder it will restore the registry files as well (regardless of whether you want them restored or not). If you do need to restore a file to that folder, restore it to the \temp folder, and then copy the file(s) you need to restore to the \Windows folder.

EXPORTING THE REGISTRY TO A TEXT FILE

If your registry explorations go bad, the Windows 95 or 98 probably won't boot. If this occurs, neither CFGBACK or the Backup utility will do much good as you need to be running Windows 95 or 98 to use them. It is not quite the Catch-22 it seems, however.

You can export the entire registry to a .reg file (or just export specific subtrees or keys) and keep the file on a floppy disk. For example, you can export HKEY_LOCAL_MACHINE and its subkeys as indicated here:

```
[HKEY_LOCAL_MACHINE\hardware]
[HKEY_LOCAL_MACHINE\hardware\devicemap]
[HKEY_LOCAL_MACHINE\hardware\devicemap\serialcomm]
"COM1"="COM1"
"COM2"="COM2"
[HKEY_LOCAL_MACHINE\hardware\DESCRIPTION]
[HKEY_LOCAL_MACHINE\hardware\DESCRIPTION\System]
[HKEY_LOCAL_MACHINE\hardware\DESCRIPTION\System\FloatingPointProcess
   or]
[HKEY_LOCAL_MACHINE\hardware\DESCRIPTION\System\FloatingPointProcess
   or\0]
```

You can then use the real-mode version of REGEDIT (found on that system startup disk you've made for emergencies – you have made one, right?) and import the complete registry backup. This is done using the command-line REGEDIT -C command, and should solve any registry induced errors.

If you haven't created that start-up disk yet, launch the Add/Remove Programs Control Panel applet, click the Startup Disk tab, and select Create Disk. You'll need a blank floppy to create the disk. You will then be prompted for the Windows 95 or 98 Distribution CD, so unmodified startup files can be copied to the Startup Disk.

BACKING UP THE REGISTRY WITH DOS

If you don't bother to make that Startup Disk (or, like most of us, can't find it two months after it was created), there is another option. You can just copy the two registry files to another directory as a backup. There's a trick to this; you can't copy the registry files while Windows 95 or 98 is running. The following procedure enables you to copy those files:

1. Reboot the computer.

2. While Windows 95 or 98 is booting, press F8 to bring up the Windows 95 or 98 Boot options menu.

3. Select "Safe Mode Command Prompt Only" from the pick list. This launches the DOS shell without loading the Registry.

4. Change to the \Windows directory, and use the ATTRIB command to remove the System, Hidden, and Read-only attributes from SYSTEM.DAT and USER.DAT. (Type **attrib -s -h -r *.dat** to do this.)

5. Copy SYSTEM.DAT and USER.DAT to the directory of your choice on a local hard drive.

6. Restore the file attributes to the .DAT files (**attrib +h +s +r *.dat**).

You can now reboot into Windows 95 or 98 with an accurate copy of the registry available for future mishaps. If need be, repeat steps 1 through 3, and then copy your backed-up registry files to the \Windows directory. This will restore the registry to its prehacked state.

Controlling the Size of the NT 4 Registry

While it is unlikely that the registry will grow to an unmanageable size, Windows NT 4 provides the capability to limit, or raise, the maximum size of the registry. To perform this function:

1. Open the System icon in the Control Panel.

2. Select the Performance Tab.

3. Click the Change button in the Virtual Memory section of the dialog box.

4. Modify the Maximum Registry Size figure in that section of the dialog box (see Figure 1-15).

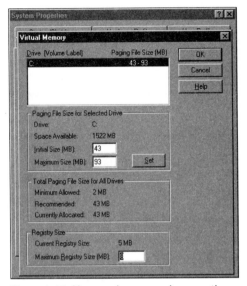

Figure 1-15: You can decrease or increase the maximum size of the registry.

To get an idea of registry sizes, I inspected a couple of my NT 4 computers:

◆ In a computer with 128MB RAM and 7GB of storage, with about 40 installed applications, the registry size was 6MB with the maximum size defaulting to 26MB.

◆ In a computer with 32MB RAM and 2GB of storage, with about 12 installed applications, the registry size was 5MB with the maximum size defaulting to 8MB.

Summary

This chapter has provided a brief overview of the registry, its history, and its use. The specific keys of the registry and their relationships to your system's configuration and behavior are discussed in the remaining chapters.

Chapter 2

Using the Registry Editors

WINDOWS 95, WINDOWS 98, AND WINDOWS NT 4 are equipped with a tool that enables the user to edit the registry; it's called, surprisingly enough, the Registry Editor. Windows NT actually has two Registry Editors. The first is REGEDIT.EXE, which Windows NT shares with Windows 95 and 98; it is identical to the application found in Windows 95 and 98. The second is REGEDT32.EXE, which it inherited from the previous versions of Windows NT, and which enables you to modify the Windows NT registry in ways that Windows 95 or 98 does not support. You'll notice that REGEDIT shows the same keys in Windows 95, Windows 98, and Windows NT, but REGEDT32 is missing HKEY_DYN_DATA.

Although both Registry Editors are installed by default in NT 4, and REGEDIT is installed in Windows 95 and 98, neither Editor gets an icon or a listing anywhere in the Start menu's Programs listing of the Windows launch menus. Both operating systems can launch the applications from the Run command. If you plan to do a lot of registry editing, you may want to add the Editor to the Start menu. To do so, right-click the taskbar, select Properties, and then click the Start Menu Programs tab. In the Customize Start Menu box, click the Add button. Then, in the provided dialog box, simply type the name of the Registry Editor you want to launch. You don't need a fully qualified pathname because both of the Editors are in the default paths configured by either operating system.

An important note: Keep in mind that the information displayed in the Registry Editor is static. It's an accurate picture of the registry at the time you opened the Registry Editor, but if the operating system or an application makes a change to the registry while it's open, the changes won't be reflected. This is not likely to be a problem on the local system, unless you are using the Registry Editor as part of your software development tool kit. But if you are running the Registry Editor to examine or modify any remote registries, there's always the possibility that the locally attached users are installing software or performing some task that can modify their registry.

Using REGEDIT

Like almost every browsing tool currently available for Windows, Registry Editor uses an Explorer-like, two-pane view of the registry contents (see Figure 2-1).

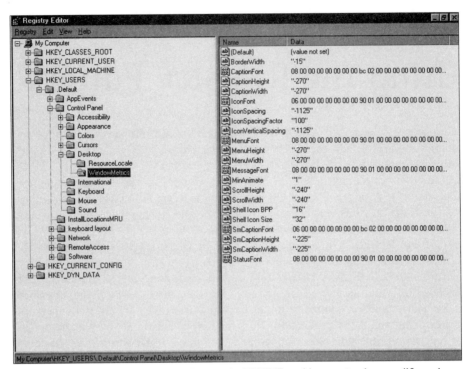

Figure 2-1: Using the appropriate registry tools, REGEDIT enables you to view, modify, and manipulate the contents of the Windows 95, Windows 98, and Windows NT registries.

In fact, the similarity to Explorer goes further. You can create new entries using the same keystrokes or menu commands, and you can use right-click capabilities to manipulate the objects.

Using the REGEDIT Commands

You'll find only four entries on the REGEDIT menu bar. Additional REGEDIT capabilities are easily accessible via shortcut menus in the appropriate screen locations.

IMPORTING AND EXPORTING REGISTRY FILES
Instead of the traditional File menu that holds commands for manipulating files, REGEDIT has the Registry menu (see Figure 2-2).

The six options on the Registry menu are pretty much self-explanatory. But for clarity's sake, I'll expand on importing and exporting registry contents, and on using REGEDIT across the network.

IMPORTING REGISTRY FILES   This option enables you to select an already created .REG file and import it into the registry. The Import Registry File dialog box appears so you can select the file you want to import (see Figure 2-3).

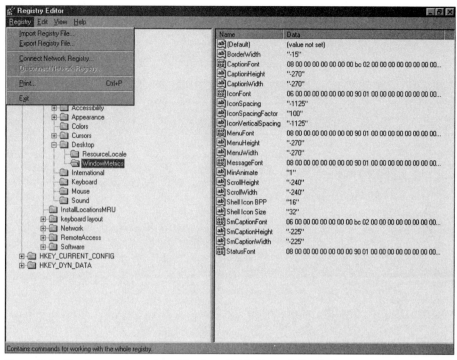

Figure 2-2: Direct access to registry files is available through the Registry menu.

Figure 2-3: Most of the time, you'll be looking for
a registry backup file to import, so you can correct
a mistake you made when you worked in the registry.

You'll find .REG files all over your system, because software applications use
them to import registry information. You can't tell just by looking at a filename
what the contents of the .REG file are for, or what they'll do to your system, but
.REG files are ASCII text and can be opened in any text editor.

Whatever you do, don't just double-click a .REG file. It will automatically merge
with the existing registry, without any additional prompting. To get an idea of what

the .REG file will do, open it first in a text editor and review its contents (see Figure 2-4). In fact, if you right-click the file in Explorer, you can use the Edit command on the shortcut menu (which opens Notepad).

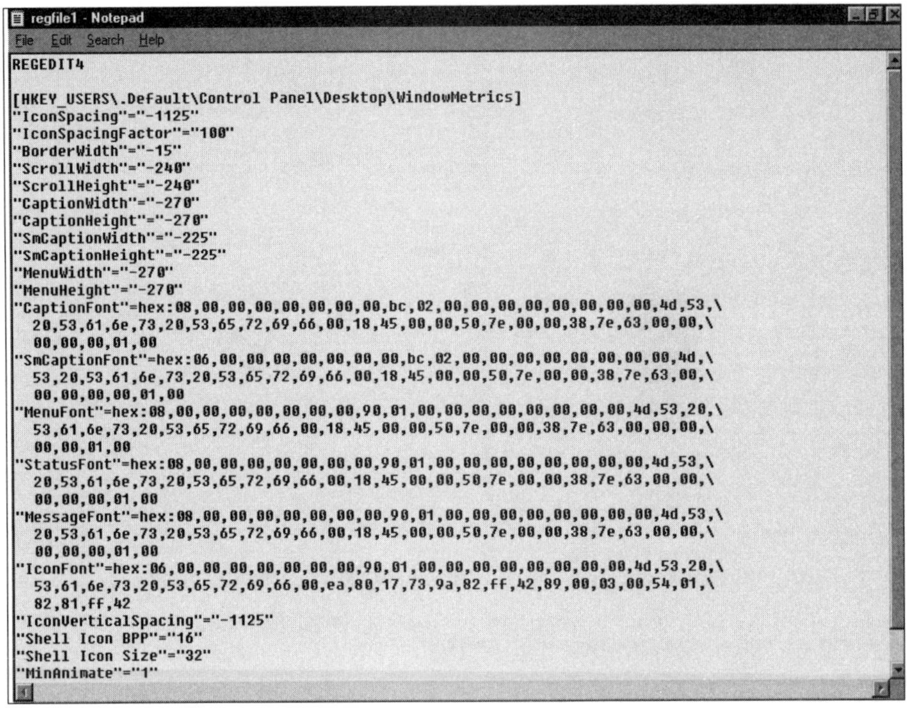


```
REGEDIT4

[HKEY_USERS\.Default\Control Panel\Desktop\WindowMetrics]
"IconSpacing"="-1125"
"IconSpacingFactor"="100"
"BorderWidth"="-15"
"ScrollWidth"="-240"
"ScrollHeight"="-240"
"CaptionWidth"="-270"
"CaptionHeight"="-270"
"SmCaptionWidth"="-225"
"SmCaptionHeight"="-225"
"MenuWidth"="-270"
"MenuHeight"="-270"
"CaptionFont"=hex:08,00,00,00,00,00,00,00,bc,02,00,00,00,00,00,00,00,00,4d,53,\
  20,53,61,6e,73,20,53,65,72,69,66,00,18,45,00,00,50,7e,00,00,38,7e,63,00,00,\
  00,00,00,01,00
"SmCaptionFont"=hex:06,00,00,00,00,00,00,00,bc,02,00,00,00,00,00,00,00,00,4d,\
  53,20,53,61,6e,73,20,53,65,72,69,66,00,18,45,00,00,50,7e,00,00,38,7e,63,00,\
  00,00,00,00,01,00
"MenuFont"=hex:08,00,00,00,00,00,00,00,90,01,00,00,00,00,00,00,00,00,4d,53,20,\
  53,61,6e,73,20,53,65,72,69,66,00,18,45,00,00,50,7e,00,00,38,7e,63,00,00,00,\
  00,00,01,00
"StatusFont"=hex:08,00,00,00,00,00,00,00,90,01,00,00,00,00,00,00,00,00,4d,53,\
  20,53,61,6e,73,20,53,65,72,69,66,00,18,45,00,00,50,7e,00,00,38,7e,63,00,00,\
  00,00,00,01,00
"MessageFont"=hex:08,00,00,00,00,00,00,00,90,01,00,00,00,00,00,00,00,00,4d,53,\
  20,53,61,6e,73,20,53,65,72,69,66,00,18,45,00,00,50,7e,00,00,38,7e,63,00,00,\
  00,00,00,01,00
"IconFont"=hex:06,00,00,00,00,00,00,00,90,01,00,00,00,00,00,00,00,00,4d,53,20,\
  53,61,6e,73,20,53,65,72,69,66,00,ea,80,17,73,9a,82,ff,42,89,00,03,00,54,01,\
  82,81,ff,42
"IconVerticalSpacing"="-1125"
"Shell Icon BPP"="16"
"Shell Icon Size"="32"
"MinAnimate"="1"
```

Figure 2-4: This registry file is designed to change registry information about your desktop window metrics.

As you can see in the third line of this sample file, this .REG file holds the contents of the `HKEY_USERS\.Default\Control Panel\Desktop\WindowMetrics` subkey. You can compare it to the existing entries by opening the subkey in the Registry Editor. If the changes it makes are minor, you may want to enter them by hand, rather than merging this file with the existing registry information.

EXPORTING REGISTRY FILES You can export the contents of the registry, either in its entirety or by selecting a specific branch or subkey. This is, of course, a backup of the key, which you can import back into the registry if necessary. The Export Registry File dialog box (see Figure 2-5) works like a Save dialog box. Pick a folder and a filename to export (save) the file.

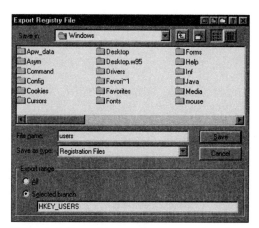

Figure 2-5: Exporting a registry or a registry key means you are saving the data in the form of a file.

In the example shown in the previous figure, the entire HKEY_USERS branch is to be exported. This resulted in a text file of almost 400K. The nearer the top of a branch you start your export operation, the larger the exported file will be; an entire registry export can reach several megabytes in size, depending on your system configuration.

TIP If you are exporting the registry (or parts of the registry) in order to experiment, or to examine the changes that were made, change the .REG extension that the Registry Editor assigned to the file to .TXT (or another extension). This will prevent your "experiment" from accidentally being merged back into the system registry, should you happen to double-click the file. Changing it to .TXT means it will be opened by Notepad or Wordpad.

CONNECTING TO NETWORK REGISTRIES It's also possible to open the registry on another computer that you can access over the network. If you are working in Windows NT 4 and the remote computer is also running Windows NT 4, you don't have to take any preliminary steps before using this feature. If your computers are running Windows 95/98, or if you are running Windows NT 4 and trying to manipulate the registry of a connected Windows 95/98 computer, you have to set up the Windows 95 or 98 system (this is covered in the next section) to enable remote registry editing, as explained here.

To open the registry of a connected computer, select Connect Network Registry, and when the Connect Network Registry dialog box appears (see Figure 2-6), type the name of the computer you want to access. You must have the appropriate rights on that computer, of course.

Figure 2-6: If you have the appropriate rights, you can connect to the registry of a remote computer and manipulate it.

If you don't know the name of the system whose registry you wish to open, click Browse to search the network for the appropriate machine. When you've finished, you can select the Disconnect Network Registry option from the registry menu to close your network remote registry connection.

Once you've opened the registry of another computer, it appears in the left pane of the Registry Editor, just below the entries for your local system. The top level is the Computer Name of the remote system, rather than the My Computer entry shown for the local machine.

The changes you make in that remote registry are as immediate as those you make to your own machine. Remember that if you export registry information to provide backup for changes made on the remote machine, the .REG file will be stored on your local machine (unless you have a share mapped to the local storage on the remote system). So if you export more information than you can store on a floppy disk, you'll need a method for getting that backup .REG file to the remote system in case your registry edits create a problem.

USING REMOTE REGISTRY SERVICES WITH WINDOWS 95 AND 98   For this to work properly on a Windows 95 or 98 computer, you first need to install and configure the remote registry services. Here's how to set up remote registry capabilities (you need the Windows 95 or 98 distribution CD):

1. Open the Network Control Panel applet and choose Add.

2. Choose Service, and then choose Have Disk.

3. Enter the path to the files you need. They are located in the \ADMIN\ NETTOOLS\REMOTREG folder on the Windows 95 CD-ROM.

4. Highlight Microsoft Remote Registry and click OK.

Once Microsoft Remote Registry Services is installed, you need to enable the service. To enable remote registry services, open the Passwords Control Panel applet, select the Enable Remote Administration of this server check box, and then add and confirm a password.

PRINTING THE REGISTRY   Use the Print command to print the entire registry or just selected branches or subkeys. Make sure you have plenty of paper if you're planning to print the entire registry or one of the large subkeys such as HKEY_LOCAL_COMPUTER.

EDITING THE REGISTRY

You can make modifications to the registry via the Edit menu, which is context sensitive. It offers different options, depending on which pane of the Registry Editor is active.

For example, the Modify option is only available when you've selected a value in the right-hand pane of the Registry Editor (see Figure 2-7). Also, the Delete and Rename options will appear grayed out unless a value is highlighted.

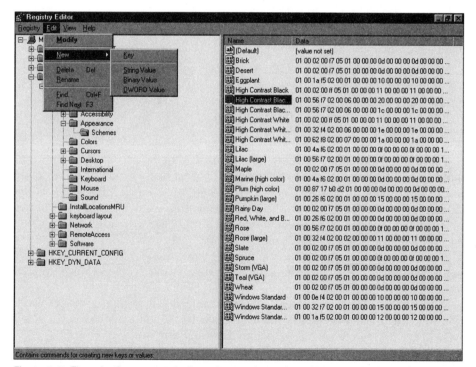

Figure 2-7: The selections you make in each pane determine which commands are available on the Edit menu.

MODIFYING DATA   The Modify command gives you the same result as double-clicking the name of any value. There are three possible results when you execute this option. If the icon for the value has the letters "ab," then it's a String value, and modifying this opens the Edit String Value dialog box. If the icon is the little binary icon (ones and zeros), then it's either a Binary value or a DWORD value. The Modify command opens the appropriate dialog box, indicating whether you need to enter a binary value or a DWORD value.

CREATING NEW ENTRIES   The New command has a submenu that offers choices for creating a new entry:

- ◆ Select Key to create a new subkey entry in the left pane of the Registry Editor.

- ◆ Select String Value, Binary Value, or DWORD Value to create a new value in the right pane of the editor (connected to the selected key in the left pane, of course).

You don't need to put data into the value you've created until later. If you don't enter data, you'll get these default values:

- ◆ String   [value not set]

- ◆ Binary   [zero-length binary value]

- ◆ DWORD 0x00000000 [0]

For a String value, the Registry Editor inserts a new value entry in the right pane and highlights it. To name the new entry, just begin typing the new value name at this point. If you hit Enter without entering a name, the entry gets the default name New Value #1. If other unnamed entries exist, the numeric value is incremented accordingly (this could create a string of entries labeled New Value #1, New Value #2, New Value #3, ad infinitum).

For a Binary entry, the entry is a numeric value, up to 64K in length. At this point, you can immediately enter data, if necessary. Otherwise, to change it later, use the Modify command.

A DWORD value entry is always a 4 byte value, also known as a double-word. You can enter data at the time you create the entry; if you enter data later, you'll have to use the Modify command to enter the value you need.

You can use either the Menu bar option or simply right-click in the right pane of the Registry Editor to create a new value (this is much like adding a new folder in Explorer). In any case, whether it's a new key in the left pane or a value in the right pane, the entry will be added under the currently highlighted entry.

There are only two real restrictions on creating keys and values:

◆ You cannot add top-level keys.

◆ Each subkey at a given level must have a unique name. You can have multiple keys with the same name (and you'll find many keys with identical names in an unmodified registry), but they can't have the same parent key – so keys at the same relative level can have the same name, but two keys of the same parent at the same level cannot.

DELETING REGISTRY ITEMS   You can use the Delete command to remove either the highlighted key or the selected value. You'll be prompted to confirm the actual delete. There is no confirmation, however, of which key or value you are deleting, so it pays to double-check the highlighted item on the screen before confirming the delete. If you are performing wholesale editing of the registry, it's safest to export the key you are editing to a backup file before performing the edits. This enables you to restore just the branch or subkey you've been working on without needing to restore the entire registry – in case you've been a little too free with the Delete key. Remember that the Undo option is not available in the Registry Editor.

You can also delete a registry object by right-clicking the item you wish to delete, and then selecting Delete from the shortcut menu.

When you delete an object, all the keys below the selected key are deleted as well. If you try to delete a default value from a top-level key, you'll get the error message, "Unable to delete all specified values." The Registry Editor should gray out the Delete option in these situations (not only should you avoid deleting here, you actually *can't* delete), but for some reason the option remains available. This is one of the few cases where the Registry Editor protects you from doing something you shouldn't. In most cases, you are on your own!

RENAMING REGISTRY ITEMS   Use the Rename command to rename either keys or values. Be careful with this, because Windows expects almost all the default keys and values to retain their default names.

CHANGING THE VIEW

The View menu enables you to change the appearance of the Registry Editor in a few minor ways. It gives you the choice of toggling the Status bar at the bottom of the screen on and off, moving the split between the two view panes of the editor, and refreshing the panes of the editor to reflect changes (which you can also do by hitting F5).

Searching the Registry

The Find command in REGEDIT enables you to search the registry for either keys, values, or the data contained therein. When the Find dialog box appears (see Figure 2-8), you can enter a few characters from the name of the item you are looking for, or you can enter the entire name. Also, you can force the match to be exact for a word you've entered, by selecting the Match whole string only check box.

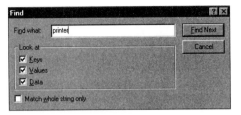

Figure 2-8: You can search for information in
the registry by examining any or all parts of it.

The search function drills down into whatever branch you've highlighted in the left pane of the Registry Editor. If you want to search the entire registry, highlight My Computer. If you know in which branch the information that you need resides, simply highlight that branch name. You can repeat the search across different branches by highlighting the branch or subkey that you want to search (after the initial search) and then hitting F3.

Using REGEDIT from the Command Line

In Windows 95 and 98, you can run REGEDIT from the DOS command line, as part of the emergency Startup disk you can create to provide a little additional system protection. As with many applications run from the command line, there are also command line switches to automate the use of REGEDIT at the DOS prompt.

You can get help for the switches by typing **REGEDIT** or **REGEDIT /?** after booting to the real-mode DOS prompt. All the other switches will also work within Windows 95 if you use the Run command on the Start menu. (If you are not at a real-mode DOS prompt, but you're using the shell to the command line from within Windows 95 or 98, you get the usual REGEDIT window.)

Running REGEDIT with these switches does not launch any user interface; instead, REGEDIT runs in the background or with no apparent user interface. Here are the valid switches:

◆ /L:*system*, where *system* specifies the path to, and filename of, the backup SYSTEM.DAT file.

◆ /R:*user*, where *user* specifies the path to, and filename of, the backup USER.DAT file.

◆ /E *filename* <*regpath*>, where *filename* specifies a .REG file you want to generate, using the <regpath> location.

◆ *filename*, which indicates you want to merge or import the .REG file identified by filename.

◆ /C *filename*, which replaces the entire registry content with the contents of filename.

You use a combination of these keys to perform the registry maintenance tasks you would want to perform from the command line. Look at some of these examples:

REGEDIT /L:*system* /R:**user** /E *filename <regpath>*

Make sure you use a fully qualified pathname for the .REG file. The <regpath> command is optional, and enables you to specify which registry branch to export. If you don't specify a branch, the command exports the entire registry.

REGEDIT /L:*system* /R:*user filename*

You need to include the filename and its extension. The command line import option won't assume the .REG file extension that the GUI version assumes.

REGEDIT /L:*system* /R:*user* /C *filename*

Once again, you need to specify path, filename, and extension. You should use this option only as a last resort, however, because it replaces the main keys of the registry with the contents of the specified filename. Even on a fast Pentium system, this can take quite a bit of time, depending on the size and complexity of the registry.

Navigating in REGEDIT

The most common way to wander through the registry when using REGEDIT is to use the mouse and click on keys and plus and minus signs; however, a number of navigational shortcuts can simplify your editing chores. Table 2-1 displays some of these navigational shortcuts.

TABLE 2-1 **Navigational Shortcuts**

Key combination	Function
F1	Provides context sensitive help
F2	Renames selected key
F3	Launches the Find command, and once that is configured, does Find Next
F5	Refreshes the display
F6	Toggles between foreground window panes
F10	Makes menu active
Shift+F10	Opens context menu (if open, it closes context menu)
Alt+Home	Opens My Computer icon
Alt+Home+←	Collapses all entries to top level, opens My Computer

continued

TABLE 2-1 **Navigational Shortcuts** *(Continued)*

Key combination	Function
↓	Opens the next key on the same level
↑	Open previous key on same level
→	Expands key or opens next level
←	Opens previous key or collapses level
Tab	Toggles between foreground window panes

Disabling Registry Access

When you're finally comfortable with the idea of editing the registry and know where to find the tools to do so, as a Windows 95/98 user you may see the message "Registry editing has been disabled by your administrator" when attempting to launch REGEDIT.

This means that your network administrator is staying a few chapters ahead of you, and has figured out how to use the Windows 95 or 98 System Policy Editor.

In fact, the network administrator has made a small change to the registry (sound familiar?). When REGEDIT launches, it attempts to open a registry key that may or may not exist. The key is `HKEY_CURRENT_USER\Software\Microsoft\Windows\CurrentVersion\Policies\System`. If the key doesn't exist, the Registry Editor is launched normally. If the key does exist, the application checks for the value of the DisableRegistryTools entry. If the value is set to 1, your network administrator is using the System Policy Editor to prevent users from running REGEDIT. If the value is set to 0, this means Policy Editor is being used, but registry editing is allowed and the Registry Editor is launched normally.

None of this applies to Windows NT, because Windows NT uses its built-in security to make the registry hive files inaccessible to users who don't have the correct system level access privileges.

Using REGEDT32

REGEDT32, which exists only in Windows NT, has a completely different interface than REGEDIT (see Figure 2-9).

Instead of the Explorer-like interface found in REGEDIT, REGEDT32 sports an interface derived from the Windows 3.*x* File Manager model. It opens an individual Window for each hive file, and doesn't use the two-pane registry view found in the newer Registry Editor. Each individual window does have two panes, but there is no context sensitivity to the location, nor are there any right-click context menus available.

REGEDT32 has a much richer choice of menu options than REGEDIT has. Shortcut menus are not available, so you can only access options via the menu choices. The following sections cover the various menu choices you can use to work with REGEDT32.

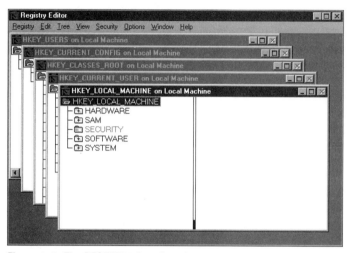

Figure 2-9: The REGEDT32 interface does not resemble the Explorer model.

Manipulating Registries and Registry Keys

You can accomplish basic manipulation of the registry via the Registry menu. It contains the fundamental tools for opening selected registries, saving and restoring hive files, and printing registry information (see Figure 2-10).

Here's how to perform some of the common tasks available on the Registry menu:

◆ Choose Open Local to open the registry hive files on the local machine (this is the default action when you launch REGEDT32).

◆ Use Close to shut the active registry windows. If you have multiple registries open, or have multiple views of the same registry, this command closes all windows (hive files) related to the currently active window.

◆ Use Load Hive to load a previously saved hive file back into the registry. This affects only the HKEY_USERS and HKEY_LOCAL_MACHINE predefined keys. The command is only active when these predefined keys are selected. When you load a hive back into the registry, the hive becomes a subkey of one of these predefined keys.

◆ Use Unload Hive to remove a hive from the registry. You must first save the hive file so you can restore it after using this command.

◆ Use Restore to restore hive information from a previously saved file. This action overwrites any existing keys in the selected hive.

◆ Use Save Key to save the selected key to a non-ASCII file.

◆ Use Select Computer to open the registry on remote NT systems. Enter the system name you wish to open, or browse the network for computers. By default, all computers visible to the network appear. You can only browse HKEY_USERS and HKEY_LOCAL_MACHINE branches on the remote systems.

◆ Use Print Subtree to send the currently selected subtree to the printer.

◆ Use Save Subtree As to save entire hives or selected parts as text files. As you can see in Figure 2-11, the format of these saved files is not the same as those saved by REGEDIT, even though it is standard ASCII text. The selected key and all subkeys are saved.

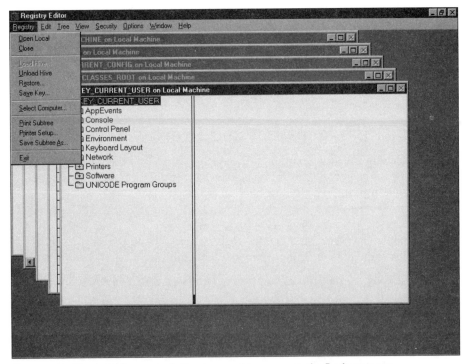

Figure 2-10: The tools for manipulating keys and trees are on the Registry menu.

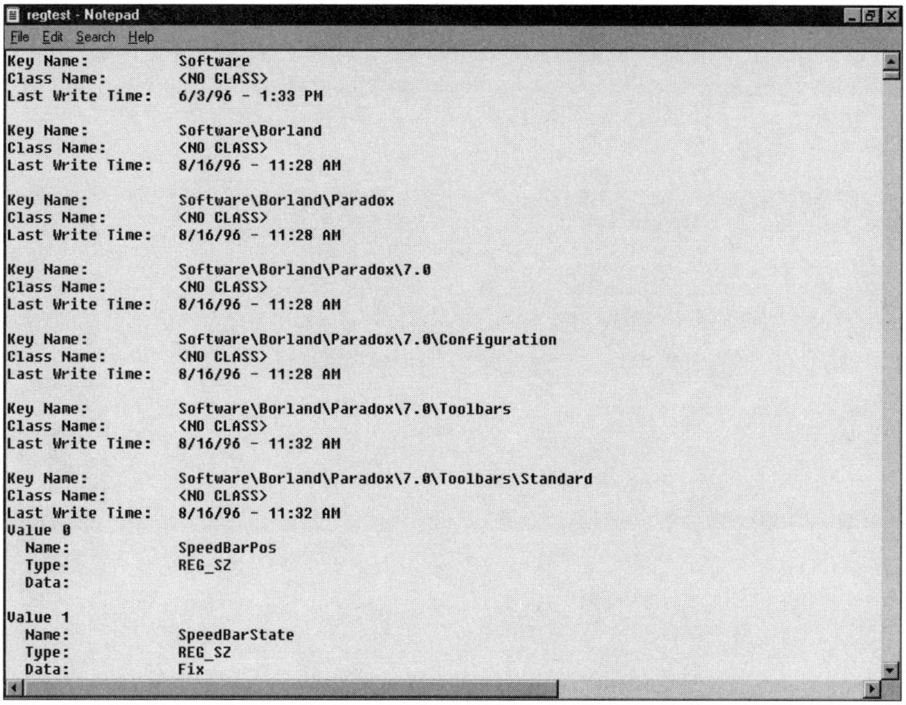

```
regtest - Notepad                                                    _ | & | X
File  Edit  Search  Help
Key Name:         Software
Class Name:       <NO CLASS>
Last Write Time:  6/3/96 - 1:33 PM

Key Name:         Software\Borland
Class Name:       <NO CLASS>
Last Write Time:  8/16/96 - 11:28 AM

Key Name:         Software\Borland\Paradox
Class Name:       <NO CLASS>
Last Write Time:  8/16/96 - 11:28 AM

Key Name:         Software\Borland\Paradox\7.0
Class Name:       <NO CLASS>
Last Write Time:  8/16/96 - 11:28 AM

Key Name:         Software\Borland\Paradox\7.0\Configuration
Class Name:       <NO CLASS>
Last Write Time:  8/16/96 - 11:28 AM

Key Name:         Software\Borland\Paradox\7.0\Toolbars
Class Name:       <NO CLASS>
Last Write Time:  8/16/96 - 11:32 AM

Key Name:         Software\Borland\Paradox\7.0\Toolbars\Standard
Class Name:       <NO CLASS>
Last Write Time:  8/16/96 - 11:32 AM
Value 0
  Name:           SpeedBarPos
  Type:           REG_SZ
  Data:

Value 1
  Name:           SpeedBarState
  Type:           REG_SZ
  Data:           Fix
```

Figure 2-11: You can save an ASCII text version of a hive by using Save Subtree As.

Modifying Keys and Values

The Edit menu contains the tools you use to add, delete, or modify keys and values (see Figure 2-12).

ADDING NEW KEYS

Choose Add Key to add keys to any hive. When this command is executed, you're prompted for the key name and class (the class refers to the data type). No pick list exists for data type in this dialog box, but you can create the key here, and then define the data type when you add a data value to the new key.

ADDING DATA VALUES TO KEYS

Choose Add Value to add a data value to any key. The dialog box offers a pick list, which enables you to select a String value (REG_SZ, REG_MULTI_SZ, and REG_EXPAND_SZ) or the Binary values (REG_DWORD and REG_BINARY).

DELETING KEYS AND DATA

Choose Delete to remove a key or to delete the value of a key. You will be prompted to confirm before the deletion is commited. You should make sure you've backed up the hives from which you are deleting keys. Once you confirm the Delete, you have no way to recover the information removed, short of restoring the key from a backup. Although we tend to think of the Registry Editors as editor programs, there is no Undo command to help you fix any editing errors that might occur.

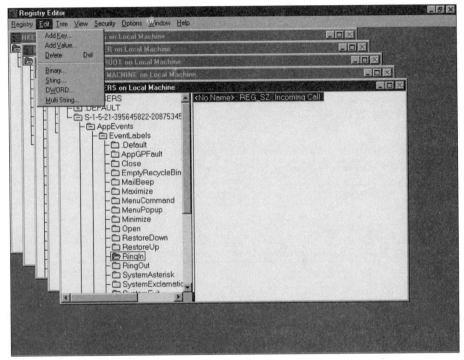

Figure 2-12: Use the Edit menu commands to work with the data in the registry.

OPENING THE BINARY EDITOR

Choose Binary to launch the Binary Editor (see Figure 2-13).

Enter data in the Data section of the window. To enter the data as binary digits, select Binary. If you need to enter the data in hexadecimal format, select Hex.

TIP   Double-clicking any REG_BINARY data type object launches the Binary
       Editor automatically.

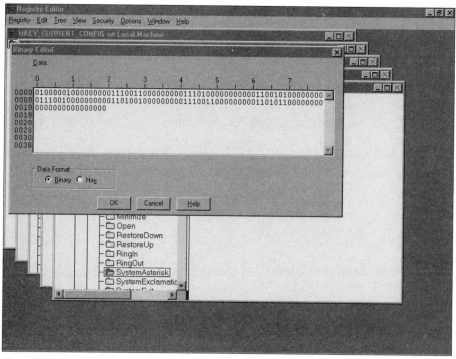

Figure 2-13: The Binary Editor enables you to edit binary value data in either binary or hexadecimal formats.

EDITING STRING VALUES

Choose String to launch the String Value Editor, a simple dialog box that enables you to enter or modify String values.

EDITING DWORD VALUES

Choose DWORD to launch the DWORD Editor. By default, all binary data defined as DWORD is displayed in hexadecimal format. You can also display the variable information in decimal or binary formats by clicking the appropriate radio button.

EDITING MULTI STRING VALUES

Choose Multi String to open the Multi String Editor. This editor's dialog box enables you to modify large and complex multi-string values.

Expanding the View

The Tree menu contains four entries you can use to expand or collapse the tree view of the registry hive file. All the commands, however, have two sets of keystroke alternatives that you are more likely to use, because most of us prefer using the keyboard rather than working with menus. For quicker action, try these:

Expand One Level	Alt+X or +
Expand Branch	Alt+B or *
Expand All	Alt+A or Ctrl+*
Collapse Branch	Alt+C or -

Controlling the View

The View menu contains the controls for the display of the registry hive data. It also includes the search function, and works just like the search function in REGEDIT's Edit menu.

You can change the view with the following commands:

◆ Tree and Data; Tree Only; Data Only defines the data displayed in the active windows (this applies only to the currently displayed hive file).

◆ Split sizes the view pane.

◆ Display Binary Data displays the currently selected Binary data value in your choice of Byte, Word or Dword format.

◆ Refresh All; Refresh Active refreshes the display after an edit. Refresh All updates all windows connected to the currently edited entry. Refresh Active only refreshes the active window.

◆ Find Key launches REGEDT32's search engine. Unlike the Find function in REGEDIT, Find Key can only search a single hive at a time. It also searches the entire hive, and can't be limited to Keys, Values, or Data. It does enable you to search both up and down a subtree – unlike REGEDIT, which only traverses down a tree or branch. It also lacks a Find Next command to simplify continuing searches.

Controlling Security

You can manipulate the security permissions and auditing features connected to the registry.

ASSIGNING RIGHTS AND PERMISSIONS

Choose Permissions to view and set control permissions on registry keys. Only three types of permissions available. The first two, Full Control and Read, are what you would expect from your experience with setting file permissions. The third type, called Special Access, enables you to create a subset of the user permissions for a specific group.

Selecting Special Access brings up a dialog box with check boxes for each type of action you can perform against the selected registry key (see Figure 2-14).

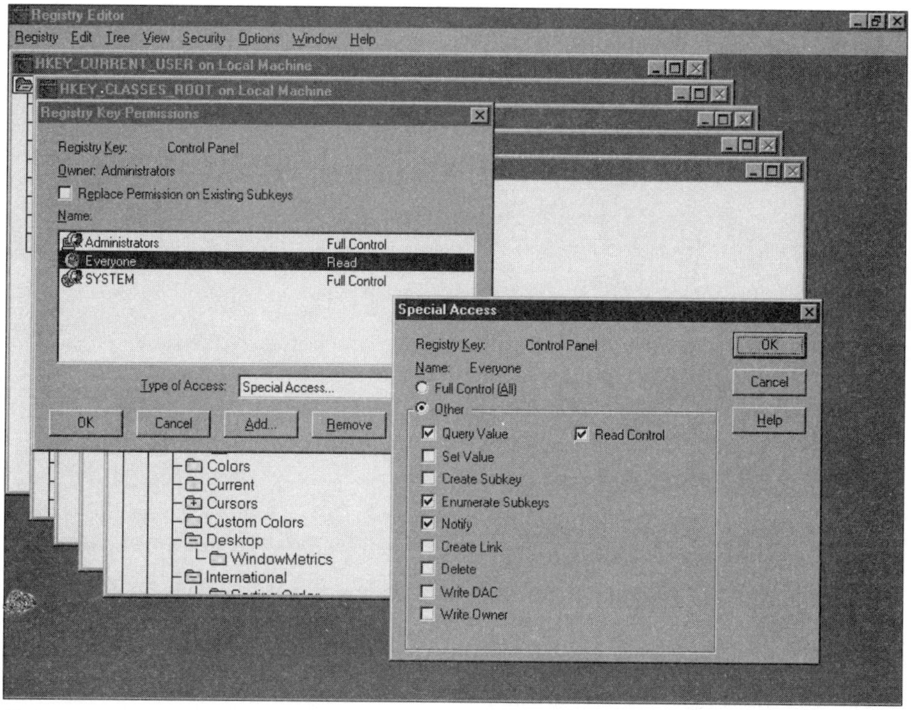

Figure 2-14: The Special Access dialog box enables you to design your own permissions for a group.

You can set ten different controls for special access. The controls and the rights attached to them are shown in Table 2-2.

TABLE 2-2 Special Access Controls

Controls	Rights
Query Value	Right to read the value entry from a registry key
Set Value	Right to set the value in a registry key
Create Subkey	Right to create subkeys of the selected registry key
Enumerate Subkey	Right to identify registry key subkeys
Notify	Right to audit registry keys
Create Link	Right to create a symbolic link in a particular registry subkey

continued

TABLE 2-2 Special Access Controls *(Continued)*

Controls	Rights
Delete	Right to delete the selected key
Write DAC	Right to access the key and create an Access Control List (ACL) for the key
Write Owner	Right to take ownership of a registry key
Read Control	Right to view the access security settings for a registry key

AUDITING REGISTRY ACCESS

The Auditing command configures the auditing of registry key actions (see Figure 2-15). All the permissions listed in Table 2-2, with the exception of Write Owner, can be audited for attempts made to operate on specific registry keys or the entire registry.

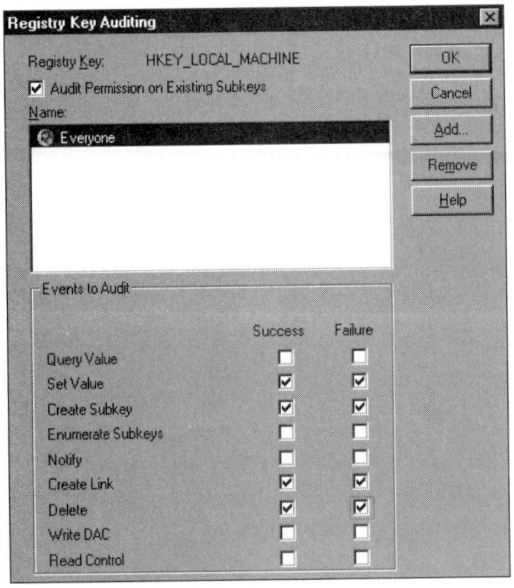

Figure 2-15: Choose the type of information you want to know, if people or applications are manipulating the registry.

You can configure this auditing procedure to apply to either failed or successful manipulations, or both. You can apply the audits to individual users or to entire groups. Only users from the Administrators group, or those who've had the Notify permission set in the Permissions command, can view the audits.

Table 2-3 describes what the Auditing functions allow.

TABLE **2-3** Auditing Functions

Function	Description
Query Value	Audits the attempt, by any system activity, to read a registry key value
Set Value	Audits the attempt, by any system activity, to set the value entry in a registry key
Create Subkey	Audits any attempt to create a registry subkey entry
Enumerate Subkeys	Audits any event that attempts to identify the subkeys of the targeted registry key
Notify	Audits the Notify event (this happens when an audited event occurs)
Create Link	Audits any event that attempts to create a symbolic link in any targeted key
Delete	Audits any attempt to delete any object in the registry
Write DAC	Audits attempts to access a key for the express purpose of changing the ACL for the key
Read Control	Audits user attempts to access the ACL on a monitored key

You can view audit events by opening the Windows NT Event Viewer from the Administrative Tools folder, or by choosing Start → Programs → Administrative Tools (Common) → Event Viewer. The events are recorded in the NT security log. Select Security from the Log menu item.

CHANGING OWNERSHIP

Choose Owner to display or change information about the ownership of a registry key. You can only change ownership if the current user is a member of the Administrators group or has the Write Owner permission granted.

Configuring Options for the Registry Editor

You can manipulate the configuration and confirmation options for the Registry Editor. Changes you make here apply across all the registry hive files.

SELECTING FONTS

The Font command launches the standard Windows Font selection and configuration dialog box. Unlike REGEDIT, REGEDT32 enables you to select and configure any of the installed fonts on the local system, for use as the standard display type for REGEDT32.

SETTING AUTO REFRESH

Auto Refresh sets the editor to refresh the registry windows automatically. If you select this, the Refresh All and Refresh Active options of the View menu will not be available.

 It is possible to select Auto Refresh when working with remote registries —
the selection is not grayed out. It won't work, however. Only Refresh All and
Refresh Active work on remote registries.

WORKING IN READ ONLY MODE

When selected, the Read Only Mode command prevents any changes from being written to the registry. If you're only browsing, this is a good setting to select because it can prevent accidental registry edits.

CONFIGURING CONFIRMATIONS ON DELETE

The Confirm on Delete option, which is selected by default, is responsible for the "Are you sure you want to do this" messages that appear when you attempt to delete registry entries. If you opt to deselect the feature, move slowly and carefully.

SAVING SETTINGS

Choose Save Settings to save the changes you've made to the options in this menu, as well as screen size and position information, so they're the defaults when you start REGEDT32 hereafter.

The Window and Help menus contain the standard Windows entries for these menus.

Summary

Becoming familiar with the operations you can perform in the Registry Editors can make troubleshooting your network easier. Although it's important to tread carefully when working in the registry, if you develop the habit of making backups before changing anything, you'll find that the editors become part of your power tools kit.

Chapter 3

Customizing With and Without the Registry

ALTHOUGH USERS CAN MAKE most modifications to their Windows 95, Windows 98, and Windows NT systems by manipulating the Control Panel applets, some changes can be accomplished only by editing the registry directly. I cover some of these modifications in this chapter, and some in other chapters dedicated to specific aspects of your system (such as the Desktop and Networking). In the previous chapter, I showed you how to use all the features of both versions of the registry Editor (REGEDIT and REGEDT32). Here, I'll show you how to apply those editing skills both within and outside the registry.

Customizing the Boot Process

Even though Windows 95, Windows 98, and Windows NT 4 configure themselves for the correct boot sequence for the hardware on which they're installed, I know you can't possibly leave well enough alone. Adding additional operating systems, changing the boot sequence, or just adding a custom logo file are all modifications many users enjoy making to their systems.

You have much more control over the Windows 95 and 98 boot process than you do over Windows NT. NT boot tinkering is an almost unknown concept, just because you can't do much to it.

While much of this section does not directly concern the registry, it's important to make sure you've done everything you can to get a clean boot of the system. Whatever can't be tweaked, fixed, or configured in the manner I describe here might be a registry issue (depending on the specifics of the problem).

Booting Windows 95 and 98

After Windows 95 and 98 begin their boot sequence, you'll see a message on the screen: "Starting Windows 95..." Almost everyone knows that you can bring up the Windows 95 or 98 character mode Start Menu if you hit F8 at this point. What you may not know is that you can hit a whole selection of function keys and key combinations at this point to cause Windows 95 and 98 to boot in different fashions.

You have seven boot choices:

◆ F4 – If you have a previous version of Windows 3.*x* or MS-DOS installed, and you've enabled it as a boot option in the MSDOS.SYS file (described later in this chapter), then hitting F4 at this point causes that previous operating system version to boot instead of Windows 95 or 98.

◆ F5 – Automatically launches Windows 95 or 98 in Safe Mode (640x480 video, no networking, and so on).

◆ CTRL+F5 – Boots directly to MS-DOS 7 without executing CONFIG.SYS or AUTOEXEC.BAT.

◆ Shift+F5 – Boots directly to MS-DOS 7, loads CONFIG.SYS and AUTOEXEC.BAT, but does not load any compressed drives.

◆ F6 – Boots into Windows 95 or 98 Safe Mode with networking support.

◆ F8 – Boots the Windows 95 or 98 character mode Startup Menu with these seven options listed as choices.

◆ Shift+F8 – Loads IO.SYS, and then continues to load CONFIG.SYS and AUTOEXEC.BAT one line at a time, giving you the opportunity to confirm each command-line option or prevent any command-line option from being executed.

If you want to restart Windows 95 or 98 to check these out, I know a shortcut. Of course, there are plenty of other good reasons to know about this shortcut, particularly if installing a program or changing a configuration option requires a reboot. No matter what the reason, this shortcut will speed up the time it takes to reboot Windows 95 and 98 (don't you sometimes feel you are actually aging while Windows reboots?). Here it is:

1. Select Shut Down from the Start Menu.

2. When the Shut Down dialog box appears, select Restart the Computer.

3. Hold down the Shift key when you click Yes.

4. The system exits the Windows 95 or 98 GUI, and then displays the message "Restarting Windows 95" (or 98).

You won't have to go through the entire system restart, which should significantly speed up your reboot time.

EDITING MSDOS.SYS

The MSDOS.SYS file that's in the root directory of your Windows 95 or 98 boot drive isn't the binary file you'd expect a .SYS file to be. Instead, it's an editable ASCII text file that looks a lot like the .INI files with which you may already be familiar.

To see the MSDOS.SYS file in the Windows Explorer, you need to have configured the Options settings on the View menu to show all files and to show file extensions for registered file types. To make changes, you need to reset the attributes (the file is Read-only, Hidden, System), and then restore the attributes after you've completed your changes.

Usually, the first entries in MSDOS.SYS are under the heading [Paths], and they contain information about boot directories and boot drives. The second section, called [Options], is the more interesting one.

The Options section may have no entries present, but it supports fifteen boot options that may interest you. With one exception, the parameters that each option supports are either a logical yes/no (1/0), or a time in seconds. Each setting is described as follows, including its default value:

- ◆ **Boot Delay=.** With a default value of 2 seconds, this is the setting that determines how long the "Windows 95 is Starting..." message remains onscreen before Windows 95 or 98 launches the GUI. If you can't seem to catch that brief window when trying to get the Windows 95 or 98 character mode Start Menu to appear, you may want to double or triple this setting. The older I get, the more time I need.

- ◆ **BootFailSafe=.** With a default value 0, this is the setting that gets changed when Windows 95 or 98 can't boot correctly and has forced a boot in Safe Mode. If you are having difficulty troubleshooting a problem, you can force the system to boot to Safe Mode (or to attempt to force a normal boot) by booting from a DOS floppy and changing this parameter. Safe Mode means that only standard VGA, mouse, and keyboard drivers are loaded, so no other drivers can interfere with the boot process.

- ◆ **BootGUI=.** With a default value of 1, this determines whether the system should boot to the Windows 95 or 98 GUI. If you have a dedicated system that's running Windows 95 or 98 as the operating system but only needs a DOS character mode interface, you can get rid of the GUI overhead by setting this parameter to 0. This is very handy if your job involves working in your company's character-based accounting system all day. Then, if you need the GUI, type **win** at the command line (reminds you of Windows 3.*x*, doesn't it?).

- ◆ **BootKeys=.** With a default value of 1, this setting enables (1=Yes) or disables (0=No) the Function Key boot settings described previously. If you are supporting users who you don't want interfering with the boot process in this manner, you can disable their capability to use the Function Keys during boot by changing this setting to 0.

- ◆ **BootMenu=.** With a default of 0, this determines whether the Windows 95 or 98 character mode Start menu appears. Change it to 1 if you want the menu; this setting can also be very useful when troubleshooting system problems.

◆ **BootMenuDefault=**. With a default value of 3, this setting determines which menu number choice is highlighted as the default option in the character mode Start Menu.

◆ **BootMulti=**. With a default of 0, this is the setting you need to change if you plan on dual-booting Windows 95 or 98 with another operating system (other than Windows NT, which uses its own Boot manager). I explain how to configure for multi-boot later in this chapter.

◆ **BootWarn=**. With a default value of 1, this setting determines whether Windows 95 or 98 warns you if it's booting into Safe Mode.

◆ **BootWin=**. With a default value of 1, this determines whether the computer will boot Windows 95 or 98 as the default operating system.

◆ **DblSpace=**. With a default value of 1, this determines whether the system loads DBLSPACE.BIN.

◆ **DoubleBuffer=**. With a default value of 1, this tells the system whether to double buffer SCSI devices.

◆ **DrvSpace=**. With a default value of 1, this determines whether the system loads DRVSPACE.BIN.

◆ **LoadTop=**. With a default value of 1, this determines whether the system loads COMMAND.COM in the high memory space (between 640K and 1MB).

◆ **Logo=**. With a default value of 1, this determines whether Windows 95 or 98 loads that annoying animated logo screen while booting. Tempting to change this one, eh?

◆ **Network=**. With a default value of 1, this determines whether Windows 95 or 98 boots into Safe Mode with Networking.

MAKING WINDOWS 95 OR 98 A DUAL-BOOT SYSTEM WITH WINDOWS 3.x OR MS-DOS

If you decide, after installing Windows 95 or 98, that you need the capability to run Windows 3.x or a previous version of MS-DOS, you can set up the system to do just that. You need the installation disks for that earlier operating system to make this process work. Windows 95 and 98 have their own dual-boot technique. Turning your system into a dual-boot system is really something Windows 95 or 98 could have done itself, had you installed it over the previous version of Windows or over MS-DOS.

Even if you want to install Windows 3.x, the first thing you need to do is install MS-DOS. Once that's done, you can just use the dual-boot to launch DOS, and then install Windows 3.x:

1. Make a copy of the MS-DOS boot disk.

2. On that disk, use the `ATTRIB` command to remove the system, hidden, and read-only bits from the IO.SYS and MSDOS.SYS files (attrib -r -h -s *.sys).

3. Rename those .SYS files as .DOS on the floppy.

4. On the floppy, rename COMMAND.COM as COMMAND.DOS

5. Copy IO.DOS and MSDOS.DOS to the root directory of your boot drive.

6. Reset the file attributes (attrib +r +h +s *.dos)

7. Copy COMMAND.DOS from the floppy to the root directory of your boot drive.

8. If you have specific commands that would go in the CONFIG.SYS and AUTOEXEC.BAT files of this operating system (such as the commands necessary to get the CD-ROM drive recognized), you can create CONFIG.DOS and AUTOEXEC.DOS, with the appropriate commands, in the root directory of the boot drive.

Reboot the computer. You can hit F4 to launch this newly installed operating system, or you can bring up the Windows 95 or 98 Start menu by hitting F8. You'll find the alternate operating system as choice 8 on the option menu.

Now that I've said all this, I'll admit it doesn't always work perfectly. Sometimes, Windows 3.*x* boots with an error message (frequently referencing a swap file problem) or fails to load devices and drivers. Sometimes Windows 95 and 98 fail to load the proper protected mode drivers.

Most of the time, Windows 95 and 98 do not need the contents of CONFIG.SYS or AUTOEXEC.BAT. The drivers needed by Windows 95 or 98 are loaded by Windows 95 or 98. However, if you have some peripheral or internal device for which no protected mode device driver is available, the old driver must be loaded for Windows 95 or 98 to recognize the device. Non-protected mode drivers are loaded in CONFIG.SYS.

So, test your Windows 95 or 98 system. Rename CONFIG.SYS and AUTOEXEC.BAT (I change the extensions to my initials, so I have CONFIG.KI and AUTOEXEC.KI in my root directory). Then, boot Windows 95 or 98. Go to the Device Manager (in the Systems applet in Control Panel) and check every device and its properties. Everything should be there — no device should have an exclamation point icon, nor a message telling you that the device is either not present or not configured properly. If this doesn't work, you can keep CONFIG.SYS, but a better idea is to contact the manufacturer of the device and demand a Windows 95 or 98 driver. Incidentally, Windows 95 and 98 ignore the stuff they don't need in CONFIG.SYS.

If you frequently boot into MS-DOS (not the same thing as going to the command prompt from within Windows 95 or 98), you still need the devices you load in CONFIG.SYS. If you get a swap file corruption message when booting into Windows 3.x, just reestablish the swap file.

One other thing to note: if you install Windows 95 or 98 over existing Windows 3.x, and you were running software applications in 3.x that you want to run in Windows 95 or 98, reinstall them while in Windows 95 or 98. The applications should go through a full Windows 95 or 98 installation to take care of all the registry notifications, installation of the proper DLLs, and other technical details.

Booting Windows NT 4

Due to Windows NT's nature as a secure, protected operating system, there aren't many files that you can actually edit to affect the way Windows NT boots. In fact, you are likely to edit only the BOOT.INI file that's in your boot drive root directory.

The BOOT.INI file has two sections. The first, [boot loader], comprises the current boot time-out value and the disk partition that contains the default boot operating system.

The second section, [operating systems], indicates which operating systems are installed on the system.

The contents of BOOT.INI reflect the operating systems in the computer. If you are running only Windows NT, the file looks similar to Figure 3-1. In this example, only the default Windows NT installations are included: the configured setup of NT, and the default VGA boot version that causes the system to boot in diagnostic mode with basic 640 x 480 video support. (In the system used for Figure 3-1, the operating system resides on the second hard disk in the system, rdisk(1), because drives are counted starting with disk 0).

For a system configured to boot Windows 95 or 98 as well as Windows NT, there would be an entry in the second section to cover the additional operating system choice (see Figure 3-2).

The simplest way to make changes in the BOOT.INI file is to launch the Control Panel System Properties applet. Select the Startup/Shutdown tab; you can then choose to make the operating system boot, and select the boot delay time from the System Startup box.

If you want to edit this file manually, you can follow these simple steps:

1. In Explorer, open BOOT.INI from the root directory of the first drive in the system.

2. Right-click the file, select Properties, and deselect the Read-only and Hidden file attributes.

3. Double-click the file; this launches the file into Notepad.

4. Edit the file and save your changes.

5. Change the attributes back to Read-only and Hidden.

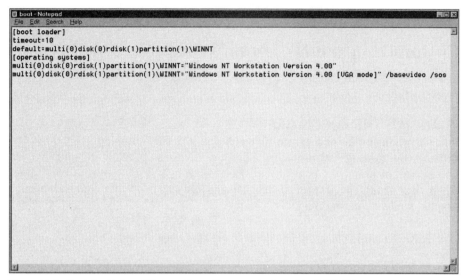

Figure 3-1: By default, two NT 4 configurations are included in BOOT.INI.

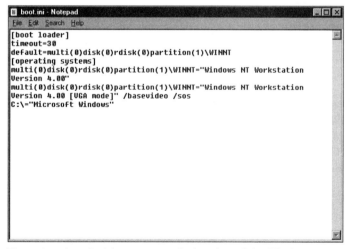

Figure 3-2: In a dual-boot system, the location of the Windows 95 or 98 operating system is included in BOOT.INI.

Don't forget about security attributes for files if you are using NTFS.

Customizing the NT Logon Process

In Windows NT, you can use the registry to change the standard, default logon process in several ways.

CHANGING THE LOGON GRAPHIC

You can change the look of the logon dialog box (the one you see behind the Ctrl+Alt+Del message), substituting a picture of your grandchild or your dog. Or, you may want to put the company logo on everyone's system (in case they forget where they work). The graphic is a bitmap, and you can substitute your own bitmap graphic file by changing the registry entry:

1. Go to `HKEY_LOCAL_MACHINE\Default\Control Panel\Desktop`.

2. Change the Wallpaper entry so it contains the path to your bitmap file.

ADDING A LOGON MESSAGE

You can also display a message to users during logon. In addition to the rather mundane dialog box that asks for Username, Domain, and Password, you may want to display a clever *bon mot*. You can have both a title and a message. When you invoke this option, a small information window will open after the user presses Ctrl+Alt+Del to begin the logon process. If you create a title, it appears in the title bar of that window. The message you create appears in the message window, along with an OK button. When the user presses OK, the logon process continues and the Logon Information dialog box appears. Here are the steps to accomplish this:

1. Go to `HKEY_LOCAL_MACHINE\SOFTWARE\Microsoft\WindowsNT\CurrentVersion\WinLogon` (see Figure 3-3).

2. Double-click the value for LegalNoticeCaption and enter a phrase for a title.

3. Double-click the value for LegalNoticeText and enter something clever, useful, or menacing (depending on your relationship with the users for which you're configuring systems). Figure 3-4 shows what users on my system see (the title bar says "Remember:").

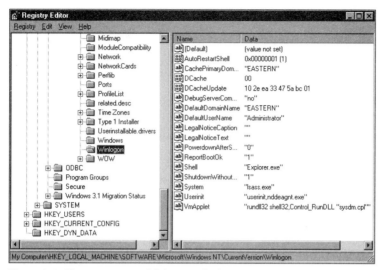

Figure 3-3: You can create additions to the logon messages in the
Winlogon subkey.

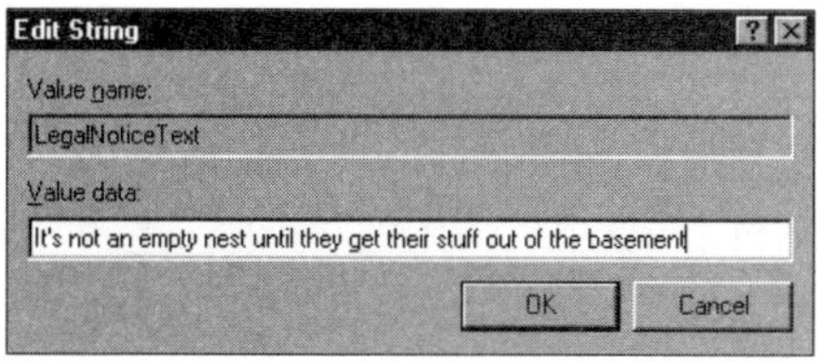

Figure 3-4: I've added an inspiring message to
the logon process.

AUTOMATING THE LOGON PROCESS

You can't bypass logon in NT (there's no Cancel button here, as there is in Windows
95 and 98) because it's an integral part of the security inherent in the operating
system. You can automate it, however, which saves the need to enter a name,
password, and domain, and to click OK. You can also do this in the HKEY_
LOCAL_MACHINE\SOFTWARE, Microsoft\WindowsNT\CurrentVersion\WinLogon
registry key, but instead of changing an existing value, you must add a new value.
It's easier and faster to do this with REGEDT32 than with REGEDIT, by the way.
Follow these steps:

1. In REGEDT32, move to the key noted in the preceding paragraph.

2. Choose Add Value from the Edit menu.

3. Name the new value AutoAdminLogon, and select a datatype of REG_SZ
   (see Figure 3-5). Choose OK.

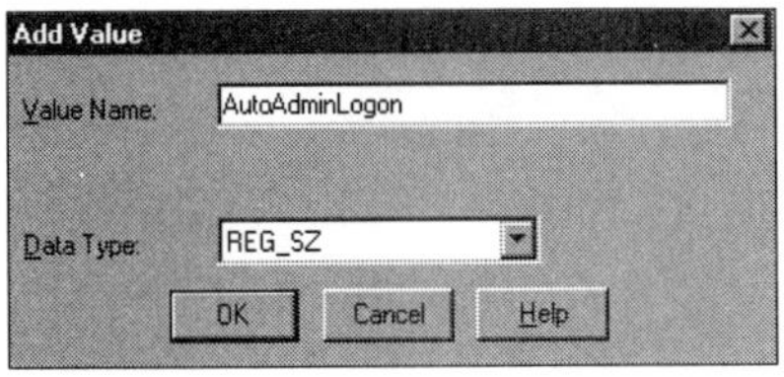

Figure 3-5: The creation of a new value
starts with a name and a data type.

4. In the String Editor dialog box, enter 1 as the value and choose OK.

5. Open DefaultDomain, DefaultUserName, and DefaultPassword, and enter
the appropriate information for the user who is being logged on
automatically (probably you).

The user will sail right through the next logon for this computer, without having
to fill in any information.

Of course, this process may involve some serious security issues, and you
shouldn't configure a computer for automatic logon unless you know it won't cause
security concerns.

In fact, the best place to use this process is on computers that have server-type
functions, such as a print server, or peer web services. This way, if a power problem
occurs, the computer will boot into its function automatically when the power
returns. Don't add a customized message to the computer's logon process, because
the message dialog box waits for an OK before proceeding to the logon.

If you decide to eliminate this function, return to the key and change the value
of AutoAdminLogon to 0; you don't have to delete the value. (If you want to put it
back, just make the value 1).

HIDING THE LAST LOGGED-ON USER

One nifty security trick is to eliminate the display of the name of the last logged-on
user (which prevents someone else from using that information). This is another
value that resides in the registry key discussed for the last several configuration
options – and again, it's a bit faster and easier to use REGEDT32.

1. Follow the steps described in the preceding section to add a value entry.

2. Name the entry **DontDisplayLastUserName** and choose a data type of
REG_SZ.

3. Set the string to 1. If you want to disable this function later, change it to 0.

Configuring the System Folders

If you are editing all the system files, you may decide at some point to relocate some of the system folders. Imagine your surprise – after you've carefully relocated the Favorites directory so that you can play with the browser entries – when you boot up and find that another copy of the folder is right back where it started!

This happens because Windows 95, Windows 98, and Windows NT 4 store the location of that folder in the registry, and will not let you move the folder without changing its location in the registry. Microsoft Office also adds its folder preferences to this location (which is why you can't get rid of that My Documents folder in the root). You'll find these folders set as values in the `HKEY_CURRENT_USER\SOFTWARE\Microsoft\Windows\CurrentVersion\Explorer\Shell Folders` subkey.

For Windows 95 and 98, the entries (and their default locations) that you're likely to find are:

Desktop	`C:\WINDOWS\Desktop`
Favorites	`C:\WINDOWS\Favorites`
Fonts	`C:\WINDOWS\Fonts`
NetHood	`C:\WINDOWS\NetHood`
Personal	`DriveOfficeIsInstalledOn\My Documents`
Programs	`C:\WINDOWS\Start Menu\Programs`
Recent	`C:\WINDOWS\Recent` (though some apps will change this)
SendTo	`C:\WINDOWS\SendTo`
Start Menu	`C:\WINDOWS\Start Menu`
Startup	`C:\WINDOWS\Start Menu\Programs\Startup\`
Templates	`C:\WINDOWS\ShellNew`

For Windows NT 4, the shell folders and default locations are:

AppData	`C:\WINNT\Profiles\username\Application Data`
Common Desktop	`C:\WINNT\Profiles\All Users\Desktop`
Common Programs	`C:\WINNT\Profiles\All users\Start Menu\Programs`
Common Start Menu	`C:\WINNT\Profiles\All Users\Start Menu`
Desktop	`C:\WINNT\Profiles\username\Desktop`
Favorites	`C:\WINNT\Profiles\username\Favorites`

Fonts	`C:\WINNT\Fonts`
NetHood	`C:\WINNT\Profiles\`*`username`*`\NetHood`
Personal	`C:\WINNT\Profiles\`*`username`*`\Personal`
Programs	`C:\WINNT\Profiles\`*`username`*`\Start Menu\Programs`
Recent	`C:\WINNT\Profiles\`*`username`*`\Recent`
SendTo	`C:\WINNT\Profiles\`*`username`*`\Sendto`
Start Menu	`C:\WINNT\Profiles\`*`username`*`\Start Menu`
Startup	`C:\WINNT\Profiles\`*`username`*`\Start Menu\Programs\Startup`
Templates	`C:\WINNT\Profiles\`*`username`*`\ShellNew`

Customizing Shortcut Menus

In case you've been asleep in a cave somewhere since August '95, shortcut menus (also called Context menus) are the menus that appear when you right-click in Windows 95, Windows 98, and Windows NT 4. Though they're used throughout the operating system, and within some applications, they are most commonly modified to add actions for use with Windows Explorer.

Shortcut menus are quick shortcuts to common commands. They are context-sensitive (hence the double name). The options on the shortcut menus change based on the type of file you select.

Some third-party applications take advantage of the capability to make changes and additions to the menus. Norton AntiVirus adds a command so you can check a file for an infection simply by right-clicking it, and WinZip adds an Add to Zip option so you can create Zipped files (it also adds an Extract To command for .ZIP files).

Opening a Single File Type with Different Programs

One of the most annoying things I've come across in recent months is the difficulty I face when I want to open an HTML file in my editor, rather than in my Web browser. The .HTM and .HTML extensions will be associated with your Web browser after you've installed any of them, so when you want to edit a file for your Web site, the document loads into your browser. Well, I'm going to show you how to click these files to open them in your editor of choice, without messing up your Web browser file associations:

1. Launch Windows Explorer and select View → Options → File Types. Scroll down until you find the association for your browser. In Figure 3-6, it shows up as a Netscape Hypertext Document, because Netscape is the registered browser.

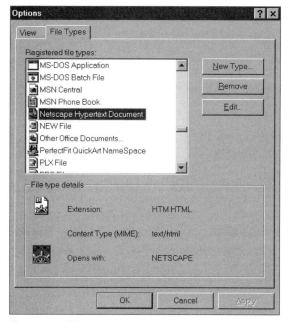

Figure 3-6: File extensions and their associated applications appear in the Explorer Options dialog box.

2. Highlight the entry and click the Edit button. This launches the Edit File Type dialog box. You'll now add a new action.

3. In the New Action dialog box, name the action **Open with HTML editor.**

4. In the box labeled Application Used to Perform Action, identify the application that you want to use as the editor. If the system knows where the executable resides, you'll only need to enter the name of the executable, in quotes, followed by "%1". You're using the Textpad editor, so your entry could read "textpad32.exe" "%1".

5. If you try to path to a nonexistent application or to the wrong location, you'll get an error message when you click OK. If everything's satisfactory, you can OK your way out of the application.

You can determine whether you need to add a fully qualified pathname, such as "e:\textpad\textpad32.exe", by attempting to run the application from the Start Menu Run command. If it launches from there, it will work without the full pathname.

A quick check of the shortcut menu for an HTML file shows you that the entry named Open with HTML editor has now been added to this registered file type.

Creating a Default Application for Opening Unknown File Types

Here's a little twist on the previous tip. How often have you double-clicked a file that you know you should be able to view, such as a file named READ.ME accompanying an application? You know that it's ASCII text, but you either have to open an editor first or go through the whole file association process. The preceding tip won't work because it requires that the file extension be registered, and that's the whole problem here. We'll show you how to edit the registry so those unknown file types get opened.

This can be particularly useful if you have an editor that can open both binary and text files—this way, you'll never get an error message. But for the sake of simplicity, use the Windows accessory program Wordpad (it's more capable than Notepad, and doesn't have the small file size limitations).

1. Launch REGEDIT.

2. Expand the key `HKEY_CLASSES_ROOT\Unknown\shell`.

3. In the left-hand pane, right-click the key and add a new key. Name the key **OpenWpad**.

4. In the right-hand pane, double-click the Default entry and change the value to **wordpad.exe %1**. For other applications, you may need to use a fully qualified pathname (in this case, that would be `C:\Program Files\accessories\wordpad.exe`).

5. Restart Windows.

Now, whenever you double-click an unregistered file type, it will immediately open in WordPad.

Adding Actions to the Send To Menu

You can add any application or container you want to the Send To application list. It's easy—just follow these steps:

1. Open Windows Explorer.

2. Select a folder or an application you want to add to the Send To menu.

3. Create a shortcut to the folder or application.

4. Right-click the shortcut and select Cut.

5. Open the folder `\Windows\SendTo` and paste the Shortcut in the folder.

That's it. Your new SendTo is immediately active.

Enhancing a Three-button Mouse

If you are one of the many users who have a Logitech three-button mouse, you've probably wondered what to do with that middle button. Logitech does offer software to reconfigure the buttons, but Windows 95 and 98 are so tied to the right-click shortcut menu that it would be counterproductive to change that. So, how about configuring the middle button to act as a single-click double-click button? For this to work, you first need to make sure that the Logitech mouse driver for Windows 95 is installed. Then, follow these steps:

1. Launch REGEDIT.

2. Expand the `HKEY_LOCAL_MACHINE\Software\MouseWare\Current Version` subkey.

3. This key contains several subkeys. Expand the `Global configuration settings` key.

4. In the left-hand pane, select the key labeled 0000.

5. In the right-hand pane, select the value DoubleClick and change its value to 1.

6. Exit the registry and restart Windows 95 or 98.

You can now save milliseconds per day by hitting the middle button once, rather than the left button twice, when you need to double-click.

Creating Other Common Customizations

You can make several other changes to the way your operating system behaves. This section presents some of the less dangerous, more common changes. These are commonly performed because they're useful.

Creating Your Own "Welcome to Windows 95" Tips

Remember that annoying "Welcome to Windows 95" message that popped up when you first started using it? Well, you can replace the tips the message presented (or simply add new tips) with your own thought for the day, or your favorite Dilbert quote. And it's really easy – simply follow these steps:

1. Launch the Registry Editor.

2. Open the subkey HKEY_LOCAL_MACHINE\SOFTWARE\Microsoft\Windows\CurrentVersion\explorer\tips.

3. Right-click in the right-hand pane of the Registry Editor and select New → String Value.

4. Name the new value (the last tip is number 47, so start with 48), hit Enter, and then double-click the new value.

5. The Edit String dialog box appears, so you can enter new value data. Type in whatever annoying platitude you'd like to impose on the system's user. Click OK.

6. If you prefer to replace the existing tips, just click the tip name (number) and edit the Value field in the dialog box that appears.

Of course, if the user has stopped using the Welcome window (by deselecting the Show This Welcome Screen Next Time You Start Windows options), aren't your efforts wasted? Of course not – just bring the window back. Find WELCOME.EXE in your Windows 95 or 98 directory and double-click it to open the screen and admire your work (see Figure 3-7). Then, click the option that causes it to appear whenever you start Windows.

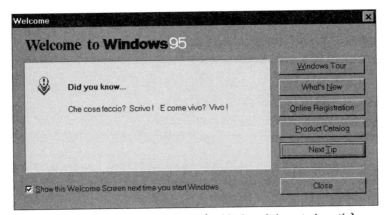

Figure 3-7: Enter a welcoming message (and it doesn't have to be a tip).

Stopping AutoRun from Launching CD-ROMs

One of the most annoying things that Windows 95, Windows 98, and Windows NT do is to AutoRun CDs. Oh sure, it's handy when you're launching CD-based games, or installing a new product. But if you're just trying to get a single file from an application CD or the operating system CD, you'll find yourself waiting for the AutoRun to execute, and then you'll have to deal with the pop-up screen that AutoRun has launched.

This is even worse when you are using a notebook computer and running on batteries. In this case, AutoRun is just eating up battery life for very little gain. Turning AutoRun off in Windows 95 and 98 is easy, and in Windows NT 4, it's only a minor pain. So I'll show you how to do it.

In Windows 95 and 98, you can accomplish this from the desktop — you don't need to use the registry:

1. Launch the System applet from Control Panel.

2. Select the Device Manager tab.

3. Scroll down to the CD-ROM entry and double-click it to expand the branch.

4. Select the CD-ROM drive on which you'd like to disable AutoRun (yes, you can have more than one CD-ROM drive listed).

5. Click the Properties button, and then select the Settings tab.

6. Under Options, deselect the Auto Insert Notification option (this tells Windows 95 or 98 not to scan CD-ROMs for autorun.inf files).

7. Click OK, and then click OK once more.

You'll need to restart Windows 95 or 98 for this to take effect.
In Windows NT 4, you have to use the registry to disable AutoRun:

1. Launch REGEDIT.

2. **Expand** `HKEY_LOCAL_MACHINE\System\CurrentControlSet\Services\Cdrom`.

3. In the right-hand pane, double-click the AutoRun icon.

4. Change the number in the Value Data field from 1 to 0.

Restart Windows NT 4 for this change to take effect.

Getting Rid of Shor~t Fil~e Name~s

When Windows 95 and 98 create the 8.3 DOS compatible filename, they're really only giving you a six-character name plus a tilde and a number. If you'd rather just see the first 8 characters of the filename, here's a little trick to slow down Windows' use of the tilde. And don't worry—if you have two long filenames that share the first 8 characters, Windows will revert to the six-character/tilde/number format. Follow these steps:

1. Launch REGEDIT.

2. Expand `HKEY_LOCAL_MACHINE\System\CurrentControlSet\Control\FileSystem`.

3. In the right-hand pane, create a new Binary value.

4. Name the value **NameNumericTail** and set its value to 0.

Bye-bye, tilde!

You should be aware, however, that you have a much higher risk of overwriting existing files when you do this, so if your system tends to accumulate many files with the same or similar names, don't make this registry change.

Creating an Object for a File

Applications often create empty file objects that you can click to launch the application. Then, you can open a file with preselected file properties that you or the application has chosen. You can create your own empty objects and link them to a specific application by following these steps:

1. Create an empty file (a document or spreadsheet, for example) for the program you want to use.

2. Copy that file to the `C:\Windows\ShellNew` folder.

3. Launch REGEDIT, open the `HKEY_CLASSES_ROOT` key, and then scroll down to the file extension used by the application.

4. In the left-hand pane of REGEDIT, right-click the selected extension and choose to create a new key. It will be created as a subkey of the extension you've selected. Name this new key `ShellNew`.

5. Switch to the right-hand pane, right-click the background, and create a new String Value. Name the value **FileName**.

6. Double-click the new FileName entry and enter the name of the empty file you created in step 1, in the Value data field of the Edit String dialog box.

Close REGEDIT, and this addition takes effect immediately.

Preventing Changes to Your Desktop

Are you sharing your computer with your children? And every time you come home from work, do you find yourself having to reconfigure the desktop because the kids have moved things around, or made changes to the desktop? (Nothing like booting up and finding 26 shortcuts to the latest Barbie game.)

Maybe your workstation at the office is shared by another user who has absolutely no sense of order and adds shortcuts to your desktop in a sloppy manner (or maybe you like haphazard arrangements, and the other user is incredibly, compulsively neat, which drives you nuts).

Well, here's a trick for making Windows 95, Windows 98, and Windows NT forget those changes and reboot with the desktop look you worked so hard to create.

1. Launch REGEDIT.

2. Expand the key `HKEY_CURRENT_USER\Software\Microsoft\Windows\CurrentVersion\Policies\Explorer`.

3. In the right-hand pane, double-click the entry NoSaveSettings. Set its value to 1. If this value doesn't exist, right-click and add the new value (it's a string value).

That's all it takes. When you want to change the desktop, change the value to 0, make any other changes you want, and reboot. Then, change the value back to 1 to prevent additional changes.

Summary

This chapter covered different ways you can customize your system, using either the registry or the control panel. You learned how to customize boot folders, system folders, and shortcut menus. Chapter 4 will cover more customization options.

Chapter 4

Customizing Desktops

ALL THE WINDOWS DESKTOPS in your network can be customized for users, for the convenience of administrators, or to enhance security. The parts of the registry you use for desktop customization are a bit less risky to hack, because most of the changes you make won't cause severe system problems. It's unlikely that a system will fail to boot if you make errors in desktop configurations. However, the work involved in fixing errors that cause the loss of a desktop function can be considerable – so back up the registry, or the key you're planning to work on, before you open the registry editor.

Customizing the Default Icons

All Windows desktops present a number of default icons after installation of the operating system. My Computer and the Recycle Bin always appear on the desktop; other icons may also appear, depending on the installation options or the configuration of the computer.

You can change the name, the icon, or both, of any of the default icons; in fact, you could remove any of them (although there's rarely a reason to do so).

Changing or Removing Default Icons

To get to the keys for the desktop icons, expand HKEY_CLASSES_ROOT and find the key named CLSID, which means Class ID. The keys are listed alphabetically, but don't worry if you don't see CLSID as you begin to browse – there are two separate alphabetic lists, one after the other. The first list includes the registered file types (you're actually looking at a list of file extensions). Then, the alphabet starts over again after the last entry in the first set (which may be .zip if you use WinZip, or perhaps .xlw, which is an Excel Workspace file).

Expand CLSID and you'll see a number of subkeys – a vast number, even an overwhelming number of subkeys, in fact. Figure 4-1 shows just a small portion of the CLSID listing, none of which have English names (these are all system ID's).

The Briefcase information is in the following subkey:

```
{85BBD920-42A0-1069-A2E4-08002B30309D}
```

The data for this subkey shows the name of the resource, "Briefcase". You can change the name if you wish. Just double-click the data item in the right-hand pane and enter a new name in the Edit String dialog box (see Figure 4-2).

If you want to change the icon for the Briefcase, expand the key and select the `DefaultIcon` subkey. The data item that you see in the right pane is the path to the DLL file that has the icon, and indicates the specific icon assigned to the Briefcase. The syntax of this information is:

```
"%SystemRoot%\system32\syncui.dll,0"
```

where `%SystemRoot%` is the name of the directory in which your Windows operating system software resides (usually Windows for Windows 95 and 98, and WINNT for Windows NT 4), and `system` or `system32` is the subdirectory that holds the DLL file, respectively.

`Syncui.dll,0` is the name of the DLL file that contains the icon (many .DLL files contain icons), and 0 is the first icon available in this file (computers start counting with zero).

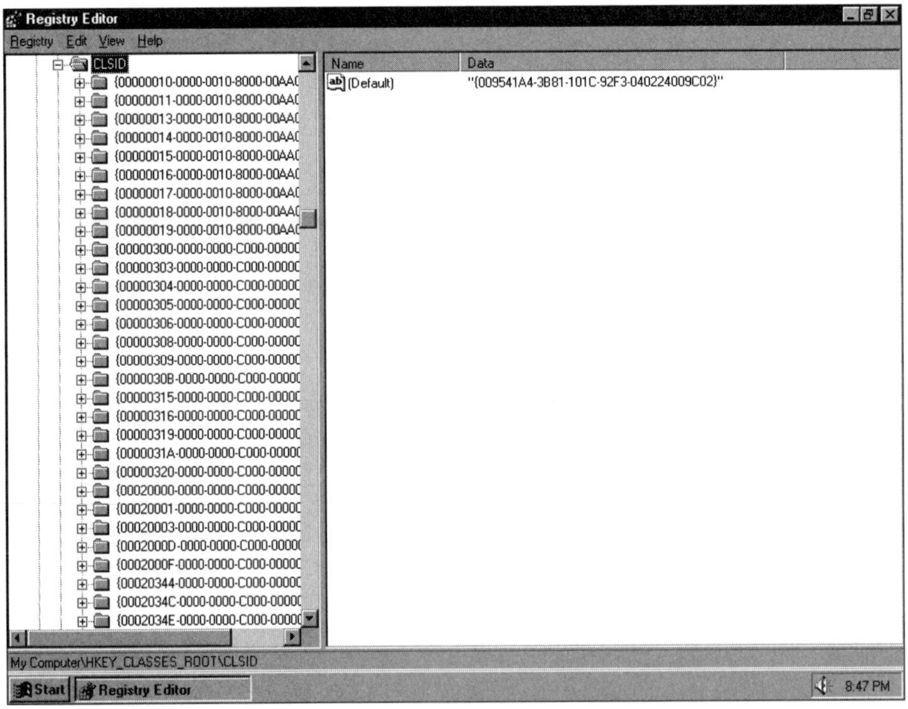

Figure 4-1: The `CLSID` subkeys contain system information that the operating system and applications need.

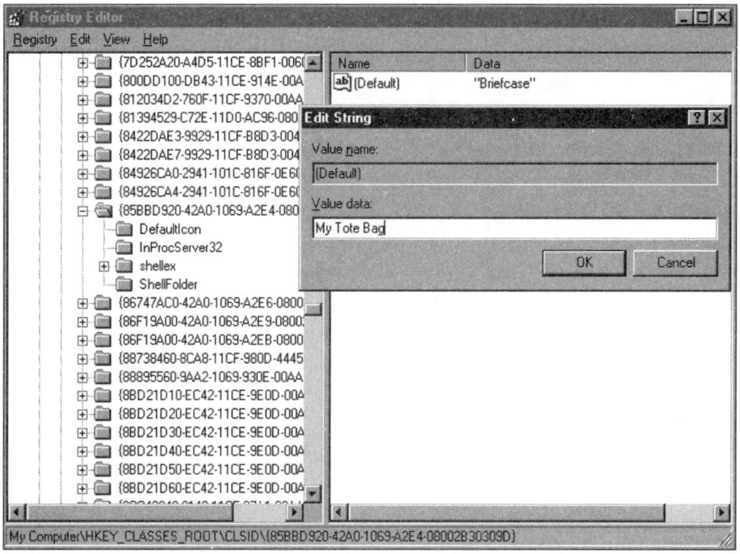

Figure 4-2: Enter a new name for the Briefcase and don't worry about the quote marks — they'll be added when you choose OK.

You can perform the same manipulations for the other desktop icons, which you'll find in the following \CLSID subkeys:

◆ Control Panel {21EC2020-3AEA-1069-A2DD-08002B30309D}

◆ Dial Up Networking {992CFFA0-F557-101A-88EC-00DD010CCC48}

◆ Inbox {00020D75-0000-0000-C000-000000000046}

◆ My Computer {20D04FE0-3AEA-1069-A2D8-08002B30309D}

◆ Network Neighborhood {208D2C60-3AEA-1069-A2D7-08002B30309D}

◆ Printers {2227A280-3AEA-1069-A2DE-08002B30309D}

◆ Recycle Bin {645FF040-5081-101B-9F08-00AA002F954E}

◆ The Internet {FBF23B42-E3F0-101B-8488-00AA003E56F8}

◆ Microsoft Network {00028B00-0000-0000-C000-000000000046}

Now, if you want to change the name of your Recycle Bin to something else (perhaps "Dustbin" if you're from England), you can.

Understanding the Default Icon Subkeys

Subkeys exist under each of the CLSID keys, and the number of subkeys varies depending on the key. The following list describes the most common subkeys:

♦ DefaultIcon, which is the icon used for objects managed by this CLSID.

♦ InprocServer, which is the DLL associated with objects of this type.

♦ InprocHandler, which is the DLL that manages these object types.

♦ InprocServer32, which is used if the object is a 32-bit process server.

♦ LocalServer, which is the path and filename of the server program.

♦ ShellEx, which defines shell extensions associated with the CLSID.

♦ ProgID, which is the name of the associated ProgID or File Type.

Changing the Desktop Values

The appearance and behavior of the desktop are controlled within the registry, and a small difference exists between Windows 95/98 and Windows NT 4 in the way the data is stored.

In Windows 95 and 98, HKEY_CURRENT_USER\Control Panel\Desktop includes entries similar to the following (your entries will vary depending on the configuration options you've chosen):

♦ Wallpaper, which is the path and filename of the .BMP file you're using as wallpaper.

♦ TileWallpaper, with an entry of 1 or 0, which indicates whether the bitmap you're using for wallpaper should be tiled over your screen.

♦ ScreenSaveLowPowerActive, with an entry of 1 or 0, which indicates whether Low Power Standby is enabled (if you have a power-saving monitor).

♦ ScreenSaveLowPowerTimeout, which is the time delay before your monitor switches to low-power standby mode. The data for time delay is in seconds and the entry exists only if the previous entry has "1" as the data.

♦ ScreenSavePowerOffActive, with an entry of 1 or 0, which indicates whether automatic powering off is enabled (for power-saving monitors).

♦ ScreenSavePowerOffTimeout, with an entry indicating the number of seconds before power off takes effect (only exists if the feature is enabled).

Optimizing Explorer's Refresh

Most of the time, when you make changes to the currently open directory of an open Windows Explorer screen, you have to press F5 to refresh the screen. But this is the '90s, and you shouldn't have to perform a task manually that you could easily automate. So, let's enable the automatic screen refresh feature:

1. Launch REGEDIT.

2. Expand the `HKEY_LOCAL_MACHINE\System\CurentControlSet\Control\ Update` subkey.

3. In the right-hand pane, double-click the Update Mode entry. This brings up the Edit Binary Value data entry screen. The last two digits will be 01 (in Windows 95 and 98, 01 are the only digits). Change the last digit to any value between 2 and 7.

4. Save the change and exit REGEDIT.

5. Restart Windows.

This change is global and will now automatically update any screen for which you previously used the F5 Refresh command, as soon as there's any change.

Customizing Shortcuts

Desktop shortcuts are terrific because they save time and energy. You can customize them with just a few steps.

To get rid of the little arrow on a shortcut (which for some reason really annoys me, and if it annoys you too, you'll appreciate this), follow these steps:

1. Open `HKEY_CLASSES_ROOT` and move to the second alphabetic section of entries to find the subkey `lnkfile`.

2. When you select `lnkfile`, the data in the right-hand pane appears. Select the entry IsShortcut.

3. Press F2 to change the name of the entry, and enter any letter in place of the initial letter I.

4. Press Enter to complete the edit of the entry name.

Reboot, and when your desktop reappears, all those little arrows will be gone.

If you don't like the words "Shortcut to" on the icon title for all your desktop shortcuts, and you always edit the title to get rid of it, you can train Windows to stop putting that phrase in the title. I refer to it as "training" Windows because you have to do it a few times until the operating system gets the idea. Create at least seven shortcuts, one after the other. As you create each shortcut, edit the title to remove the words "Shortcut to," and then go on to create the next shortcut. The easiest way to do this is to open Explorer to a folder containing several executable files, and drag each file to the desktop (you can delete these after the training session is over). After you've done this at least seven times, Windows suddenly makes the next shortcut without the words "Shortcut to" in the title. Windows finally "got it" and will never use those words again.

See Chapter 6 for information about Microsoft's PowerToys, which contains a software solution for this problem.

Incidentally, if you find your desktop shortcuts aren't terribly useful because they're hard to get to when you have applications open, you can put the desktop on your taskbar. To do this, follow these steps:

1. Open My Computer.

2. Make sure the toolbar is displayed (if it's not, choose View → Toolbar).

3. Click the arrow to the right of the list box on the toolbar, and then scroll up and select Desktop (see Figure 4-3).

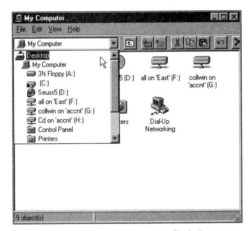

Figure 4-3: Click the up arrow to find the entry for the Desktop.

4. Minimize the window; an icon for it appears on your taskbar.

When you restart your computer, the Desktop icon will remain on the taskbar. Whenever you need to double-click a shortcut, click the Desktop icon to find the shortcut.

Customizing the Start Menu

You can control the way a user accesses the items on the Start menu. In REGEDIT, move to `HKEY_CURRENT_USER\Software\Microsoft\Windows\CurrentVersion\Policies\Explorer`. Then, add REG_DWORD entries to configure the user's Start Menu. To add such an entry, follow these steps:

1. Right-click in the right-hand pane of REGEDIT and choose New → DWORD Value (see Figure 4-4).

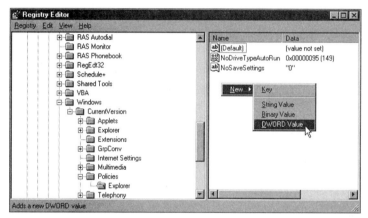

Figure 4-4: Add a new value to a key by choosing the correct data type from the shortcut menu.

2. A new value entry appears in the right-hand pane, with the default name New Value. The entry is highlighted (in edit mode) so you can type in the value name (see the choices under Step 4). Press Enter to complete the edit.

3. Double-click the entry to bring up the Edit DWORD Value dialog box (see Figure 4-5). Enter the Value data as described in the list of options in the next step.

4. Click OK to complete the procedure.

Some of the Start menu restrictions you may want to impose are listed as follows. In each case, a value of 1 imposes the restriction, and a value of 0 gives the Start menu option back to the user:

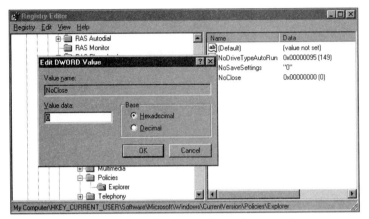

Figure 4-5: Change the Value data to configure the new entry.

- ◆ **NoClose,** which disables the Shut Down command on the Start menu. (The user can still use the Shut Down command in the Logon dialog box.)

- ◆ **NoCommonGroups,** which eliminates the menu choices in the common programs group section of the Start menu. Because this group includes administrative tools, it's often a good idea to restrict the group.

- ◆ **NoFind,** which eliminates the Find command.

- ◆ **NoRun,** which eliminates the Run command.

- ◆ **NoSetFolders,** which eliminates the Control Panel and Printers choices from the Settings menu item. These choices are also eliminated from My Computer and Explorer.

- ◆ **NoSetTaskbar,** which eliminates the Taskbar menu choice in the Settings menu item. This also prevents the user from right-clicking the taskbar to set properties (an error message appears).

You can perform all of these changes and more with the System Policy Editor (see Chapter 12 for more information about the Policy Editor).

Creating a Submenu for the Control Panel

If you want to find an applet in the Control Panel, you need to open the Start menu, choose Settings, choose Control Panel, wait for the Control Panel to open, scroll through the icons to find the applet you need, and double-click on the applet's icon to open it. That's just too many keystrokes. Why not make the applet a submenu item on your Start menu, so you can move your pointer to it and click once?

To do this, you need to create a new group named Control Panel on the Start menu; this way, all the applets in the Control Panel will be parts of that group. Follow these steps to accomplish this:

1. Right-click the Start button and choose Open.

2. When the Start Menu folder opens, choose File → New, and then choose Folder from the submenu.

3. Enter the folder name exactly as follows: **Control Panel. {21EC2020-3AEA-1069-A2DD-08002B30309D}** and then press Enter. (The period after Panel is necessary.)

Your Start menu presents the Control Panel with a cascading menu for every applet in the Control Panel (see Figure 4-6). You have one-click access from here on.

Figure 4-6: A click of the mouse is all that's needed now to configure any Control Panel applet.

When you press Enter after filling in the characters, you should see only the name Control Panel on the folder title. If you see all those characters, you've made a typing error, and you should go back and try it again (a frequent mistake is forgetting to type the closing curly brackets, so check for that first).

The period after the name of the folder (Control Panel) is a signal to Windows to use the characters following the period as a CLSID registry item, not as a title. In fact, you don't have to call the menu entry "Control Panel"; you can call it anything you wish (perhaps Configuration Apps), just make sure you enter the characters you want to use in front of the period.

You should have recognized the characters after the period as the CLSID for system icons that I mentioned earlier in this chapter (okay, you probably didn't memorize this CLSID as the Control Panel, but the format should have looked familiar). Now that you're reminded of this, think about providing one-click access to the objects in your Dial Up Networking folder or your Printers folder. To do this, repeat the same process but use the appropriate CLSID after the period.

Speeding Up Icon Display

Almost everything you look at from your desktop, including the Start menu, Explorer, My Computer, or any folders, displays icons. Windows stores the icons it displays in a cache file called ShellIconCache. This enables the icons to appear quickly because Windows doesn't have to fetch the icons from programs that contain them.

However, the cache is limited to 512 icons. When the cache gets filled, Windows doesn't start a process of eliminating one icon to make room for the next. Instead, the cache is destroyed and starts all over again, filling itself as you access objects. At that point, your desktop activities slow down (in fact, you may see your desktop redraw itself).

You can tell Windows to hold a larger number of icons in the icon cache by changing the registry:

1. In REGEDIT, go to `HKEY_LOCAL_MACHINE\SOFTWARE\Microsoft\` `Windows\CurrentVersion\Explorer`.

2. Right-click in the right-hand panel and choose New → String Value to create a new entry (see Figure 4-7).

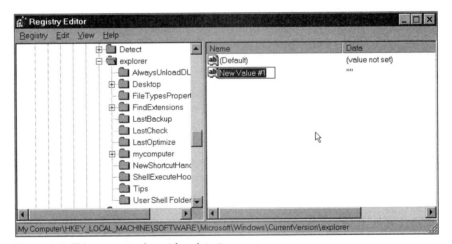

Figure 4-7: This new entry is a string data type.

3. Name the entry **Max Cached Icons** and press Enter.

4. Double-click the entry to open the Edit String dialog box (see Figure 4-8) and set the value at any high number (I used 3000).

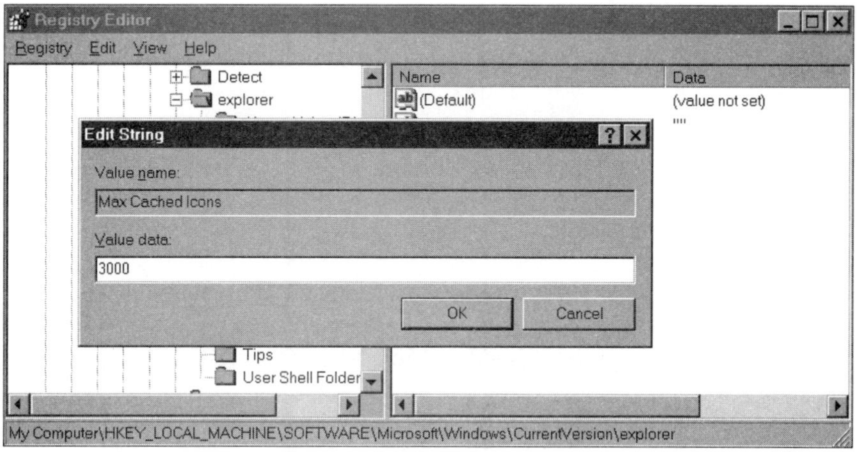

Figure 4-8: It's probably a good idea to quadruple the size of the icon cache.

5. Close REGEDIT.

Hiding Drives

You can restrict users' access to other computers in several ways.

Find the key HKEY_CURRENT_USER\Software\Microsoft\Windows\CurrentVersion\ Policies\Explorer and add a new DWORD value, NoNetHood, and set the value to 1 (it's a REG_DWORD data type). The Network Neighborhood icon is removed from the user's desktop, and connected computers do not appear in Explorer or My Computer.

In the same subkey, you can also limit the drives displayed in Network Neighborhood, My Computer, and Explorer. The new value is named NoDrives and the default value is 0, meaning the option is turned off and all drives are displayed. However, the lower 26 bits of the 32-bit word represent all the possible drives in the system. The bit farthest to the right is Drive A (there are a lot of useful reasons to keep users away from Drive A), and then you move to the left for each possible drive letter all the way to Z. Just set the bit to 1 for each drive you want to hide.

In the key HKEY_CURRENT_USER\Software\Microsoft\Windows you can also enter the following, setting a value of 1 to enforce the policy:

◆ NoEntireNetwork, which eliminates the Entire Network icon in Network Neighborhood, limiting the display in Network Neighborhood to the local workgroup or domain.

◆ NoWorkgroupContents, which eliminates from Network Neighborhood the icons that display the computers in the local workgroup.

However, users can still access the computers previously available in Network Neighborhood with the Run command, using the UNC (Universal Naming Convention) for any existing share: `\\computer_name\share_name`.

Summary

Most of the work you do in the registry to reconfigure desktops should be aimed at user productivity or computer security. Most administrators find that they don't need to make these changes globally—the changes are frequently user-dependent.

Chapter 5

The Control Panel and the Registry

MANY OF THE CONFIGURATION OPTIONS you perform in Control Panel applets are written back to the registry. Because of this, you have to restart Windows after a certain number of changes; the configuration doesn't take effect until the registry is read at bootup. In this chapter, you learn some of the Control Panel configuration options and link them back to the registry.

Windows 95 and 98 Hardware Information

The Windows 95 and 98 registries are more easily matched against the Control Panel applets, especially for hardware. The Plug and Play features of Windows 95 and 98 use the registry to examine the hardware during bootup and then match it against known information, which you can view in the System applet of the Control Panel.

As you boot into Windows 95 or 98, the operating system (OS) checks the hardware devices and identifies them. All the hardware-related resources are checked so you can be alerted about a conflict in I/O addresses, DMA channels, and IRQs. This process is called the *hardware enumeration process* (it checks bus enumerators) and the resulting data is used to build a tree of hardware. That tree is stored in the registry, which has keys and subkeys for it in HKEY_LOCAL_MACHINE\Enum.

The tree is built during the bootup process and by the time Windows 95 or 98 is running, this information is collected and fixed. Almost none of it is dynamic, so you can't hack the registry to change anything on the fly. It is, however, a good source of information about your system.

The following registry information is for a typical Windows 95 hardware setup. There are a few things you should know about this listing before you look at it:

◆ A lot of the lengthy Hex data has been removed, as few people could read it. The word "hex" appears in the value listed below, and in your registry that word is followed by a colon and the hex value itself.

- ◆ ConfigFlags values (hex data) are used by the OS and should rarely – if ever – be touched.

- ◆ The hardware items with multiple subkey entries are those items that have had more than one hardware configuration during the life of the registry. That's what happens when people change peripherals.

- ◆ This machine has an SCSI adapter with a number of drives attached to it. Computers with IDE or EIDE drives would have different subkeys.

- ◆ The subkey for `LogConfig` is a history of each configuration process performed for some items. I've deleted the data from the listing displayed (which is hex) because it doesn't add much to your examination of this listing.

Another interesting thing to note in this listing, as well as your own registry entries, is the number of entries in the subkey `HKEY_LOCAL_MACHINE\Enum\Root`. These are legacy hardware devices, not Plug and Play devices. Usually the newer the machine, the fewer entries appear in this subkey (this registry listing is from an older 486 of no particular brand).

Descriptions of the keys and subkeys appear below the particular key or subkey listing.

```
[HKEY_LOCAL_MACHINE\Enum]
```

This key is the beginning of information about hardware devices collected through Windows 95 *bus enumerators*. These are software programs designed to look at hardware during booting of the OS during installation and configuration.

```
[HKEY_LOCAL_MACHINE\Enum\Monitor]
[HKEY_LOCAL_MACHINE\Enum\Monitor\Default_Monitor]
```

The subkeys beneath the above key contain information about monitors, which have been configured for your computer. Often there is only one entry, but if you have changed monitors and reconfigured your system for a new monitor, both entries are here.

```
[HKEY_LOCAL_MACHINE\Enum\Monitor\Default_Monitor\0001]
"DeviceDesc"="(Unknown Monitor)"
"Class"="Monitor"
"Driver"="Monitor\\0000"
"Mfg"="(Standard monitor types)"
"HardwareID"="Monitor\\Default_Monitor"
"ConfigFlags"=hex
[HKEY_LOCAL_MACHINE\Enum\Root]
```

This is where the registry stores details about any devices in your computer that are not Plug and Play (Microsoft calls these *legacy devices*). The number of entries below this key is determined by the number of legacy devices you've installed. A Plug and Play BIOS and motherboard also influence this number. As a result, the number of entries in this section of the registry can vary greatly from computer to computer.

```
[HKEY_LOCAL_MACHINE\Enum\Root\*PNP0000]
```

This key is a container for the subkey which holds the settings for a computer's programmable interrupt controller. As a container subkey, it holds no specific values. The subkey under this one exists only if the computer has a non-Plug and Play motherboard.

```
[HKEY_LOCAL_MACHINE\Enum\Root\*PNP0000\0000]
"InfName"="MACHINE.INF"
"DeviceDesc"="Programmable interrupt controller"
"Class"="System"
"HardwareID"="*PNP0000"
"DetFunc"="*:DETECTPIC"
"NoSetupUI"="1"
"DetFlags"=hex:00,00,00,00
"BootConfig"=hex
"VerifyKey"=hex
"Driver"="System\\0000"
"Mfg"="(Standard system devices)"
"ConfigFlags"=hex
```

These are the settings for the non-Plug and Play motherboard in a computer. The number is 0000 because computers usually start numbering at 0.

```
[HKEY_LOCAL_MACHINE\Enum\Root\*PNP0000\0000\LogConfig]
```

Values in the LogConfig subkey offer a historical record of the various configurations created for the device. Because this particular subkey is for motherboard information (not a device configured by a user), there isn't any history.

```
[HKEY_LOCAL_MACHINE\Enum\Root\*PNP0200]
```

The preceding key lists the container for the subkeys for the DMA controller.

```
[HKEY_LOCAL_MACHINE\Enum\Root\*PNP0200\0000]
"InfName"="MACHINE.INF"
"DeviceDesc"="Direct memory access controller"
"Class"="System"
"HardwareID"="*PNP0200"
"DetFunc"="*:DETECTDMA"
"NoSetupUI"="1"
"DetFlags"=hex:00,00,00,00
"BootConfig"=hex
```

```
"VerifyKey"=hex
"Driver"="System\\0001"
"Mfg"="(Standard system devices)"
"ConfigFlags"=hex
```

The preceding shows settings for the system's DMA controller.

```
[HKEY_LOCAL_MACHINE\Enum\Root\*PNP0200\0000\LogConfig]
```

The preceding line is the configuration history for the DMA controller (another device that should not have any values in this subkey).

```
[HKEY_LOCAL_MACHINE\Enum\Root\*PNP0B00]
```

The preceding line is the container for the subkey for the CMOS clock.

```
[HKEY_LOCAL_MACHINE\Enum\Root\*PNP0B00\0000]
"InfName"="MACHINE.INF"
"DeviceDesc"="System CMOS/real time clock"
"Class"="System"
"HardwareID"="*PNP0B00"
"DetFunc"="*:DETECTCMOS"
"NoSetupUI"="1"
"DetFlags"=hex
"BootConfig"=hex
"VerifyKey"=hex
"Driver"="System\\0002"
"Mfg"="(Standard system devices)"
"ConfigFlags"=hex
```

The previous line includes the settings for the CMOS clock.

```
[HKEY_LOCAL_MACHINE\Enum\Root\*PNP0B00\0000\LogConfig]
```

The preceding offers the configuration history for the CMOS clock (this subkey should not have data).

```
[HKEY_LOCAL_MACHINE\Enum\Root\*PNP0100]
```

The previous line is the container for the subkey for the system timer.

```
[HKEY_LOCAL_MACHINE\Enum\Root\*PNP0100\0000]
"InfName"="MACHINE.INF"
"DeviceDesc"="System timer"
"Class"="System"
"HardwareID"="*PNP0100"
"DetFunc"="*:DETECTTIMER"
"NoSetupUI"="1"
"DetFlags"=hex
```

```
"BootConfig"=hex
"VerifyKey"=hex
"Driver"="System\\0003"
"Mfg"="(Standard system devices)"
"ConfigFlags"=hex
```

The preceding code represents settings for the system timer on this computer's motherboard.

```
[HKEY_LOCAL_MACHINE\Enum\Root\*PNP0100\0000\LogConfig]
```

The previous line offers the configuration history of the system timer (there should be no entries for this subkey).

```
[HKEY_LOCAL_MACHINE\Enum\Root\*PNP0800]
```

The preceding line is the container for the settings for the system speaker.

```
[HKEY_LOCAL_MACHINE\Enum\Root\*PNP0800\0000]
"InfName"="MACHINE.INF"
"DeviceDesc"="System speaker"
"Class"="System"
"HardwareID"="*PNP0800"
"DetFunc"="*:DETECTSPEAKER"
"NoSetupUI"="1"
"DetFlags"=hex
"BootConfig"=hex
"VerifyKey"=hex
"Driver"="System\\0004"
"Mfg"="(Standard system devices)"
"ConfigFlags"=hex
```

The preceding settings are for the system speaker—not related to any sound controller you may have installed in the computer. This is for the native, built-in speaker. These settings include the driver that the OS uses to communicate with, and control, the speaker.

```
[HKEY_LOCAL_MACHINE\Enum\Root\*PNP0800\0000\LogConfig]
```

The previous line represents the configuration history of the system speaker (another empty subkey).

```
[HKEY_LOCAL_MACHINE\Enum\Root\*PNP0C04]
```

The container for the subkey for numeric data processor is shown in the preceding line.

```
[HKEY_LOCAL_MACHINE\Enum\Root\*PNP0C04\0000]
```

```
"InfName"="MACHINE.INF"
"DeviceDesc"="Numeric data processor"
"Class"="System"
"HardwareID"="*PNP0C04"
"DetFunc"="*:DETECTNDP"
"NoSetupUI"="1"
"DetFlags"=hex
"BootConfig"=hex
"VerifyKey"=hex
"Driver"="System\\0005"
"Mfg"="(Standard system devices)"
"ConfigFlags"=hex
```

The previously listed settings are for the numeric data processor.

```
[HKEY_LOCAL_MACHINE\Enum\Root\*PNP0C04\0000\LogConfig]
```

The configuration history of the numeric data processor (another value-free subkey) is shown in the preceding line.

```
[HKEY_LOCAL_MACHINE\Enum\Root\*PNP0C01]
```

The previous line displays the container for the subkey for motherboard parameters.

```
[HKEY_LOCAL_MACHINE\Enum\Root\*PNP0C01\0000]
"InfName"="MACHINE.INF"
"DeviceDesc"="System board"
"Class"="System"
"HardwareID"="*PNP0C01"
"DetFunc"="*:DETECTSYSTEM"
"NoSetupUI"="1"
"DetFlags"=hex
"VerifyKey"=hex
"CPU"="80486DX"
"ConvMem"=hex
"ExtMem"=hex
"MachineType"="IBM PC/AT"
"Model"=hex
"Submodel"=hex
"Revision"=hex
"BIOSName"="American Megatrends"
"BIOSVersion"=""
"BIOSDate"="07/25/94"
"BusType"="ISA"
"Driver"="System\\0006"
"Mfg"="(Standard system devices)"
"ConfigFlags"=hex
"SetupMachineType"="Standard PC"
```

This information in this key is used during Setup. It is the only key that exists in this section of the registry, regardless of whether or not the motherboard is Plug and

Play. In addition, this subkey has no companion \LogConfig subkey — no history of configuration is kept.

If you upgrade your motherboard, you cannot rely on this subkey to change its information dynamically. You must reinstall Windows in order to rewrite this information to the registry.

```
[HKEY_LOCAL_MACHINE\Enum\Root\*PNP0303]
```

The preceding is the container for the subkey for the keyboard.

```
[HKEY_LOCAL_MACHINE\Enum\Root\*PNP0303\0000]
"InfName"="KEYBOARD.INF"
"DeviceDesc"="Standard 101/102-Key or Microsoft Natural Keyboard"
"Class"="Keyboard"
"HardwareID"="*PNP0303"
"DetFunc"="*:DETECTKBD"
"DetFlags"=hex
"BootConfig"=hex
"VerifyKey"=hex
"KeyboardID"=hex
"Driver"="Keyboard\\0000"
"Mfg"="(Standard keyboards)"
"ConfigFlags"=hex
```

The previously listed settings are for the keyboard attached to this computer.

```
[HKEY_LOCAL_MACHINE\Enum\Root\*PNP0303\0000\LogConfig]
```

The preceding shows the configuration history for the keyboard.

```
[HKEY_LOCAL_MACHINE\Enum\Root\*PNP0A00]
```

The container for the subkey, which holds information about the ISA bus system, is displayed in the foregoing code.

This computer is ISA, but other computers may have different bus systems. In this case, you would be looking at keys with the following identification:

- ◆ PNP0A01 for EISA bus systems

- ◆ PNP0A02 for MCA bus systems

- ◆ PNP0A03 for PCI bus systems

- ◆ PNP0A04 for ISA with VESA local bus systems

```
[HKEY_LOCAL_MACHINE\Enum\Root\*PNP0A00\0000]
"InfName"="MACHINE.INF"
"DeviceDesc"="ISA Plug and Play bus"
```

```
"Class"="System"
"HardwareID"="*PNP0A00"
"DetFunc"="*:DETECTBUS"
"NoSetupUI"="1"
"DetFlags"=hex
"VerifyKey"=hex
"Driver"="System\\0007"
"Mfg"="(Standard system devices)"
"ConfigFlags"=hex
```

The preceding settings are for the bus.

In this section of the registry you may also find information about non-Plug and Play devices that are not displayed here (because this computer does not have those devices). The following two subkeys are found here, and are usually restricted to laptop computers:

◆ PNP0C05 for advanced power management (APM) devices

◆ PNP0E00 for PCMCIA sockets

Also in this section of the registry you may find the following subkey:

◆ PNP0F0E for a generic PS/2 mouse

Following are some of the other mouse subkeys you might find:

◆ PNP0F0C for generic serial mouse

◆ PNP0F11 for standard (generic) bus mouse

◆ PNP0F00 for Microsoft bus mouse

◆ PNP0F01 for Microsoft serial mouse

◆ PNP0F03 for Microsoft PS/2 mouse

◆ PNP0F08 for Logitech serial mouse

◆ PNP0F09 for Microsoft Ballpoint Mouse (sometimes carries an ID of PNP0F0F)

Particular brands and connection types have their own IDs, which may not be listed in the previous examples.

```
[HKEY_LOCAL_MACHINE\Enum\Root\*PNP0903]
```

This is the container for the video controller subkey. The last two digits of this key's ID vary according to the specific device found. During installation, Windows 95 and 98 write the appropriate ID and settings information to the registry. They get the ID number from a file named MSDISP.INF, which you can find in your \%*SystemRoot*%\Inf **subdirectory.**

```
[HKEY_LOCAL_MACHINE\Enum\Root\*PNP0903\0000]
"InfName"="MSDISP.INF"
"DeviceDesc"="Trident 9320/9440/9660/968X/938X, Linear Accelerated
 For ISA/VL V1.31.04"
"Class"="DISPLAY"
"HardwareID"="*PNP0903"
"DetFunc"="*:DETECTTRIDENT"
"DetFlags"=hex
"BootConfig"=hex
"VerifyKey"=hex
"Driver"="Display\\0000"
"Mfg"="Trident Microsystems,Inc."
"ConfigFlags"=hex
```

The previously listed settings are for the video controller in the computer.

```
[HKEY_LOCAL_MACHINE\Enum\Root\*PNP0903\0000\LogConfig]
```

The preceding configuration history is for the video controller.

```
[HKEY_LOCAL_MACHINE\Enum\Root\*PNP0700]
```

The container key for the floppy disk controller is displayed in the preceding line.

```
[HKEY_LOCAL_MACHINE\Enum\Root\*PNP0700\0000]
"InfName"="MSFDC.INF"
"DeviceDesc"="Standard Floppy Disk Controller"
"Class"="fdc"
"HardwareID"="*PNP0700"
"DetFunc"="*:DETECTFLOPPY"
"NoSetupUI"="1"
"DetFlags"=hex
"BootConfig"=hex
"VerifyKey"=hex
"Driver"="fdc\\0000"
"Mfg"="(Standard floppy disk controllers)"
"ConfigFlags"=hex
```

The foregoing settings are for the floppy disk controller.

```
[HKEY_LOCAL_MACHINE\Enum\Root\*PNP0700\0000\LogConfig]
```

The configuration history for the floppy disk controller is displayed in the preceding line.

```
[HKEY_LOCAL_MACHINE\Enum\Root\*PNP0500]
```

The previously listed container subkey is for information about serial ports. There is a subkey for each serial port on the computer, the numbering begins at 0000. This computer has four serial ports.

```
[HKEY_LOCAL_MACHINE\Enum\Root\*PNP0500\0000]
"InfName"="MSPORTS.INF"
"DeviceDesc"="Communications Port (COM1)"
"Class"="Ports"
"HardwareID"="*PNP0500"
"DetFunc"="*:DETECTCOM"
"NoSetupUI"="1"
"DetFlags"=hex
"BootConfig"=hex
"VerifyKey"=hex
"PortName"="COM1"
"Driver"="Ports\\0000"
"Mfg"="(Standard port types)"
"ConfigFlags"=hex
"FRIENDLYNAME"="Communications Port (COM1)"
"Settings"=hex
```

The settings for COM1 are listed in preceding code.

```
[HKEY_LOCAL_MACHINE\Enum\Root\*PNP0500\0000\LogConfig]
```

The foregoing line shows the configuration history for COM1.

```
[HKEY_LOCAL_MACHINE\Enum\Root\*PNP0500\0001]
"InfName"="MSPORTS.INF"
"DeviceDesc"="Communications Port (COM2)"
"Class"="Ports"
"HardwareID"="*PNP0500"
"DetFunc"="*:DETECTCOM"
"NoSetupUI"="1"
"DetFlags"=hex
"BootConfig"=hex
"VerifyKey"=hex
"PortName"="COM2"
"Driver"="Ports\\0001"
"Mfg"="(Standard port types)"
"ConfigFlags"=hex
"FRIENDLYNAME"="Communications Port (COM2)"
```

The preceding settings are for COM2.

```
[HKEY_LOCAL_MACHINE\Enum\Root\*PNP0500\0001\LogConfig]
```

The configuration history for COM2 is displayed in the previous line.

```
[HKEY_LOCAL_MACHINE\Enum\Root\*PNP0500\0002]
```

```
"InfName"="MSPORTS.INF"
"DeviceDesc"="Communications Port (COM3)"
"Class"="Ports"
"HardwareID"="*PNP0500"
"DetFunc"="*:DETECTCOM"
"NoSetupUI"="1"
"DetFlags"=hex
"BootConfig"=hex
"VerifyKey"=hex
"PortName"="COM3"
"Driver"="Ports\\0002"
"Mfg"="(Standard port types)"
"ConfigFlags"=hex
"FRIENDLYNAME"="Communications Port (COM3)"
```

The foregoing code reveals the settings for COM3.

```
[HKEY_LOCAL_MACHINE\Enum\Root\*PNP0500\0002\LogConfig]
```

The configuration history for COM3 is displayed in the preceding line.

```
[HKEY_LOCAL_MACHINE\Enum\Root\*PNP0500\0003]
"InfName"="MSPORTS.INF"
"DeviceDesc"="Communications Port (COM4)"
"Class"="Ports"
"HardwareID"="*PNP0500"
"DetFunc"="*:DETECTCOM"
"NoSetupUI"="1"
"DetFlags"=hex
"BootConfig"=hex
"VerifyKey"=hex
"PortName"="COM4"
"Driver"="Ports\\0003"
"Mfg"="(Standard port types)"
"ConfigFlags"=hex
"FRIENDLYNAME"="Communications Port (COM4)"
```

The settings for COM4 are displayed in preceding code.

```
[HKEY_LOCAL_MACHINE\Enum\Root\*PNP0500\0003\LogConfig]
```

The previous line reveals the configuration history for COM4.

```
[HKEY_LOCAL_MACHINE\Enum\Root\*PNP0F08]
```

The preceding container key is for a Logitech serial mouse.

```
[HKEY_LOCAL_MACHINE\Enum\Root\*PNP0F08\0000]
"InfName"="MSMOUSE.INF"
"DeviceDesc"="Logitech Serial Mouse"
"Class"="Mouse"
```

```
"HardwareID"="*PNP0F08"
"DetFunc"="*:DETECTSERIALMOUSE"
"DetFlags"=hex
"VerifyKey"=hex
"ComInfo"=hex
"Driver"="Mouse\\0000"
"Mfg"="Logitech"
"ConfigFlags"=hex
```

The previously listed settings are for a Logitech serial mouse.

```
[HKEY_LOCAL_MACHINE\Enum\Root\*ADP1540]
```

This section of the registry contains information about the hard drive controller. This is the container key for an SCSI adapter. If you are not using an SCSI adapter for your hard drive, you won't see this particular key. Instead, you may see a key for an IDE hard drive controller (PNP0600).

```
[HKEY_LOCAL_MACHINE\Enum\Root\*ADP1540\0000]
"InfName"="SCSI.INF"
"DeviceDesc"="Adaptec AHA-154X/AHA-164X SCSI Host Adapter"
"Class"="SCSIAdapter"
"HardwareID"="*ADP1540"
"DetFunc"="*:DETECTAHA154X"
"NoSetupUI"="1"
"DetFlags"=hex
"BootConfig"=hex
"VerifyKey"=hex
"SCSIID"=hex
"Driver"="SCSIAdapter\\0000"
"Mfg"="Adaptec"
"ConfigFlags"=hex
```

Previously listed settings are for the SCSI controller.

```
[HKEY_LOCAL_MACHINE\Enum\Root\*ADP1540\0000\LogConfig]
```

The configuration history for the SCSI controller is displayed in preceding line.

```
[HKEY_LOCAL_MACHINE\Enum\Root\*PNP0400]
```

This is the container key for the parallel port. There is a subkey for each parallel port on the computer, starting with 0000. This particular computer has two parallel ports.

```
[HKEY_LOCAL_MACHINE\Enum\Root\*PNP0400\0000]
"InfName"="MSPORTS.INF"
"DeviceDesc"="Printer Port (LPT1)"
"Class"="Ports"
```

```
"HardwareID"="*PNP0400"
"DetFunc"="*:DETECTLPT"
"NoSetupUI"="1"
"DetFlags"=hex
"BootConfig"=hex
"VerifyKey"=hex
"PortName"="LPT1"
"Driver"="Ports\\0004"
"Mfg"="(Standard port types)"
"ConfigFlags"=hex
"FRIENDLYNAME"="Printer Port (LPT1)"
"DeviceStatus"=hex
```

The preceding settings are for LPT1.

```
[HKEY_LOCAL_MACHINE\Enum\Root\*PNP0400\0000\LogConfig]
```

The configuration history for LPT1 is shown in previous line.

```
[HKEY_LOCAL_MACHINE\Enum\Root\*PNP0400\0001]
"InfName"="MSPORTS.INF"
"DeviceDesc"="Printer Port (LPT2)"
"Class"="Ports"
"HardwareID"="*PNP0400"
"DetFunc"="*:DETECTLPT"
"NoSetupUI"="1"
"DetFlags"=hex
"BootConfig"=hex
"VerifyKey"=hex
"PortName"="LPT2"
"Driver"="Ports\\0005"
"Mfg"="(Standard port types)"
"ConfigFlags"=hex
"FRIENDLYNAME"="Printer Port (LPT2)"
"DeviceStatus"=hex
```

The settings for LPT2 are demonstrated in the previous code.

```
[HKEY_LOCAL_MACHINE\Enum\Root\*PNP0400\0001\LogConfig]
```

The preceding configuration history is for LPT2.

```
[HKEY_LOCAL_MACHINE\Enum\Root\*PNPB003]
```

This is the container key for a sound card. The last two digits of the ID vary according to the specific sound card. The information-linking sound cards and IDs are found in the WAVE.INF file, which is in your \%*SystemRoot*%\Inf subdirectory.

Incidentally, if you haven't installed a sound card, Windows 95 and 98 use your native sound system as a sound emulator, and insert a subkey here with the ID of PNPB007.

```
[HKEY_LOCAL_MACHINE\Enum\Root\*PNPB003\0000]
"InfName"="WAVE.INF"
"DeviceDesc"="Creative Labs Sound Blaster 16 or AWE-32"
"Class"="MEDIA"
"HardwareID"="*PNPB003"
"DetFunc"="*:DETECTSB"
"NoSetupUI"="1"
"DetFlags"=hex
"BootConfig"=hex
"VerifyKey"=hex
"Driver"="MEDIA\\0000"
"Mfg"="Creative Labs"
"ConfigFlags"=hex
```

The previous settings are for the sound card.

```
[HKEY_LOCAL_MACHINE\Enum\Root\*PNPB003\0000\LogConfig]
```

The preceding configuration history is for the sound card.

If you've installed a game port (joystick), this section of the registry holds the subkeys for it. The ID is PNPB02F.

```
[HKEY_LOCAL_MACHINE\Enum\Root\Net]
```

This is the container key for NICs. Assuming one NIC in the system, you may still see multiple subkeys because the registry separates the settings for network access from the settings for Dial-Up Networking.

```
[HKEY_LOCAL_MACHINE\Enum\Root\Net\0001]
"Class"="Net"
"Driver"="Net\\0001"
"DeviceDesc"="NE2000 Compatible"
"CompatibleIDs"="*PNP80D6"
"Mfg"="Novell/Anthem"
"ConfigFlags"=hex
"ForcedConfig"=hex
```

The network settings for the NIC are listed in previous code.

```
[HKEY_LOCAL_MACHINE\Enum\Root\Net\0001\Bindings]
"NWLINK\\0002"=""
"NETBEUI\\0001"=""
"MSTCP\\0000"=""
```

The preceding shows network bindings for the NIC.

```
[HKEY_LOCAL_MACHINE\Enum\Root\Net\0000]
"Class"="Net"
```

```
"Driver"="Net\\0000"
"DeviceDesc"="Dial-Up Adapter"
"CompatibleIDs"="*PNP8387"
"ConfigFlags"=hex
```

The Dial-Up Networking settings previously listed are for the NIC.

```
[HKEY_LOCAL_MACHINE\Enum\Root\Net\0000\Bindings]
"MSTCP\\0001"=""
"NWLINK\\0000"=""
"NETBEUI\\0000"=""
```

The Dial-Up Networking bindings for the NIC are listed in the preceding text.

```
[HKEY_LOCAL_MACHINE\Enum\Root\printer]
```

This is the container key for printers that have been installed on this computer. There is a subkey for each printer.

Note that the subkey 0000 is missing from this listing, as the original printer installed with this computer has been deleted. As printers are added and deleted the numbering system doesn't "fill in." It is possible to have quite a few identification numbers for printers, depending on how often you add or delete them.

```
[HKEY_LOCAL_MACHINE\Enum\Root\printer\0002]
"Class"="printer"
"Driver"="printer\\0002"
"Mfg"="Okidata"
"HardwareID"="Okidata_ML_320-IBM"
"DeviceDesc"="Okidata ML 320-IBM"
"ConfigFlags"=hex
"PrinterID"=hex
```

You'll find the settings for one of the printers installed on this computer in the preceding code.

```
[HKEY_LOCAL_MACHINE\Enum\Root\printer\0001]
"Class"="printer"
"Driver"="printer\\0001"
"Mfg"="Okidata"
"HardwareID"="Okidata_ML_520-IBM"
"DeviceDesc"="Okidata ML 520-IBM"
"ConfigFlags"=hex
"PrinterID"=hex
```

Here are the settings for one of the printers installed on this computer.

```
[HKEY_LOCAL_MACHINE\Enum\Root\printer\0003]
"Class"="printer"
```

```
"Driver"="printer\\0003"
"Mfg"="HP"
"HardwareID"="HP_LaserJet_Series_II"
"DeviceDesc"="HP LaserJet Series II"
"ConfigFlags"=hex
"PrinterID"=hex
```

The preceding settings are for one of the printers installed on this computer.

```
[HKEY_LOCAL_MACHINE\Enum\Root\UNIMODEM5A28D161]
```

This is the container key for any non-Plug and Play modems installed that conform to the UNIMODEM standard.

```
[HKEY_LOCAL_MACHINE\Enum\Root\UNIMODEM5A28D161\COM1]
"Class"="Modem"
"HardwareID"="UNIMODEM5A28D161"
"DetFlags"=hex
"DeviceDesc"="Sportster 28800"
"Driver"="Modem\\0000"
"Mfg"="U.S. Robotics, Inc."
"ConfigFlags"=hex
"FriendlyName"="Sportster 28800"
```

The previous settings are for the modem installed on the computer. Note that the subkey includes the serial port to which the modem is attached.

```
[HKEY_LOCAL_MACHINE\Enum\Network]
```

This section of the registry holds settings, generated by the bus enumerators, that investigate network devices and network services.

```
[HKEY_LOCAL_MACHINE\Enum\Network\NETBEUI]
```

The preceding is the container key for NetBEUI protocol, if installed. There are subkeys for each instance of the NetBEUI protocol, along with the bindings.

Each computer will have different subkeys depending on the protocols installed. Following are some of the protocols you might see subkeys for:

- NetBEUI

- NWLink (for Novell Netware IPX/SPX)

- NWREDIR

- NWSERVER (NetWare File and printer sharing)

- VREDIR (Microsoft Network Client)

- VSERVER (for Microsoft File and Printer sharing)

```
[HKEY_LOCAL_MACHINE\Enum\Network\NETBEUI\0001]
"Class"="NetTrans"
"Driver"="NetTrans\\0003"
"MasterCopy"="Enum\\Network\\NETBEUI\\0001"
"DeviceDesc"="NetBEUI"
"CompatibleIDs"="NETBEUI"
"Mfg"="Microsoft"
"ConfigFlags"=hex
```

The preceding settings are for a specific installed protocol.

```
[HKEY_LOCAL_MACHINE\Enum\Network\NETBEUI\0001\Bindings]
"VREDIR\\0005"=""
"VSERVER\\0011"=""
```

The bindings for the parent key's protocol are displayed in the previous code.

```
[HKEY_LOCAL_MACHINE\Enum\Network\NETBEUI\0000]
"Class"="NetTrans"
"Driver"="NetTrans\\0001"
"MasterCopy"="Enum\\Network\\NETBEUI\\0000"
"DeviceDesc"="NetBEUI"
"CompatibleIDs"="NETBEUI"
"Mfg"="Microsoft"
"ConfigFlags"=hex
```

The foregoing settings are for a specific installed protocol.

```
[HKEY_LOCAL_MACHINE\Enum\Network\NETBEUI\0000\Bindings]
"VREDIR\\0004"=""
"VSERVER\\0009"=""
```

The previous bindings are for the parent key protocol.

```
[HKEY_LOCAL_MACHINE\Enum\Network\VREDIR]
```

This is the container key for settings for the Microsoft Network Client protocol.

```
[HKEY_LOCAL_MACHINE\Enum\Network\VREDIR\0002]
"Class"="NetClient"
"Driver"="NetClient\\0000"
"MasterCopy"="Enum\\Network\\VREDIR\\0000"
"DeviceDesc"="Client for Microsoft Networks"
"CompatibleIDs"="VREDIR"
"Mfg"="Microsoft"
"ConfigFlags"=hex
```

The preceding settings are for a specific installed protocol.

```
[HKEY_LOCAL_MACHINE\Enum\Network\VREDIR\0002\Bindings]
"VSERVER\\0000"=""
```

The bindings for the parent key protocol are displayed in the previous code.

```
[HKEY_LOCAL_MACHINE\Enum\Network\VREDIR\0005]
"Class"="NetClient"
"Driver"="NetClient\\0000"
"MasterCopy"="Enum\\Network\\VREDIR\\0000"
"DeviceDesc"="Client for Microsoft Networks"
"CompatibleIDs"="VREDIR"
"Mfg"="Microsoft"
"ConfigFlags"=hex
```

The preceding settings are for a specific installed protocol.

```
[HKEY_LOCAL_MACHINE\Enum\Network\VREDIR\0005\Bindings]
"VSERVER\\0010"=""
```

The foregoing bindings are for the parent key protocol.

```
[HKEY_LOCAL_MACHINE\Enum\Network\VREDIR\0000]
"Class"="NetClient"
"Driver"="NetClient\\0000"
"MasterCopy"="Enum\\Network\\VREDIR\\0000"
"DeviceDesc"="Client for Microsoft Networks"
"CompatibleIDs"="VREDIR"
"Mfg"="Microsoft"
"ConfigFlags"=hex
```

The previously listed settings are for a specific installed protocol.

```
[HKEY_LOCAL_MACHINE\Enum\Network\VREDIR\0000\Bindings]
"VSERVER\\0002"=""
```

The bindings for the parent key protocol are shown in previous code.

```
[HKEY_LOCAL_MACHINE\Enum\Network\VREDIR\0001]
"Class"="NetClient"
"Driver"="NetClient\\0000"
"MasterCopy"="Enum\\Network\\VREDIR\\0000"
"DeviceDesc"="Client for Microsoft Networks"
"CompatibleIDs"="VREDIR"
"Mfg"="Microsoft"
"ConfigFlags"=hex
```

The foregoing settings are for a specific installed protocol.

```
[HKEY_LOCAL_MACHINE\Enum\Network\VREDIR\0001\Bindings]
"VSERVER\\0004"=""
```

The bindings for the parent key protocol are shown in preceding code.

```
[HKEY_LOCAL_MACHINE\Enum\Network\VREDIR\0003]
"Class"="NetClient"
"Driver"="NetClient\\0000"
"MasterCopy"="Enum\\Network\\VREDIR\\0000"
"DeviceDesc"="Client for Microsoft Networks"
"CompatibleIDs"="VREDIR"
"Mfg"="Microsoft"
"ConfigFlags"=hex
```

The settings for a specific installed protocol are listed in preceding code.

```
[HKEY_LOCAL_MACHINE\Enum\Network\VREDIR\0003\Bindings]
"VSERVER\\0006"=""
```

The previous bindings are for the parent key protocol.

```
[HKEY_LOCAL_MACHINE\Enum\Network\VREDIR\0004]
"Class"="NetClient"
"Driver"="NetClient\\0000"
"MasterCopy"="Enum\\Network\\VREDIR\\0000"
"DeviceDesc"="Client for Microsoft Networks"
"CompatibleIDs"="VREDIR"
"Mfg"="Microsoft"
"ConfigFlags"=hex
```

The preceding settings are for a specific installed protocol.

```
[HKEY_LOCAL_MACHINE\Enum\Network\VREDIR\0004\Bindings]
"VSERVER\\0008"=""
```

The bindings for the parent key protocol are shown in previous code.

```
[HKEY_LOCAL_MACHINE\Enum\Network\NWREDIR]
```

This is the container key for the NetWare client, if it is installed.

```
[HKEY_LOCAL_MACHINE\Enum\Network\VSERVER]
```

This is the container key for the settings for File and Printer sharing for Microsoft networks, if that service is enabled. There may be multiple subkeys (each with a number) under this container key, and also a subkey for bindings for each of those numbered subkeys. Many of the subkeys have identical information. I think the OS may install a subkey every time you open the configuration dialog box to check, or change, your settings (I'm unable to get any real explanation from Microsoft).

```
[HKEY_LOCAL_MACHINE\Enum\Network\VSERVER\0000]
"Class"="NetService"
"Driver"="NetService\\0000"
"MasterCopy"="Enum\\Network\\VSERVER\\0003"
"DeviceDesc"="File and printer sharing for Microsoft Networks"
"CompatibleIDs"="VSERVER"
"Mfg"="Microsoft"
"ConfigFlags"=hex

[HKEY_LOCAL_MACHINE\Enum\Network\VSERVER\0000\Bindings]

[HKEY_LOCAL_MACHINE\Enum\Network\VSERVER\0001]
"Class"="NetService"
"Driver"="NetService\\0000"
"MasterCopy"="Enum\\Network\\VSERVER\\0003"
"DeviceDesc"="File and printer sharing for Microsoft Networks"
"CompatibleIDs"="VSERVER"
"Mfg"="Microsoft"
"ConfigFlags"=hex

[HKEY_LOCAL_MACHINE\Enum\Network\VSERVER\0001\Bindings]

 [HKEY_LOCAL_MACHINE\Enum\Network\VSERVER\0002]
"Class"="NetService"
"Driver"="NetService\\0000"
"MasterCopy"="Enum\\Network\\VSERVER\\0003"
"DeviceDesc"="File and printer sharing for Microsoft Networks"
"CompatibleIDs"="VSERVER"
"Mfg"="Microsoft"
"ConfigFlags"=hex

[HKEY_LOCAL_MACHINE\Enum\Network\VSERVER\0002\Bindings]

[HKEY_LOCAL_MACHINE\Enum\Network\VSERVER\0003]
"Class"="NetService"
"Driver"="NetService\\0000"
"MasterCopy"="Enum\\Network\\VSERVER\\0003"
"DeviceDesc"="File and printer sharing for Microsoft Networks"
"CompatibleIDs"="VSERVER"
"Mfg"="Microsoft"
"ConfigFlags"=hex

[HKEY_LOCAL_MACHINE\Enum\Network\VSERVER\0003\Bindings]


[HKEY_LOCAL_MACHINE\Enum\Network\NWLINK]
```

This is the container key for settings for the IPX/SPX protocol.

```
 [HKEY_LOCAL_MACHINE\Enum\Network\NWLINK\0002]
"Class"="NetTrans"
"Driver"="NetTrans\\0005"
```

```
"MasterCopy"="Enum\\Network\\NWLINK\\0002"
"DeviceDesc"="IPX/SPX-compatible Protocol"
"CompatibleIDs"="NWLINK"
"Mfg"="Microsoft"
"ConfigFlags"=hex

[HKEY_LOCAL_MACHINE\Enum\Network\NWLINK\0002\Bindings]
"VREDIR\\0002"=""
"VSERVER\\0001"=""

[HKEY_LOCAL_MACHINE\Enum\Network\NWLINK\0000]
"Class"="NetTrans"
"Driver"="NetTrans\\0002"
"MasterCopy"="Enum\\Network\\NWLINK\\0000"
"DeviceDesc"="IPX/SPX-compatible Protocol"
"CompatibleIDs"="NWLINK"
"Mfg"="Microsoft"
"ConfigFlags"=hex

[HKEY_LOCAL_MACHINE\Enum\Network\NWLINK\0000\Bindings]
"VREDIR\\0003"=""
"VSERVER\\0007"=""
[HKEY_LOCAL_MACHINE\Enum\HTREE]
```

The preceding container key always has at least one data subkey beneath it. I have been unable to discover the purpose for this key.

```
[HKEY_LOCAL_MACHINE\Enum\HTREE\RESERVED]
```

```
[HKEY_LOCAL_MACHINE\Enum\HTREE\RESERVED\0]
```

```
[HKEY_LOCAL_MACHINE\Enum\ISAPNP]
```

This is the container key for ISA bus Plug and Play Devices.

```
[HKEY_LOCAL_MACHINE\Enum\ISAPNP\READDATAPORT]
```

```
[HKEY_LOCAL_MACHINE\Enum\ISAPNP\READDATAPORT\0]
"HardwareID"="ISAPNP\\READDATAPORT"
"Class"="System"
"Driver"="System\\0008"
"Mfg"="(Standard system devices)"
"DeviceDesc"="IO read data port for ISA Plug and Play enumerator"
"ConfigFlags"=hex

[HKEY_LOCAL_MACHINE\Enum\ISAPNP\READDATAPORT\0\LogConfig]
```

```
[HKEY_LOCAL_MACHINE\Enum\FLOP]
```

The preceding container key is for floppy disk controller settings.

```
[HKEY_LOCAL_MACHINE\Enum\FLOP\GENERIC_NEC__FLOPPY_DISK_]
```

```
[HKEY_LOCAL_MACHINE\Enum\FLOP\GENERIC_NEC__FLOPPY_DISK_\ROOT&*PNP070
 0&000000]
"RevisionLevel"="    "
"ProductId"="NEC  FLOPPY DISK"
"Manufacturer"="GENERIC "
"DeviceType"=hex
"Int13"=hex
"Removable"=hex
"CurrentDriveLetterAssignment"="A"
"HardwareID"="GENERIC_NEC__FLOPPY_DISK_,GenDisk,FLOP\\GENERIC_NEC__F
 LOPPY_DISK_"
"Class"="DiskDrive"
"Driver"="DiskDrive\\0000"
"Mfg"="(Standard disk drives)"
"DeviceDesc"="GENERIC NEC  FLOPPY DISK"
"ConfigFlags"=hex

[HKEY_LOCAL_MACHINE\Enum\SCSI]
```

This is the container key for the subkeys holding information about devices attached to an SCSI controller (if one is installed). For this computer, you'll see subkeys for four devices: hard drive, CD-ROM, Tape Drive, and Jaz Drive. There is a parent and child subkey for each device, the child holds the actual settings.

Notice that each device has a unique target ID, which is how the SCSI card identifies each device when it confirms its presence during the boot. This SCSI card has its own BIOS and boot process, and you configure the card and attached devices by pressing keys (Ctrl+A) during its boot. All of this occurs before the OS boots.

```
[HKEY_LOCAL_MACHINE\Enum\SCSI\QUANTUM_XP32150_____8]

[HKEY_LOCAL_MACHINE\Enum\SCSI\QUANTUM_XP32150_____8\ROOT&*ADP154
 0&000000]
"SCSITargetID"="0"
"SCSILUN"="0"
"RevisionLevel"="81HB"
"ProductId"="XP32150          "
"Manufacturer"="Quantum "
"DeviceType"=hex
"Int13"=hex
"CurrentDriveLetterAssignment"="C"
"HardwareID"="QUANTUM_XP32150_____8,GenDisk,SCSI\\QUANTUM_XP3215
 0_____8"
"Class"="DiskDrive"
"Driver"="DiskDrive\\0001"
"Mfg"="(Standard disk drives)"
"DeviceDesc"="Quantum XP32150          "
"ConfigFlags"=hex

[HKEY_LOCAL_MACHINE\Enum\SCSI\CHINON__CD-ROM_CDS-535__Q]

[HKEY_LOCAL_MACHINE\Enum\SCSI\CHINON__CD-ROM_CDS-
 535__Q\ROOT&*ADP1540&000030]
```

```
"AutoInsertNotification"=hex:01
"UserDriveLetterAssignment"="EE"
"SCSITargetID"="3"
"SCSILUN"="0"
"RevisionLevel"="Q20 "
"ProductId"="CD-ROM CDS-535   "
"Manufacturer"="CHINON   "
"DeviceType"=hex:05
"Removable"=hex:01
"CurrentDriveLetterAssignment"="E"
"HardwareID"="CHINON__CD-ROM_CDS-535__Q,GenCD,SCSI\\CHINON__CD-
 ROM_CDS-535__Q"
"Class"="CDROM"
"Driver"="CDROM\\0000"
"Mfg"="(Standard CD-ROM device)"
"DeviceDesc"="CHINON CD-ROM CDS-535   "
"ConfigFlags"=hex

[HKEY_LOCAL_MACHINE\Enum\SCSI\CONNER__CTMS__3200_____7]

[HKEY_LOCAL_MACHINE\Enum\SCSI\CONNER__CTMS__3200_____7\ROOT&*ADP154
 0&000040]
"SCSITargetID"="2"
"SCSILUN"="0"
"RevisionLevel"="7.10"
"ProductId"="CTMS  3200        "
"Manufacturer"="CONNER   "
"DeviceType"=hex:01
"CurrentDriveLetterAssignment"=""
"HardwareID"="GenTape"
"Class"="Tape"
"DeviceDesc"="CONNER CTMS  3200        "
"ConfigFlags"=hex
"Driver"="Tape\\0000"
"Mfg"="CONNER   "
"HWRevision"="7.10"

[HKEY_LOCAL_MACHINE\Enum\SCSI\IOMEGA__JAZ_1GB_____H]

[HKEY_LOCAL_MACHINE\Enum\SCSI\IOMEGA__JAZ_1GB_____H\ROOT&*ADP154
 0&000040]
"SCSITargetID"="4"
"SCSILUN"="0"
"RevisionLevel"="H.72"
"ProductId"="jaz 1GB          "
"Manufacturer"="iomega   "
"DeviceType"=hex:00
"Removable"=hex:01
"CurrentDriveLetterAssignment"="D"
"HardwareID"="IOMEGA__JAZ_1GB_____H,GenDisk,SCSI\\IOMEGA__JAZ_
 1GB_____H"
"Class"="DiskDrive"
"Driver"="DiskDrive\\0002"
```

```
"Mfg"="(Standard disk drives)"
"DeviceDesc"="iomega jaz 1GB          "
"ConfigFlags"=hex
```

The relationship between these Windows 95 registry items and the Control Panel becomes clear when you look at the System applet in the Control Panel for the same machine, as shown in Figure 5-1.

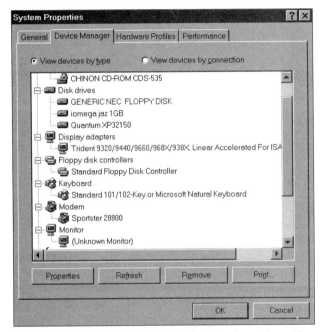

Figure 5-1: The Windows 95 Device Manager shows the settings for the system's hardware (the unknown monitor is an NEC MultiSync).

Windows NT 4 Hardware Information

Unlike Windows 95 and 98, the Windows NT 4 registry doesn't put all this hardware information in one place. Of course, NT 4 doesn't have a single applet in the Control Panel to display the properties of all the computer's hardware. The information is contained in individual Control Panel objects.

The registry key HKEY_LOCAL_MACHINE\HARDWARE, along with its subkeys, contains most of the information about the computer's resources (see Figure 5-2).

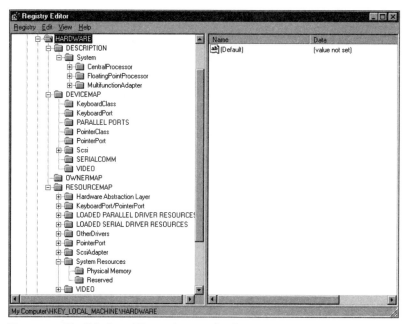

Figure 5-2: The Windows NT 4 registry entries for hardware match the setup and configuration performed in Control Panel.

The registry entries for a Pentium running NT 4 Workstation follow. Notice that the NT 4 registry values are mostly hex (the Windows 95 and 98 registries contain more English). You'll see the same pattern as shown for the Windows 95 registry: a container key with subkey(s) for the specific devices.

```
[HKEY_LOCAL_MACHINE\HARDWARE]

[HKEY_LOCAL_MACHINE\HARDWARE\DESCRIPTION]

[HKEY_LOCAL_MACHINE\HARDWARE\DESCRIPTION\System]
"Component Information"=hex
"Identifier"="AT/AT COMPATIBLE"
"Configuration Data"=hex
"SystemBiosDate"="07/15/95"
"SystemBiosVersion"=hex
"VideoBiosDate"="11/18/94"
"VideoBiosVersion"=hex

[HKEY_LOCAL_MACHINE\HARDWARE\DESCRIPTION\System\CentralProcessor]

[HKEY_LOCAL_MACHINE\HARDWARE\DESCRIPTION\System\CentralProcessor\0]
"Component Information"=hex
"Identifier"="x86 Family 5 Model 2 Stepping 12"
"Configuration Data"=hex
```

```
"VendorIdentifier"="GenuineIntel"
"~MHz"=dword:00000084

[HKEY_LOCAL_MACHINE\HARDWARE\DESCRIPTION\System\FloatingPointProcess
 or]

[HKEY_LOCAL_MACHINE\HARDWARE\DESCRIPTION\System\FloatingPointProcess
 or\0]
"Component Information"=hex
"Identifier"="x86 Family 5 Model 2 Stepping 12"
"Configuration Data"=hex

[HKEY_LOCAL_MACHINE\HARDWARE\DESCRIPTION\System\MultifunctionAdapter
 ]

[HKEY_LOCAL_MACHINE\HARDWARE\DESCRIPTION\System\MultifunctionAdapter
 \0]
"Component Information"=hex
"Identifier"="PCI"
"Configuration Data"=hex

[HKEY_LOCAL_MACHINE\HARDWARE\DESCRIPTION\System\MultifunctionAdapter
 \1]
"Component Information"=hex
"Identifier"="PNP BIOS"
"Configuration Data"=hex

[HKEY_LOCAL_MACHINE\HARDWARE\DESCRIPTION\System\MultifunctionAdapter
 \2]
"Component Information"=hex
"Identifier"="ISA"
"Configuration Data"=hex

[HKEY_LOCAL_MACHINE\HARDWARE\DESCRIPTION\System\MultifunctionAdapter
 \2\DiskController]

[HKEY_LOCAL_MACHINE\HARDWARE\DESCRIPTION\System\MultifunctionAdapter
 \2\DiskController\0]
"Component Information"=hex
"Configuration Data"=hex

[HKEY_LOCAL_MACHINE\HARDWARE\DESCRIPTION\System\MultifunctionAdapter
 \2\DiskController\0\DiskPeripheral]

[HKEY_LOCAL_MACHINE\HARDWARE\DESCRIPTION\System\MultifunctionAdapter
 \2\DiskController\0\DiskPeripheral\0]
"Component Information"=hex
"Identifier"="19371863-99d9fb65-A"
"Configuration Data"=hex

[HKEY_LOCAL_MACHINE\HARDWARE\DESCRIPTION\System\MultifunctionAdapter
 \2\DiskController\0\FloppyDiskPeripheral]
```

```
[HKEY_LOCAL_MACHINE\HARDWARE\DESCRIPTION\System\MultifunctionAdapter
 \2\DiskController\0\FloppyDiskPeripheral\0]
"Component Information"=hex
"Identifier"="FLOPPY1"
"Configuration Data"=hex

[HKEY_LOCAL_MACHINE\HARDWARE\DESCRIPTION\System\MultifunctionAdapter
 \2\KeyboardController]

[HKEY_LOCAL_MACHINE\HARDWARE\DESCRIPTION\System\MultifunctionAdapter
 \2\KeyboardController\0]
"Component Information"=hex
"Configuration Data"=hex

[HKEY_LOCAL_MACHINE\HARDWARE\DESCRIPTION\System\MultifunctionAdapter
 \2\KeyboardController\0\KeyboardPeripheral]

[HKEY_LOCAL_MACHINE\HARDWARE\DESCRIPTION\System\MultifunctionAdapter
 \2\KeyboardController\0\KeyboardPeripheral\0]
"Component Information"=hex
"Identifier"="PCAT_ENHANCED"
"Configuration Data"=hex

[HKEY_LOCAL_MACHINE\HARDWARE\DESCRIPTION\System\MultifunctionAdapter
 \2\ParallelController]

[HKEY_LOCAL_MACHINE\HARDWARE\DESCRIPTION\System\MultifunctionAdapter
 \2\ParallelController\0]
"Component Information"=hex
"Identifier"="PARALLEL1"
"Configuration Data"=hex

[HKEY_LOCAL_MACHINE\HARDWARE\DESCRIPTION\System\MultifunctionAdapter
 \2\ParallelController\1]
"Component Information"=hex
"Identifier"="PARALLEL2"
"Configuration Data"=hex

[HKEY_LOCAL_MACHINE\HARDWARE\DESCRIPTION\System\MultifunctionAdapter
 \2\SerialController]
```

This computer also has four serial ports, but there is some difference in how the registry keeps the information.

```
[HKEY_LOCAL_MACHINE\HARDWARE\DESCRIPTION\System\MultifunctionAdapte
 r\2\SerialController\0]
"Component Information"=hex
"Identifier"="COM1"
"Configuration Data"=hex

[HKEY_LOCAL_MACHINE\HARDWARE\DESCRIPTION\System\MultifunctionAdapter
 \2\SerialController\0\PointerPeripheral]
```

If you look carefully at the information in the previous listing, you'll see something interesting in the way serial ports are handled. Windows NT 4 automatically detects the mouse upon bootup (in fact, if you switch the mouse to a different serial port after shut down, Windows NT 4 will adjust the system with no error messages when you reboot).

When a mouse occupies a serial port in NT 4, the port is no longer treated as a serial port. In the registry, it's a pointer peripheral port. The registry then displays information about the remaining serial port(s). In the registry listing here, serial port 0 (COM1) contains the mouse and the remaining ports, 1 through 3 (COM2 through COM4) are displayed in the serial port section of the registry.

By opening the Mouse applet in Control Panel, you'll see there is no place to indicate the port to which the mouse is attached. In addition, if you open the Ports applet in Control Panel, there is no listing for the port to which the mouse is attached (see Figure 5-3).

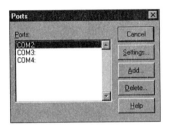

Figure 5-3: By switching the mouse to COM2, you can configure COM1, COM3, and COM4— but you cannot get to the port the mouse is on.

```
[HKEY_LOCAL_MACHINE\HARDWARE\DESCRIPTION\System\MultifunctionAdapter
  \2\SerialController\0\PointerPeripheral\0]
"Component Information"=hex
"Identifier"="MICROSOFT SERIAL MOUSE"
"Configuration Data"=hex

[HKEY_LOCAL_MACHINE\HARDWARE\DESCRIPTION\System\MultifunctionAdapter
  \2\SerialController\1]
"Component Information"=hex
"Identifier"="COM2"
"Configuration Data"=hex

[HKEY_LOCAL_MACHINE\HARDWARE\DESCRIPTION\System\MultifunctionAdapter
  \2\SerialController\2]
"Component Information"=hex
"Identifier"="COM3"
"Configuration Data"=hex
```

```
[HKEY_LOCAL_MACHINE\HARDWARE\DESCRIPTION\System\MultifunctionAdapter
 \2\SerialController\3]
"Component Information"=hex
"Identifier"="COM4"
"Configuration Data"=hex


[HKEY_LOCAL_MACHINE\HARDWARE\DEVICEMAP]

[HKEY_LOCAL_MACHINE\HARDWARE\DEVICEMAP\KeyboardClass]
"\\Device\\KeyboardClass0"="\\REGISTRY\\Machine\\System\\ControlSet
 001\\Services\\Kbdclass"

[HKEY_LOCAL_MACHINE\HARDWARE\DEVICEMAP\KeyboardPort]
"\\Device\\KeyboardPort0"="\\REGISTRY\\Machine\\System\\ControlSet
 001\\Services\\i8042prt"

[HKEY_LOCAL_MACHINE\HARDWARE\DEVICEMAP\PARALLEL PORTS]
"\\Device\\Parallel0"="\\DosDevices\\LPT1"
"\\Device\\Parallel1"="\\DosDevices\\LPT2"

[HKEY_LOCAL_MACHINE\HARDWARE\DEVICEMAP\PointerClass]
"\\Device\\PointerClass0"="\\REGISTRY\\Machine\\System\\ControlSet
 001\\Services\\Mouclass"

[HKEY_LOCAL_MACHINE\HARDWARE\DEVICEMAP\PointerPort]
"\\Device\\PointerPort0"="\\REGISTRY\\Machine\\System\\ControlSet001
 \\Services\\Sermouse"

[HKEY_LOCAL_MACHINE\HARDWARE\DEVICEMAP\SERIALCOMM]
"Serial1"="COM2"
"Serial2"="COM3"
"Serial3"="COM4"

[HKEY_LOCAL_MACHINE\HARDWARE\DEVICEMAP\VIDEO]
"\\Device\\Video0"="\\REGISTRY\\Machine\\System\\ControlSet001\\
 Services\\cirrus\\Device0"
"VgaCompatible"="\\Device\\Video0"

[HKEY_LOCAL_MACHINE\HARDWARE\DEVICEMAP\Scsi]
```

This is the top-level key for SCSI controllers. Notice that all the SCSI information is in this section of the registry. There are keys for the controller and subkeys for the devices attached to the controller. This computer has two devices attached to the SCSI controller: a hard drive and a CD-ROM.

```
[HKEY_LOCAL_MACHINE\HARDWARE\DEVICEMAP\Scsi\Scsi Port 0]
"Interrupt"=dword:0000000b
"IOAddress"=dword:00000330
"Driver"="Aha154x"
"DeviceName"="Adaptec AHA-154X/AHA-164X SCSI Host Adapter"
"Mfg"="Adaptec"

[HKEY_LOCAL_MACHINE\HARDWARE\DEVICEMAP\Scsi\Scsi Port 0\Scsi Bus 0]
```

```
[HKEY_LOCAL_MACHINE\HARDWARE\DEVICEMAP\Scsi\Scsi Port 0\Scsi Bus
  0\Initiator Id 7]

[HKEY_LOCAL_MACHINE\HARDWARE\DEVICEMAP\Scsi\Scsi Port 0\Scsi Bus
  0\Target Id 0]

[HKEY_LOCAL_MACHINE\HARDWARE\DEVICEMAP\Scsi\Scsi Port 0\Scsi Bus
  0\Target Id 0\Logical Unit Id 0]
"Identifier"="HP       C3725S          6039"
"Type"="DiskPeripheral"

[HKEY_LOCAL_MACHINE\HARDWARE\DEVICEMAP\Scsi\Scsi Port 0\Scsi Bus
  0\Target Id 3]

[HKEY_LOCAL_MACHINE\HARDWARE\DEVICEMAP\Scsi\Scsi Port 0\Scsi Bus
  0\Target Id 3\Logical Unit Id 0]
"Identifier"="NEC     CD-ROM DRIVE:2223.0i"
"Type"="CdRomPeripheral"
```

The Control Panel has the same system of configuring serial ports attached to pointing devices as the registry does. The Ports applet permits configuration only for those ports that are mouse-free (see Figure 5-3).

Future versions of Windows NT are expected to support Plug and Play. This should change the nature of Control Panel configuration (and the resulting registry information), substantially.

Summary

This chapter described how the control panel and the registry interact. The next chapter covers security for workstations.

Chapter 6

Using Microsoft PowerToys

You can take advantage of some powerful yet simple-to-use tools to configure your system, without going directly into the registry and risking disaster. One of my favorite tools is PowerToys, a collection of nifty utilities including Tweak UI, which offers a safe way to make registry changes for your desktop. This chapter concentrates on Tweak UI.

PowerToys comes from Microsoft, but it's not officially a Microsoft application. That means it was developed by Microsoft programmers, but no technical support is available. The programmers developed the utilities, probably for their own convenience, and then decided to make them available to the rest of us.

Installing the Files

The first thing you need to do is download these utilities. Go to http://www.microsoft.com/windows95/info/powertoys.htm. This document contains hyperlinks you can use to download all or some of the PowerToys.

Some of the utilities are for Windows 95, and some are for both Windows 95 and Windows NT.

The following PowerToys applications are for Windows 95 only:

◆ **CabView**, which handles CAB files (those you see in an application CD-ROM) as though they were folders. You can peek inside, move the files, and use them.

◆ **CD AutoPlay Extender**, which gives you autoplay capabilities for any software CD so you can get to the files you need quickly.

◆ **Contents Menu**, which provides access to files without the need to open folders.

◆ **FlexiCD**, which puts audio CD controls on your taskbar.

◆ **QuickRes**, which enables you to change the screen resolution from your taskbar without needing to reboot.

◆ **Round Clock**, which is an analog clock without the square frame.

◆ **Telephony Location Selector**, which enables you to change dialing locations from the taskbar.

◆ **Xmouse**, which forces the focus to follow your mouse movements (you don't have to click).

The following PowerToys applications are for both Windows 95 and Windows NT 4:

◆ **Command Prompt Here**, which enables you to open a command prompt in any folder.

◆ **Desktop Menu**, which enables you to open desktop items from a taskbar menu.

◆ **Explore From Here**, which opens Explorer at any point you want.

◆ **Find X**, which enables you to customize your Find menu.

◆ **Send To X**, which gives you Send To capabilities aimed at any folder.

◆ **Shortcut Target Menu**, which enables you to right-click to see the properties for the target instead of the shortcut.

◆ **Tweak UI**, which enables you to make changes to your user interface.

Before you download the utilities, create a target folder for them on your hard drive and direct the download process to that folder. Then, expand the file(s) you downloaded by opening them. If you obtained the full PowerToys package, your new folder will contain files for each of the applications when you open PowerToy.exe (see Figure 6-1).

Each PowerToy application has an .INF file containing setup information. To install a utility, right-click the appropriate .INF file and choose Install from the shortcut menu.

Customizing with Tweak UI

The most powerful application is Tweak UI, which works directly with registry settings to change the way your system behaves. Just as with direct registry edits, however, you must have security rights to make the changes with Tweak UI.

Where possible (meaning where I could figure it out), I'll give you the registry location for the changes that Tweak UI makes. If you change the data directly in the registry, you won't see the setting change in Tweak UI until you reboot.

Because I'm including the registry information, you could, of course, read this section and make the changes directly in the registry if you don't have a copy of Tweak UI.

Installing Tweak UI

Right-click Tweak UI.inf and choose Install from the shortcut menu to begin the process of setting up the software. When installation is complete, a message informs you of this and is accompanied by a Help File page that invites you to browse the entire help file (see Figure 6-2).

I found it useful to create a shortcut to the Tweak UI help file on my desktop. You'll probably find this helpful too, until you become familiar with the features.

Using Tweak UI

The installation program for Tweak UI creates a new applet in Control Panel. When you open the Tweak UI applet, you see a dialog box with ten tabs in Windows NT (see Figure 6-3). For Windows 95, there are eleven tabs (the extra tab is named Boot).

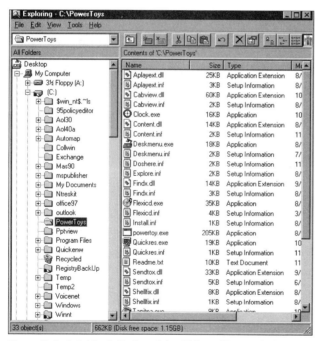

Figure 6-1: A folder full of useful utilities will come in handy on a daily basis.

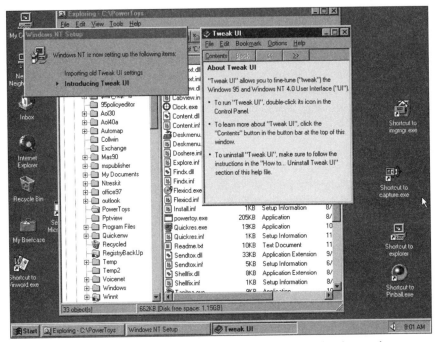

Figure 6-2: You can read the Tweak UI help file any time you need to by opening TweakUI.hlp in your PowerToys folder.

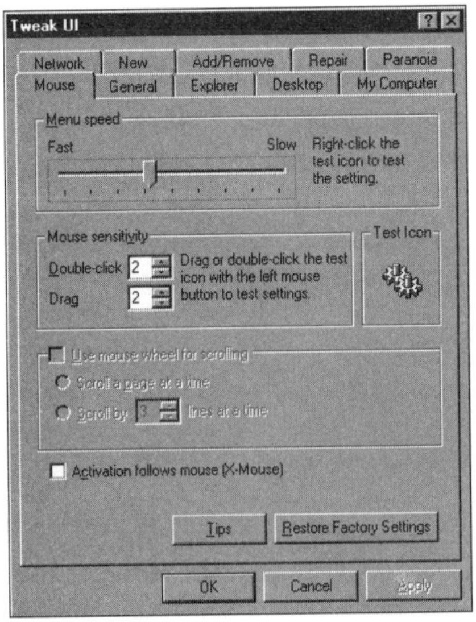

Figure 6-3: Here you'll find plenty of ways to change the way your system behaves without hacking the registry directly.

MOUSE SETTINGS

You can tweak the behavior of your mouse with more options than are available through the default Mouse applet in Control Panel. All the options discussed in this section are user options and apply only to the settings for the current logged-on user.

MENU SPEED   The Menu speed option specifies the interval that passes before the next set of menus opens, when you are working with cascading menus. Move the slider to change the speed at which the menus appear–the faster the setting, the more immediate the display. If you set the speed to slow, you'll find you can rest your mouse pointer on a menu item and have time to brew coffee before the cascading menu opens.

Test the interval by right-clicking the Test Icon (you aren't testing the speed of the mouse for right-click actions, you just use the right-click motion for this particular test). A cascading menu appears, and each menu item has another cascading menu. The speed at which the second menu appears reflects the current setting of this option.

Your changes are written back to the registry in HKEY_CURRENT_USER\Control Panel\Desktop. The data entry is named MenuShowDelay. In my registry, the original setting was "400" and my current setting is "10" (I like to see those submenus immediately).

MOUSE SENSITIVITY   You can raise or lower the current setting of the Double-click value to change the interval between two mouse clicks; this determines whether your clicking action is indeed a double click. For instance, if you frequently use two clicks (not a double-click) to rename a file or an icon title, you'll want a short interval for your real double-clicking action. Or, if you tend to be more lackadaisical or aren't incredibly well-coordinated, make the interval larger so your double-click always works. Test the new interval by double-clicking the Test Icon. If your action is recognized as a double-click, the icon will move.

The changes take effect immediately, and are written to the registry in HKEY_CURRENT_USER\Control Panel\Mouse in the data values named DoubleClickHeight and DoubleClickWidth.

You can also raise or lower the current setting of the Drag value. This value specifies how far (measured in pixels) you have to move the mouse with a button held down before the operating system realizes that you're dragging. If you tend to drag accidentally when you think you're selecting, this is a good way to solve that problem.

The changes take effect immediately, and are written to the registry in HKEY_CURRENT_USER\Control Panel\Desktop in the data values named DragHeight and DragWidth.

TIP Sometimes, users don't even realize that they've dragged instead of selected a folder. If your hand moves at all, you can drag a folder into another folder without realizing it. I've had many clients call about error messages for missing files, missing .dll's, and so on, and the first few times it happened it was a total mystery. In the absence of finding a solution, I reinstalled the application that was causing the problem. Missing data files were found using the search options in Explorer. One day, I happened to notice that a subfolder I could see in Explorer seemed out of place. A comparison with the Explorer display on another workstation showed that this subfolder should have been one level higher. The user, trying to display the contents, had moved the folder into the folder immediately above it with an inadvertent jerky motion. I learned to look for this situation when I'd hear about missing files or lost folders, and found evidence of "jerking while clicking and therefore moving a folder" in an astounding number of cases.

ACTIVATION FOLLOWS MOUSE   Usually referred to as "X-Mouse functionality," this setting creates an environment that activates the window over which your mouse moves—putting it in the foreground—without the need to click on that window. This can be extremely useful if you are viewing or moving data among multiple windows.

This setting is only available for Windows NT through Tweak UI. To activate this feature in Windows 95, you have to install and launch the Xmouse application from the PowerToys group.

The activation feature works only for the operating system. If you open an application such as a word processor and have multiple documents open in the application window, you still have to click to switch between documents.

The changes you make here take effect immediately, and are written to the registry in HKEY_CURRENT_USER\Control Panel\Mouse in the ActiveWindowTracking data entry, which is a DWORD value type (0 is off, 1 is on).

USE MOUSE WHEEL FOR SCROLLING   If your system has a mouse wheel, this option is accessible. Checking the option enables you to use the wheel to scroll through data. Once you've enabled the action, you can opt to scroll a whole page at a time, or scroll by a specified number of lines at a time. By default, scrolling is specified to occur 3 lines at a time.

Changes are written to the registry in HKEY_CURRENT_USER\Control Panel\ Desktop in the data item WheelScrollLines.

GENERAL SETTINGS

The options available in the General tab of Tweak UI are those that don't fit neatly into the categories for the other tabs – this could just as easily be called the Misc tab (see Figure 6-4).

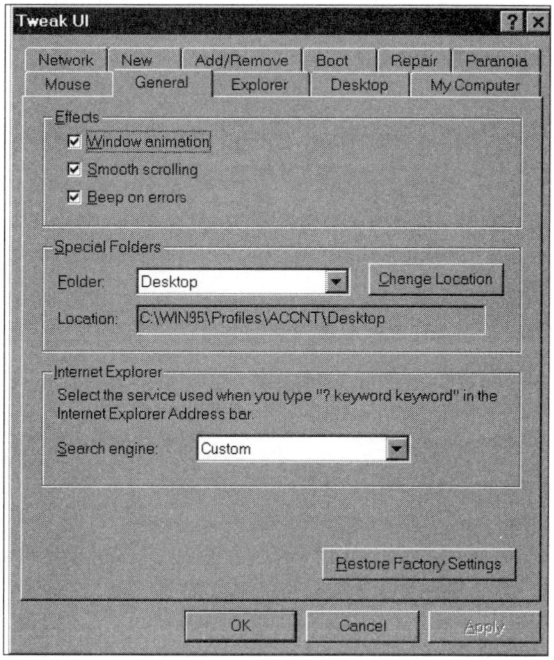

Figure 6-4: You can make a variety of miscellaneous settings in the General tab.

EFFECTS   The Effects section of this properties sheet offers three choices (by default, they are all selected).

♦ **Window animation** specifies whether you want to see the brief, animated effect of a window opening or closing when you maximize, minimize, or open a window. If you deselect the option, then a window appears suddenly when you open it, with no hint of animation. Changing the option adds the data item MinAnimate to HKEY_CURRENT_USER\Desktop\ WindowMetrics. The value is "0" when you deselect the option; if you reselect it, the value changes to "1".

◆ **Smooth Scrolling** controls the way scrolling acts in an Explorer-type view. For example, you can change the way the subkeys expand in the registry editor, from a pop-open smooth display to a less smooth display that resembles a screen repainting. (It's hard to explain, you have to see it). Changing the option adds the data item SmoothScroll to HKEY_ CURRENT_USER\Control Panel\Desktop. It's a binary value type, so if Smooth scrolling is deselected, the value is 00 00 00 00. If you reselect it, the value is 01 00 00 00.

◆ **Beep on errors** specifies whether a sound plays when an error occurs. If you decide to enable sounds, you can customize a sound using the Sounds applet in Control Panel. The setting is written to the registry in HKEY_ CURRENT_USER\Control Panel\Sound, with a data item of Beep that has a value of "yes" or "no" depending on your selection.

SPECIAL FOLDERS   You can change the location of the special folders in your system (*special* means these folders were created during the installation of the operating system or other Microsoft applications).

Click the arrow to the right of the Folder text box to display the list of available folders (see Figure 6-5).

When you select a folder, its location appears on the Tweak UI properties sheet, and you can choose Change Location to move the folder. Incidentally, I can't think of any particularly good reason (or even a valid reason) to do this. The settings are written to the registry in HKEY_CURRENT_USER\Software\Microsoft\Windows\ CurrentVersion\Explorer\Shell Folders. Figure 6-6 shows this subkey for a Windows NT 4 system; my Windows 95 registry contains fewer entries.

INTERNET EXPLORER   If you use Internet Explorer (3.0 or later), you can select a default search engine that launches if you type a question mark followed by a search word (or multiple words). Scroll through the list of search engines to pick your favorite. You can also choose Custom and enter a URL if the search engine you want isn't listed (see Figure 6-7). The option you select is written to the registry in HKEY_CURRENT_ USER\Software\Microsoft\Internet Explorer\Main in the data value named Search Page.

Incidentally, many people don't even know that you can enter ? *word* in Internet Explorer's URL box to launch a search (frequently, it's faster than going through all those steps to open a search program). Netscape Navigator doesn't have this feature (at least, not as of version 3.01).

EXPLORER

The Explorer tab has options for some of the items that make up the look of the user interface (see Figure 6-8). Don't get confused about the word Explorer – this isn't about the Explorer program you open to display files. It's the desktop interface presented by Windows 95 and Windows NT 4, which is called the Explorer Interface. Actually, Explorer is the official name for the interface.

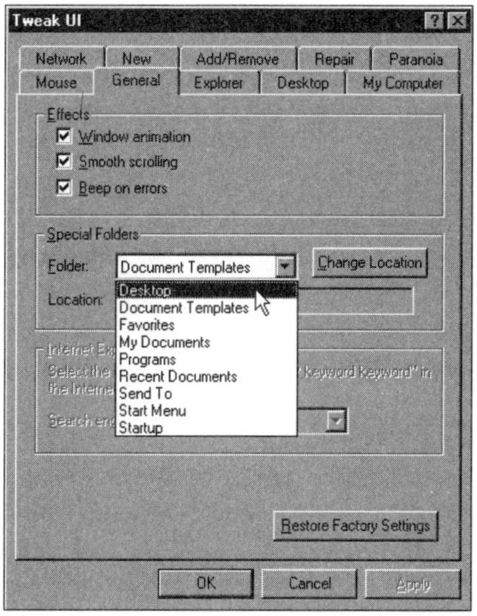

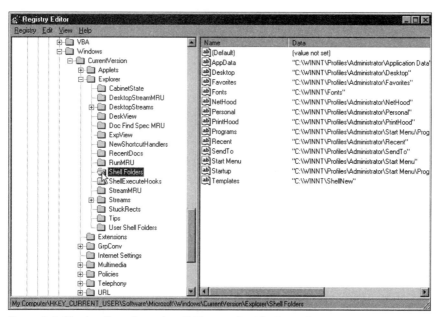

Figure 6-5: You can move the operating system folders to another place on your drive.

Figure 6-6: The locations for system folders are kept in the registry.

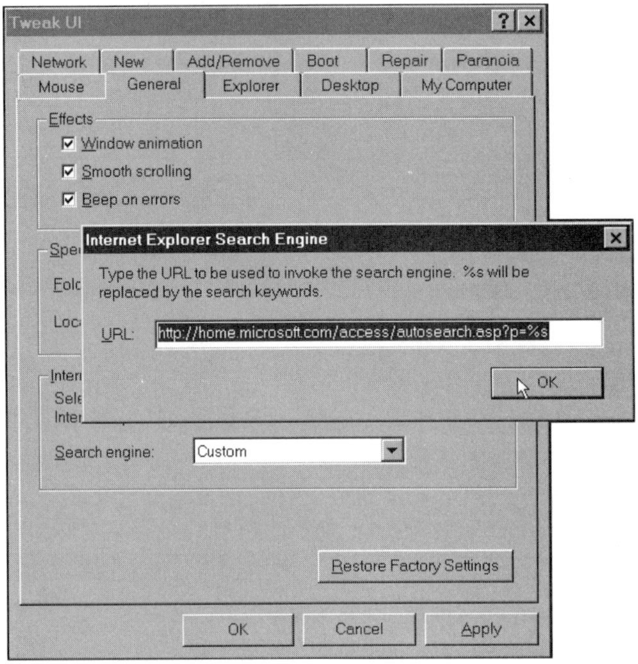

Figure 6-7: Choose a search engine to facilitate a quick search from the URL field in Internet Explorer.

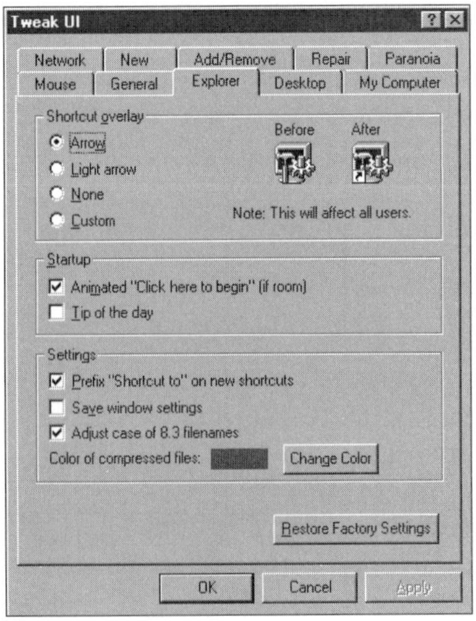

Figure 6-8: You can tweak the look and feel of your user interface with the Explorer tab.

SHORTCUT OVERLAY   You know those little curved arrows you see on the icons for shortcuts? You can change them or get rid of them. Select the option you prefer. If you choose Custom, the Change Icon dialog box appears to show you the icons available in TWEAK UI.CPL (see Figure 6-9). You can also browse your system for icon files if you want something of your own choice.

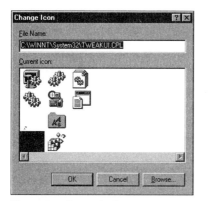

Figure 6-9: Instead of an arrow, you can use one of these images to indicate a shortcut.

Your changes are written to the registry in HKEY_LOCAL_MACHINE\Software\ Microsoft\CurrentVersion\Explorer, where a new subkey named ShellIcons is added. The value data is the path to TWEAK UI.CPL,*X* where *X* is the icon for the arrow.

Because this value is stored in HKEY_LOCAL_MACHINE, changing it means that you change it for all users who log on to this machine.

TIP If you change the arrow, and then later change the configuration to return to the original Windows arrow, the new subkey ShellIcons remains, but the data value disappears from the data pane of the registry editor.

STARTUP   Two options are available in the Startup section of this tab, and you can select or deselect either of them:

◆ Animated **"Click here to begin"**, which is that message that crawls across your taskbar from right to left.

◆ **Tip of the day**, which is a Windows tip that appears whenever you start the operating system.

Turning tips on and off results in a data value named DisplayInitialTipWindow (the values are 0 for off and 1 for on) in the subkey `HKEY_CURRENT_USER\ Software\Microsoft\Windows\CurrentVersion\Explorer\Tips`.

 The tips themselves are found in `HKEY_LOCAL_MACHINE\Software\ Microsoft\Windows\CurrentVersion\Explorer\Tips` and you can either add, change, or remove tips.

SETTINGS   The Settings section of the Explorer tab offers the following four options:

- **Prefix "Shortcut to" on new shortcuts.** Deselect this option to keep the words "Shortcut to" out of the title under your shortcut icons.

  The registry saves this setting in `HKEY_CURRENT_USER\Software\ Microsoft\Windows\CurrentVersion\Explorer` in a data entry named link (the binary data value is 00 00 00 00 when you opt to remove the prefix).

- **Save window settings.** Select this option to save the settings of any folders when you close them. The next time you open a folder, it will have the same setting it had when you closed it last. Additionally, if you leave folders open when you shut down, they will be waiting for you the next time you log on.

  The registry saves this setting in `HKEY_CURRENT_USER\Software\ Microsoft\Windows\CurrentVersion\Policies\Explorer` in a data entry named NoSaveSettings. Because the data entry is a negative, changing the option to save the settings creates a binary data value of 00 00 00 00. The default option (don't save settings) is 01 00 00 00.

- **Adjust case of 8.3 filenames.** In Windows NT 4, this option changes the display of 8.3 filenames that are uppercase (most legacy filenames fall in this category) to mixed-case when you view them in Explorer or My Computer.

- **Color of compressed files.** In Windows NT 4, if you use compression and you've configured Explorer to display compressed files and folders in a different color, this is the place to change that color.

DESKTOP

The Desktop tab enables you to manipulate the icons displayed on this tab:

♦ You can place the icon on the desktop or remove it by selecting or deselecting the check box.

♦ You can rename the icon by right-clicking it and choosing Rename from the shortcut menu.

♦ You can create a file for the icon, and then place that file in any folder in your system. Select the icon and then select Create As File.

The icons shown in Figure 6-10 are from a Windows 95 system. Your Tweak UI dialog box may show a different display, depending on the operating system and the installed applications.

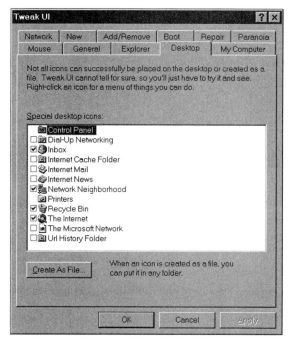

Figure 6-10: Notice that the Control Panel does not have a check box option, because you cannot place it on the desktop as an icon.

There's rarely an urgent (or good) reason to manipulate these icons, but if you think you need to do this, be sure to read the cautions in the Tweak UI Help Files under Issues and Limitations.

MY COMPUTER

Use the My Computer tab to control the drives that you can see (and access) from My Computer. The list of drives shown spans the entire alphabet (see Figure 6-11), but that bears no relationship to the drives displayed in My Computer. This properties sheet simply covers all the possibilities.

When you make changes to this tab, they are written to the registry in `HKEY_CURRENT_USER\Software\Microsoft\Windows\CurrentVersion\Policies\Explorer`. A new data item named NoDrives is placed in the data pane. The data value is binary and represents the drives that are excluded—but to tell you the truth, I can't read/translate that data value, so I have to trust Tweak UI (see Figure 6-12).

NETWORK

Use the Network tab to automate your network logon (see Figure 6-13).

Stop! Don't look at this tab and think, "How nifty, what a great time-saver." It's dangerous. Anybody can walk up to your computer and log on as you.

In a secure office or in the absence of any private files, however, you may want to log on automatically; this way, you can go to the coffee machine after you turn on your computer, and when you return you'll be ready to go to work.

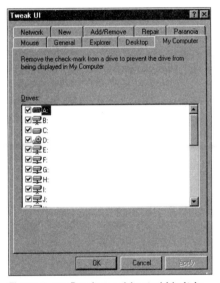

Figure 6-11: Deselect a drive to hide it in My Computer.

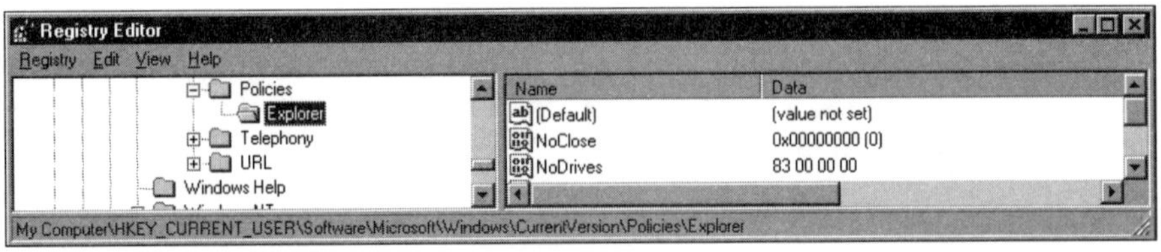

Figure 6-12: This is the binary value when I exclude drives A, B, and H from My Computer; when no drives are excluded, the value is 00 00 00 00.

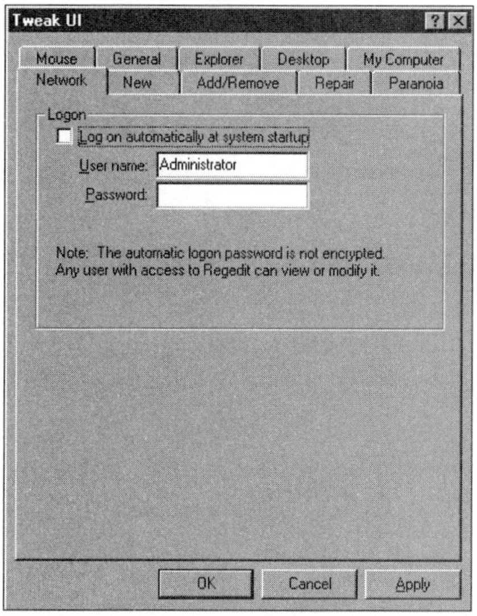

Figure 6-13: If security isn't a problem, save
time with an automatic logon.

In Windows NT 4, your settings are written to the registry in HKEY_LOCAL_
MACHINE\SOFTWARE\Microsoft\WindowsNT\CurrentVersion\WinLogon.

In Windows 95, your settings are written to the registry in HKEY_LOCAL_
MACHINE\SOFTWARE\Microsoft\Windows\CurrentVersion\WinLogon.

Automatic logon is established in the data item AutoAdminLogon, which has a
value of "1" if enabled, and "0" if not.

Your password is stored in the data item DefaultPassword, and the data value is
the password itself, in plain English so anyone can read it.

If you've created a logon banner, you'll have to click OK to get past it before
the automatic logon begins — I got rid of it for the machines that were
secure enough to warrant automatic logons (which users absolutely love).

NEW

The New tab should be named New Document Types, because that's what it controls. This setting corresponds to the shortcut menu you see when you right-click
on the desktop to create a new document (see Figure 6-14).

Click the corresponding check box to deselect a file type and remove it from the
shortcut menu list. To add a new file type to the list, create a document of that type
and drag its icon to the right side of the New tab (over the scroll bar).

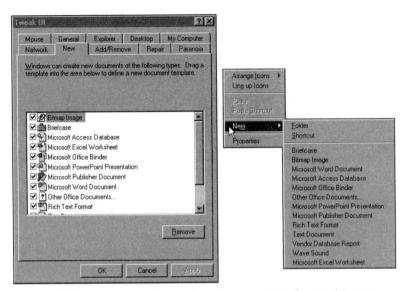

Figure 6-14: You can control the document types available for creating new documents from the desktop.

The registry settings for whether a document type is on the New shortcut menu are kept in HKEY_CLASSES_ROOT\ *file extension subkey*\ShellNew. See Chapter 7 for more information on file extension subkeys.

TIP

If you don't use the right-click desktop menu to create new documents, deselect all the document types on this tab. Your desktop shortcut menu becomes much shorter and therefore easier to navigate.

ADD/REMOVE

This tab controls the listing of software applications that appear on your Add/Remove Software applet in the Control Panel (see Figure 6-15).

♦ If you remove an entry from this tab, it will no longer appear in your Add/Remove applet in Control Panel.

♦ If you have written software with an uninstall routine, or know that an uninstall routine exists for installed software, you can add a New listing.

♦ If you move an application's uninstall program, select it and choose Edit to enter the new path.

Changes are written to `HKEY_LOCAL_MACHINE\Software\Microsoft\Windows\CurrentVersion\Uninstall`, where a subkey exists for each program that has registered an uninstall program (see Figure 6-16).

REPAIR

This is a housekeeping/fix-up tab you can use when things go awry. The choices differ between Windows NT 4 (see Figure 6-17) and Windows 95 (see Figure 6-18).

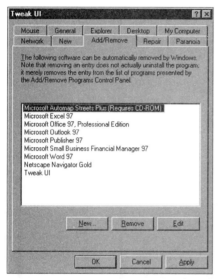

Figure 6-15: Add, remove, or edit the uninstall features of installed software.

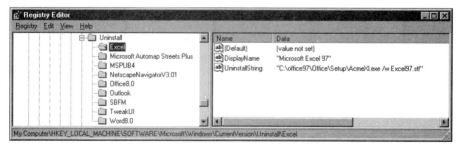

Figure 6-16: The path for the uninstall program is the data value for each application's subkey.

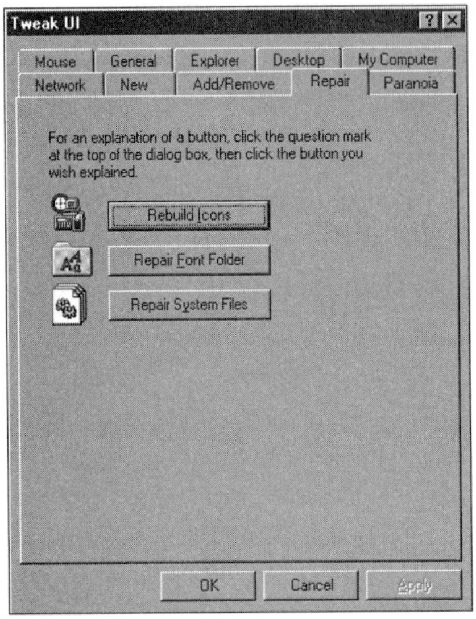

Figure 6-17: Clean up a messy NT 4 system
with the Repair tab.

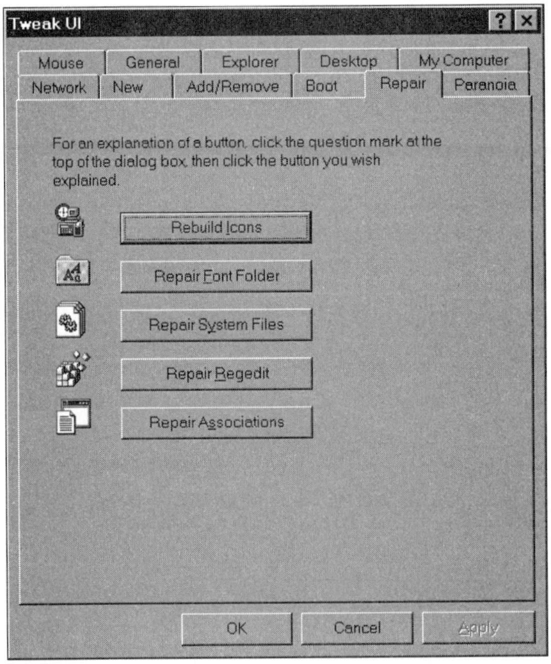

Figure 6-18: The Repair tab for a Windows 95 machine
has more choices for cleanup/fix-up.

Use **Rebuild Icons** when you find that some of the icons appearing in Explorer are incorrect. The rebuilding process isn't complete until you restart the operating system. (By the way, this happens most frequently when users change icons for file types).

Use **Repair Font Folder** when the font folder isn't working properly. Extra functions are available on the menu bar and the shortcut menu for this folder, and sometimes they disappear.

Use **Repair System Files** to restore system files that have been replaced by application setup programs. The operating system checks all system files against the originals, which are stored in the hidden directory \%SystemRoot%\Sysbckup. If that directory is not on the system, this repair tool fails.

For what it's worth, the \%SystemRoot%\Sysbckup directory was available on all my Windows 95 machines, but not on my Windows NT machines (neither server nor workstation). I know I didn't delete the directory, so I suspect it's not placed there during a normal installation, and this feature may be available only for Windows 95.

Use **Repair Regedit** in Windows 95 to fix the display of the REGEDIT window. As you work in the editor and you move, change, or otherwise alter columns, you may lose some of them. This feature resets the REGEDIT window to its original settings so that all the view options are available again.

Use **Repair Associations** in Windows 95 to reassociate files and icons. The most common symptom you'll see indicating that you need to run this program is that the shortcut menus for files don't present the appropriate choices.

PARANOIA

What a great name for a tab! And this one is perfectly named (see Figure 6-19). If you've ever worked in a large corporation, you know about creating "paper trails." Of course, if you're the one being "trailed," it would be nice to be able to get rid of the paper. This is what this tab does for you — it eliminates any trail of your activities.

Select one or all of the options in the **Covering Your Tracks** section to hide your tracks.

In the **Things That Happen Behind Your Back** section, just relax — there's nothing to worry about, nothing that anybody knows about your computer activities (and this section probably shouldn't be in a tab named Paranoia).

By default, the operating system plays a CD automatically when you insert it in the CD-ROM drive (the registry entry controlling this is HKEY_LOCAL_MACHINE\

System\CurrentControlSet\Services\Cdrom, with a data item named Autorun, and a DWORD value of "1" for on and "0" for off).

If you find this as annoying as I do, turn it off. I like having control of the drives on my machine (do you think maybe the control issue is why this choice is on the Paranoia tab)?

Windows 95 machines offer an additional choice on this tab called **Log Application Errors to FAULTLOG.TXT**. Select that option to keep track of errors generated by applications. The errors are sent to a text file named FAULTLOG.TXT, which you can examine in an effort to do some investigation and troubleshooting.

BOOT

This tab is available only in Windows 95. It provides a way to set options for system startup. Figure 6-20 shows the Boot tab for a Windows 95 computer that has a previous operating system; when Windows 95 was installed, it did not overwrite the existing Windows for Workgroups 3.11.

The items on this properties sheet are self-explanatory, and your options for booting are stored in a hidden file under C:\ named MSDOS.SYS, which you can view in a text editor (see Figure 6-21).

For detailed information about all the boot options, function key actions, and options for MSDOS.SYS, see Chapter 3.

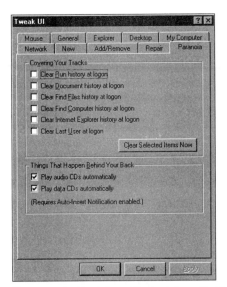

Figure 6-19: Check 'em off, check 'em all off—
then nobody will know where you've been
or what you've done.

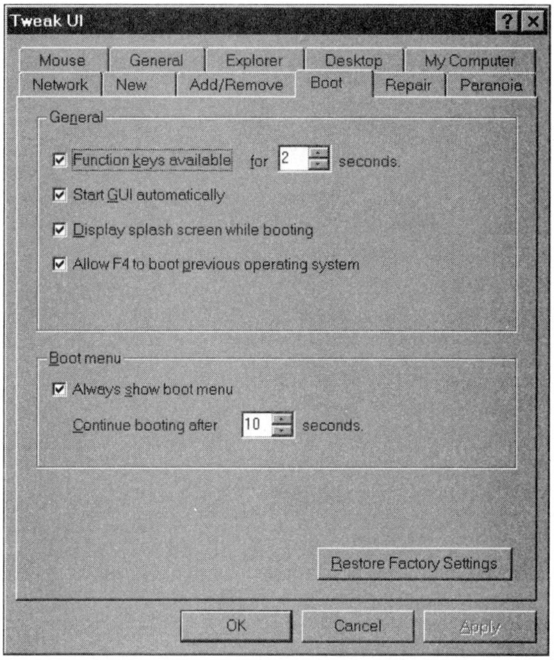

Figure 6-20: Set your boot process to match the way you want to work.

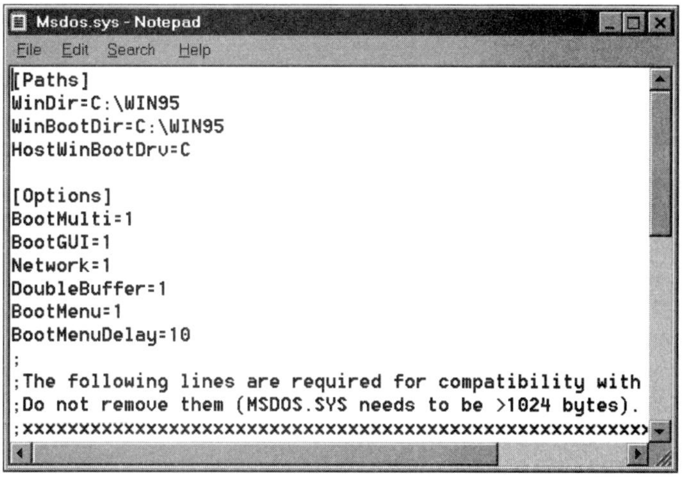

Figure 6-21: If you want to edit MSDOS.SYS directly, change the read-only attribute so you can save the changes—and don't forget to set it back the way it was.

Customizing with Other PowerToys

Try some of the other utilities that come with PowerToys – remember that you need to install most of them by right-clicking the .INF file.

DosPromptHere

I love this utility. I'm old and I've been around computers for a long time (my first computer ran the brand new DOS version 2.1). I still drop to a command prompt to perform many tasks – I type fast, I know the commands, and I find it faster than waiting for folders and windows to open. And you can still do some things better with DOS, such as renaming or deleting a group of files that share a common characteristic in their current names. In fact, for mass deletes I use DOS so I don't have to hold down the Shift key to avoid the Recycle Bin (have you noticed that Shift key thing doesn't always work?).

Install this utility by right-clicking Doshere.inf and choosing Install. It takes about three seconds to install. Then, right-click a folder and notice the new command on the shortcut menu (see Figure 6-22).

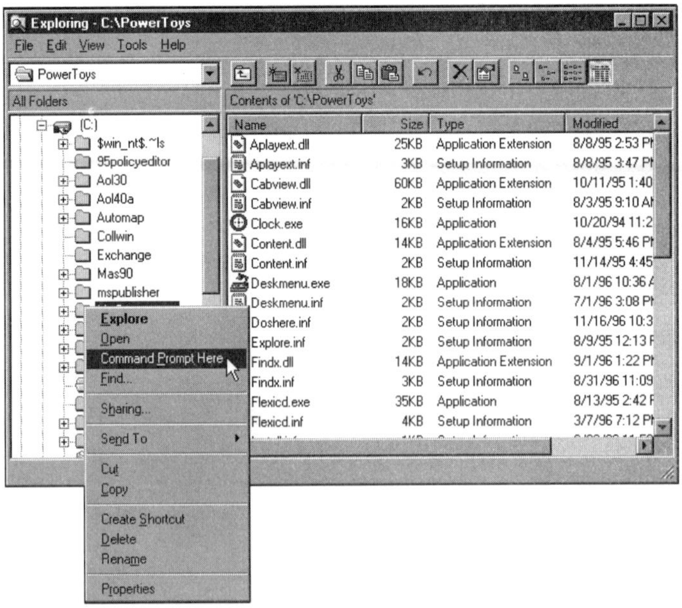

Figure 6-22: Now I don't have to navigate to the directory I need when I want to use a command prompt – this is so much easier than typing all those tildes (~).

Send To Extensions

This is another utility you'll wonder how you lived without. Install this to enhance the Send To option on the shortcut menu. If you move files around (especially after downloading them) this is so much better than cutting or copying, and then pasting, in Explorer. And it's even easier than dragging in Explorer.

Right-click Sendtox.inf and choose Install. Wait for the "Okay, it's installed and here's what it does" message, and then right-click any file and choose Send To (see Figure 6-23).

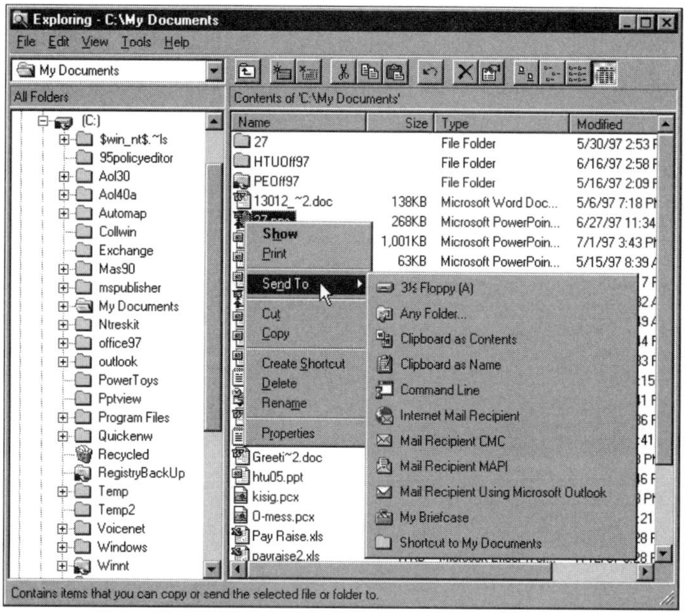

Figure 6-23: Now, this is what I call having options that match my work habits.

Choose Any Folder to see a dialog box that lets you name the target folder for the selected file (see Figure 6-24).

You can choose either to copy or to move the file. Here are some additional guidelines:

◆ Use the complete path of an existing folder to copy or move the selected file.

◆ Enter the complete path of a folder that doesn't exist; the folder is then created, and the file is sent there.

◆ If you enter a folder name without a path (for instance, **letters**), that folder is created under the current folder, and the file is sent there.

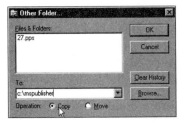

Figure 6-24: The dialog box keeps a history
of the folders you use, so after a while
this is really a quick operation.

Explore From Here

This is another wonderful time and motion saver, especially if you are on an NT network. This utility opens another Explorer window starting at any point you choose, so you don't have to scroll up and down as you view (or exchange files between) local and connected folders.

Right-click Explore.Inf to install the utility, and then right-click a folder and choose the new command Explore From Here. Another instance of Explorer opens, with that folder at the top of the All Folders panel (see Figure 6-25). To move files, just move to the source folder or file in one window and drag it to the target in the other window.

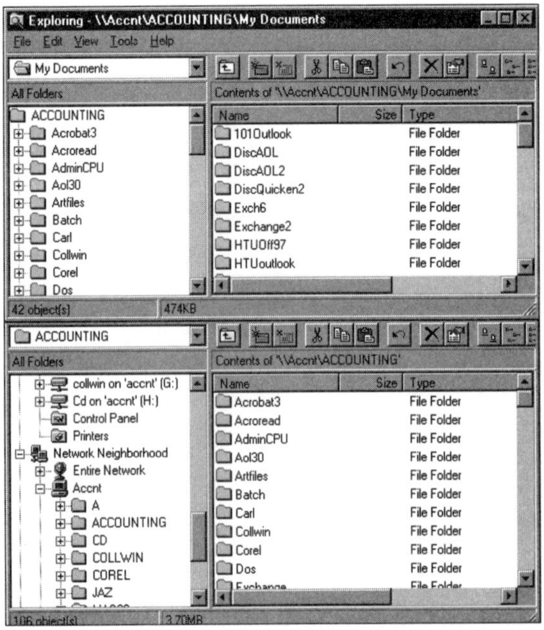

Figure 6-25: Look Ma, no scrolling—moving files between
computers is a piece of cake.

Contents Menu

Only available for Windows 95, this is another addition to the shortcut menu for folders. The new entry is named Contents, and selecting it displays a list of the subfolders and files in the selected folder (see Figure 6-26). Except you don't really have to select that particular folder – you can have one folder selected and then right-click another folder to see the contents. Click a file, and its associated application launches to open the file. Click a subfolder, and a window opens to display the files.

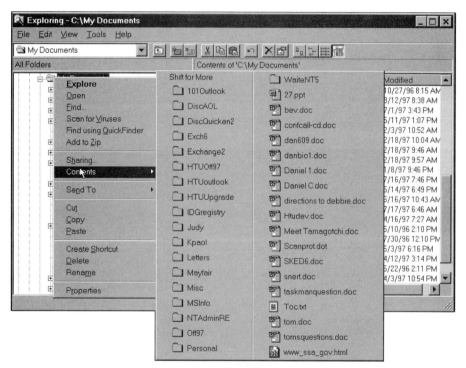

Figure 6-26: Quick access to folders and files with the shortcut menu makes me more productive.

Summary

You learned about Tweak UI and a few other PowerToys in this chapter. Depending on the way you work, you'll find some PowerToys more exciting than others. Read the descriptions, install the software you want to try, and have fun. The PowerToys all register themselves with the Add/Remove applet in the Control Panel, so it's easy to uninstall any you don't find useful.

Chapter 7

File Associations

FILE ASSOCIATIONS ASSOCIATE a file extension to a file type. The file type is usually associated with an icon and an application (or multiple applications). File associations are kept in the registry in HKEY_CLASSES_ROOT, and are displayed in Explorer and My Computer (click View → Options, then move to the File Types tab of the Options dialog box). You can add, delete, or change file associations from any of those three places.

In addition, file types are associated with other system features such as Object Linking and Embedding (OLE) and Dynamic Data Exchange (DDE). All the information for achieving successful OLE and DDE functions are contained in the registry.

Registering File Types

File types are registered in one of two ways:

◆ Programs register the file types they use.

◆ Users register file types that are not registered by programs.

When you install programs that are written for Windows 95, Windows 98, or Windows NT, part of the installation process is a registry import that puts the program's file types in the registry. (Other information, such as DLLs used by the program, is also imported).

However, legacy software, DOS software, and most programs that are developed in-house don't register file types during installation. In addition, many companies have house rules about file extensions for certain types of documents. For example, user-created reports from a company database may require specific extensions (perhaps .cus for customer reports, .inv for inventory reports, and so on). If you register the association, you can double-click the data file to launch the software.

Another common company rule is that text files should be edited and saved in the word processing program adopted by the company. This means you'll want to change the association for text files.

TIP

In many organizations, internal conventions dictate that word processing documents must have an extension that identifies the document type, such as .ltr for letters, or .mmo for memos. These extensions do not need to be registered, because the file header contains information about the creating application (usually the icon also matches the associated application).

Using Explorer or My Computer

It's easy to add new file types or configure existing file types with Explorer or My Computer, instead of doing it directly in the registry.

ADDING A FILE TYPE

To create a new file type, follow these steps:

1. Open Explorer or My Computer and choose View → Options. Move to the File Types tab of the Options dialog box.

2. Choose New Type to bring up the Add New File Type dialog box (see Figure 7-1).

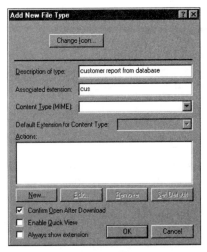

Figure 7-1: Add a new file type to your system and configure its association.

3. Fill out the options in the dialog box as follows:

- In the Description of type box, enter a description of this file type. The description you use will appear in Explorer and My Computer when you use the Details view for displaying files.

- In the Associated extension box, enter the three-letter filename extension for this file type.

- In the Content Type (MIME) box, specify the Multipurpose Internet Mail Extension (MIME) type you want to associate with this file (this is optional). When you open a file over the Internet, your browser will use this association. Click the arrow to the right of this field to see the available options.

- In the Default Extension for Content Type box, choose a filename extension for the MIME association (this is optional). This becomes the default extension (since most MIME types permit more than one choice for extensions).

- In the Actions box, specify the action you want to occur upon double-clicking this file listing (see the section that follows, "Associating an Action").

- Click the Confirm Open After Download check box if you want a confirmation dialog box to appear before this file type is opened automatically following downloading. The confirmation dialog box queries you about whether you want to open the file.

- Click the Enable Quick View check box if this file type is supported by Quick View.

- Click the Always show extension check box if you want to display the file type's extension in folder windows (even if you have configured the view to eliminate extensions for registered file types).

ASSOCIATING AN ACTION

The Action box in the Add New File Type dialog box is where you make things happen. When any file of your new file type is opened from Explorer or My Computer, the action you specify takes place. The action is a command—an executable file—and when you attach that file as an action, the executable file becomes the software association for the new file type.

1. To begin, click New, which opens the New Action dialog box (see Figure 7-2).

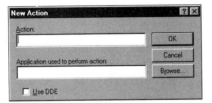

Figure 7-2: Any action you add will be associated with all files of the specified type.

2. In the Action box, specify the command you want to appear on the shortcut menu. Most of the time this would be Open.

3. In the Application used to perform action box, enter the path and filename of the executable file you want to associate with this file type (use the Browse button to find it if you need to).

4. If the application can use DDE, select the Use DDE check box. Choose OK when you are finished.

If you want the shortcut menu to display an underlined letter that you can use with the Alt key (a hot key), precede the appropriate letter with an ampersand (&). Don't use a letter that is already in use on shortcut menus.

 TIP You can also add startup parameters to the executable file you've inserted in the Action box.

If you don't add an action to the file type, when you double-click on it the Open With dialog box will open so you can pick the software you want to use. Select the Always Use This check box if you want to establish a permanent association.

ASSOCIATING MULTIPLE ACTIONS

You could associate two actions to any file type to give yourself or other users a choice about which application to use. To do so, repeat the steps for adding an action, but use a different name for the second action in the Action box (otherwise you're replacing the first action you added). For example, if you used Open (or if the registered file type has a shortcut menu choice of Open), call the new action OpenWithWord or OpenWithWordPerfect.

You can set one of these actions as the default by selecting it and choosing Set Default. If you don't set a default, the actions are listed alphabetically and the first choice on the list becomes the default.

When you right-click a file type with two associated actions, both choices are displayed and the default choice is bold (see Figure 7-3). If you double-click this file type the default choice application launches.

Figure 7-3: This database report was saved to disk and now can be opened with either of two applications.

Another good idea for an additional action is Print. Usually there's a parameter for software for printing (/p), so you only need to enter the path and filename for the executable file and include the parameter. For example, for a text file you could add Print as an action, then use NOTEPAD.EXE /p for the application. When you choose Print from the shortcut menu, the application opens, prints the file, then closes.

EDITING EXISTING FILE TYPES

You can select an existing file type and add another action to it by selecting it and choosing Edit. In this case, however, it's usually a good idea to keep the original association as the default action.

There are times when you might want to replace the existing action or create another action and make that the default. For instance, if you routinely receive text files that have to be formatted and otherwise handled by your word processing program, it's easier to open them right in your word processing program.

Using the Registry

You can also add new file types directly into the registry. In fact, there's one additional thing you can do when you work directly in the registry: you can register the file type for creation. That means when a user right-clicks on the desktop and chooses New, this file type will appear as one of the choices.

To work directly in the registry when adding file types, you have to register the extension, and then create the file type.

REGISTERING AN EXTENSION

To register the extension, launch REGEDIT and follow these steps:

1. Select HKEY_CLASSES_ROOT, then right-click in the right pane and choose New → Key (you can also use Edit → New → Key from the menu bar). The key expands and a new key is inserted at the bottom of the list of subkeys.

2. Enter the extension with a period in front of the three-letter extension and press Enter.

3. Press F5 to refresh the display, and your new key displays in the proper place (in the first alphabetic section of the expanded key).

4. With the new key selected, double-click the Default item to enter a description of the new file type in the Value data field (see Figure 7-4)

REGISTERING THE FILE TYPE

Now you have to register the file type. This entry (the technical name for this is ProgID) goes into the second set of alphabetic subkeys in HKEY_CLASSES_ROOT and is configured for associations. Follow these steps to complete this process:

1. Select HKEY_CLASSES_ROOT and right-click in the right pane. Choose New → Key.

2. When the new key appears in the left pane, name it to match the Default entry you just entered for the new extension. Then press F5 to refresh the screen so your new entry appears in its proper alphabetic place.

3. With the new key selected, double-click the Default object in the right pane, then enter a description of this file type in the Value data field. This description appears in Explorer and My Computer when you are looking at the Details view.

4. To establish the association for software, you must create a new key `\Newtype\Shell\Open\Command`, where `Newtype` is the name of your new file type. Just keep creating keys until you get there.

5. Select the `Command` subkey and double-click the Default object in the right pane. Then enter the path and filename of the application you want to associate with this file type. Add the parameter %1 to pass the name of the file that is double-clicked to the software. The complete setup for my new vendor database report file type is shown in Figure 7-5.

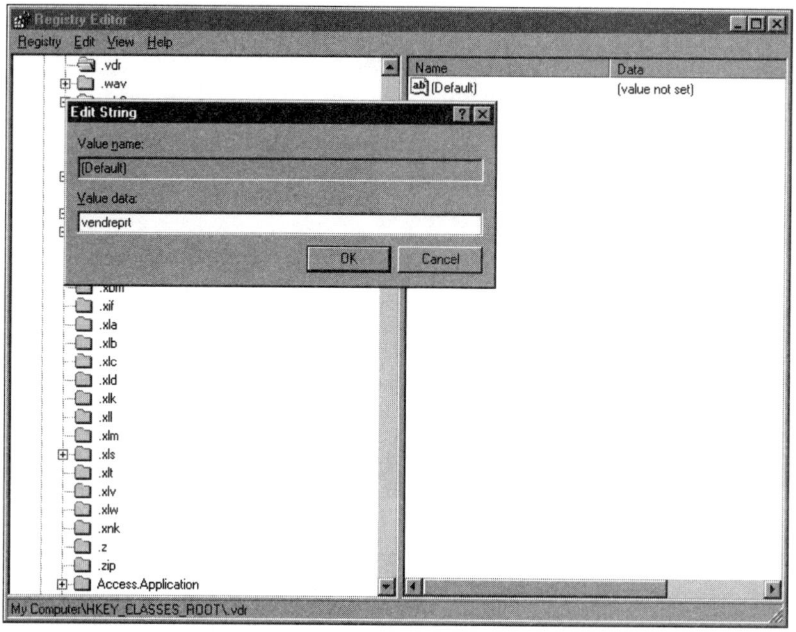

Figure 7-4: The new file extension is .vdr, which is for the vendor reports from our database.

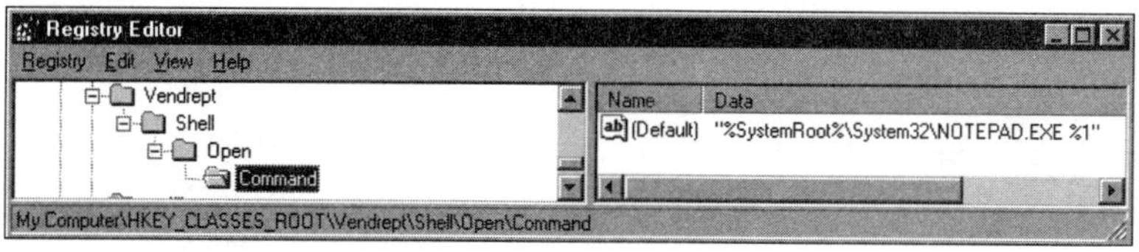

Figure 7-5: All files of the vendor database report type will now launch Notepad when they're double-clicked.

REGISTERING A CREATION FILE TYPE

This action places your file type on the drop down menu that displays when you right-click the desktop and choose New. You cannot configure a creation file type from Explorer or My Computer; you must use the registry for this. Here are the steps for creating this subkey:

1. Move to the extension subkey you entered to register the extension (in this case, it's .vdr) and create a subkey named ShellNew.

2. Select ShellNew and right-click in the right pane . Choose New → String Value from the shortcut menu.

3. Fill in the String Value data as follows:

   - **NullFile,** to indicate that an empty file will be created (this is the most common value for ShellNew).

   - *Filename,* where the filename you enter is a template file that will be copied to the associated application so it can be used as the basis for a new file. You must specify a path for the template file.

   - **Data,** where the data in the value entry is copied into the new file.

4. The new value appears in the right pane. After your next bootup, when you right-click on the desktop and choose New, this file type will appear on the list (see Figure 7-6).

Class Identifiers

Every document type has a unique class identifier (CLSID) and all of its information is in the subkey HKEY_CLASSES_ROOT\CLSID. When you view a CLSID subkey, you can learn about its OLE class and the location of the file that is used for the implementation of OLE.

The actual CLSID subkey isn't English, it is a 16-byte number that is formatted as 32 hexadecimal digits. It's also a Globally Unique Identifier (GUID), and that definition is literal, as each object carries its GUID on every PC in the world (you can think of it as similar to a social security number).

If you're a programmer and you've introduced a new object type, you must create a GUID for it. The Microsoft SDK has a program that does this for you, named Uuuidgen.exe. And in the DDK there's a program named Guidgen.exe that also generates GUIDs. The way GUID creation works is to generate the first 8 digits as random numbers, then the next 4 digits use the current date and time on your computer, and the last 20 digits are generated using information from your computer's hardware setup. It would be an incredible coincidence if two GUIDs ended up the sam—the odds are so far against it that it's not a problem.

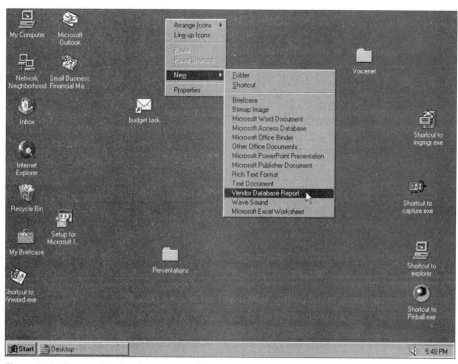

Figure 7-6: The vendor database report file type is on the New menu and works exactly like all the other file types on this list.

The subkeys under each `CLSID` key vary according to the type of object. But there are some subkeys that occur in most of the `CLSID` keys. Figure 7-7 shows the GUID for the Microsoft Excel executable file (EXCEL.EXE) in a Windows NT 4 system.

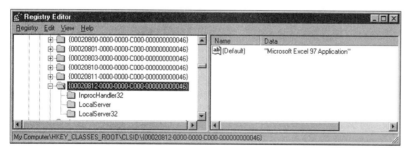

Figure 7-7: The subkeys for a handler and/or a server are found under most `CLSID` keys.

Here's the information you'll find under most of the `CLSID` subkeys:

- ◆ `InprocServer`, which is a pointer to the In-Process Server, the .DLL that handles this object.

- ◆ `InprocServer32`, for object types that use a 32-bit In-Process Server.

- ◆ `DefaultIcon`, which specifies the icon attached to the object type.

- ◆ `InprocHandler`, which is a pointer to the .DLL file that works as an Object Handler (meaning it works in connection with an .EXE file) to manage objects of this type.

- ◆ `LocalServer`, which holds the path\filename of a server application that handles objects of this type.

- ◆ `LocalServer32`, for object types that use a 32-bit server application.

- ◆ `ProgID`, which is usually the short name for the object type (txtfile, for example).

- ◆ `Shellex`, which holds additional subkeys, defining the .DLL files and commands that are used to get to the object's shortcut menu and/or Properties dialog box.

Viewing Files with Quick View

Quick View is a utility that provides a way to look at a file without opening the software that created that file. In fact, you don't even have to have the software associated with the file on your computer.

It's a complicated feature and is dependent upon the registry in order to work. When you right-click a document file in Explorer or My Computer, the shortcut menu offers the Quick View command if the file type is supported by Quick View.

How Quick View Works

Quick View works by launching QUIKVIEW.EXE, which is not the viewer but a software application that locates and launches an appropriate viewer. In Windows NT QUIKVIEW.EXE is usually found in `\%SystemRoot%\System32\Viewers`. In Windows 95 and 98, it is usually located in `\%SystemRoot%\System\Viewers`.

A separate instance of a viewer is opened for each file selected by the user. If you select multiple files and choose Quick View, the shell starts QUIKVIEW.EXE for each selected file (using the Win32 CreateProcess or WinExec function) and a viewer will open for each file type that is supported.

QUIKVIEW.EXE checks the registry to locate the viewer that should be used with a particular file type. It starts the search at `HKEY_CLASSES_ROOT\QuickView\*` to locate all registered viewers (see Figure 7-8). You'll usually find that the viewer is SCC Quick Viewer.

QUIKVIEW.EXE checks the file extension for the selected file and finds the viewer for that file type.

If there is only one registered viewer, all the file extension subkeys will display the default viewer (see Figure 7-9).

If the file type has no viewer installed, Quick View displays a message saying that there is no viewer attached to this file type and asking if you want to try the default viewers. If you say No, all processing stops. If you respond affirmatively, the filename is passed to the default viewers, one at a time. (If a file viewer is able to handle the file, it may be a hex dump of the data). If none of the default viewers displays the file, Quick View displays an error message indicating there was an error opening or reading the file.

Quick View must have a target path and filename to pass to the viewer. Without that information, it is assumed that Quick View was launched as if it were a software program and it is terminated without any error messages. This means if you double-click on QUIKVIEW.EXE nothing will happen. It is meant to be used as a command associated with a selected file.

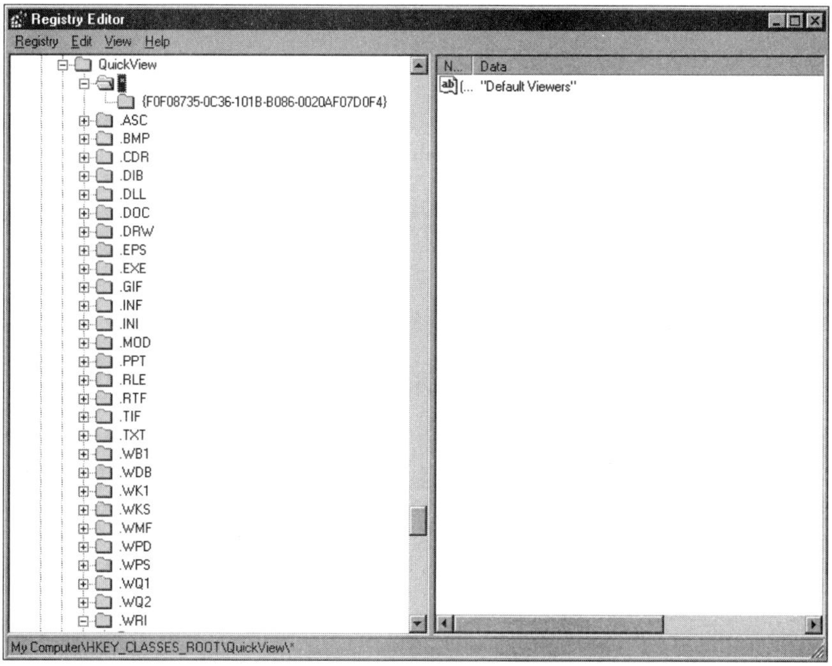

Figure 7-8: This system, like most systems, has one viewer installed, and its CLSID appears as the subkey (click the subkey to learn that the viewer is SCC Quick Viewer).

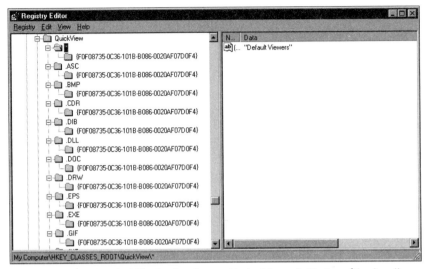

Figure 7-9: There is a `CLSID` for the viewer attached to each file type (they're all identical if you only have one viewer installed).

How a File Viewer Works

When a file viewer is installed, it registers itself for all the file types it can handle. If a file type has more than one registered file viewer, the most recently registered viewer for that file type is used when you choose Quick View from a shortcut menu.

A file viewer is an OLE object in an in-process server DLL. The way it functions is that the in-process server exports the DllGetClassObject and DllCanUnloadNow functions, and then the object implements the interfaces. This design takes advantage of the fact that a DLL loads faster than an executable file and is usually much smaller.

Sometimes a file viewer object needs to display pop-up windows and/or process messages. The DLL structure allows the object to use its own message loop if it is employing a stub process (Quick View fits this description).

It's quite probable that eventually other functions may be added to the DLL object, and the object may have to handle a request to sort or index the contents of a file. This would likely occur with a different interface, not a file viewer. In order to build additional functions, the file loading functions are separated from the operation that is performed on the file.

Here's what is checked in the registry: `HKEY_CLASSES_ROOT\QuickView \<file extension>\{<CLSID>}` is where the viewer name is checked. Then, in order to use the DLL, that viewer name `CLSID` is checked in `HKEY_CLASSES_ROOT\CLSID\`

InprocServer32 to find the path for the file viewer DLL (the subkey \InprocServer is used when it is not a 32-bit DLL).

Unknown File Types

Sometimes you open Explorer and find a file type that is unknown to your operating system. There are several explanations for this, and the most common are:

◆ You installed a software application that uses this file extension but didn't register it during the installation process. This sometimes happens if you are beta testing software, by the way.

◆ You downloaded a file from the Internet.

◆ You program in-house applications and you've devised file types that you didn't register.

When you double-click on such a file, Windows checks the registry, starting with a search for the extension subkey under HKEY_CLASSES_ROOT. If the extension isn't found, the registry is checked at HKEY_CLASSES_ROOT\Unknown\shell\openas\ command for instructions on handling unknown file types (see Figure 7-10).

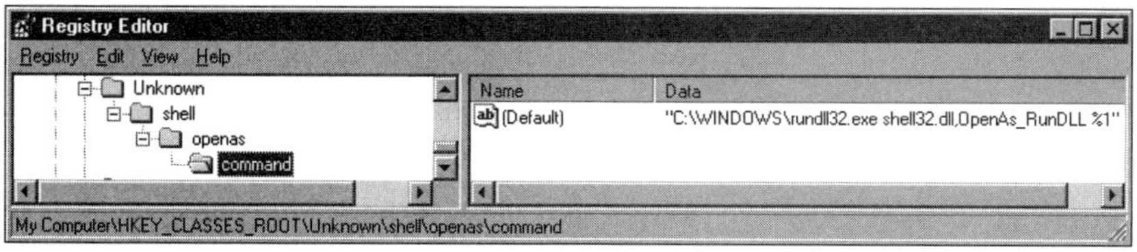

Figure 7-10: The path to the .DLL that handles unknown file types is found in the registry.

By default, the command is "%SystemRoot\rundll32.exe shell32.dll,OpenAs_ RunDLL%1", which opens the Open With dialog box (see Figure 7-11).

From the dialog box, select a program to use to open this file. If you try Quick View, you'll be told there are no viewers registered for this file type, and there will be an offer to try the default viewers. Answer Yes, and you'll frequently end up with the ability to view some or all of the file contents, or at least enough readable English to figure out where this file came from.

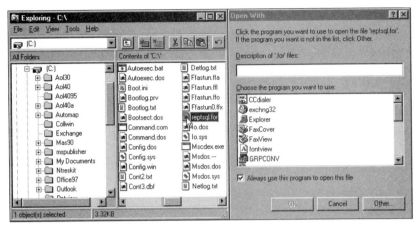

Figure 7-11: Double-clicking an unknown file type launched the Open With dialog box.

Summary

You learned about file associations in this chapter, including how to register file types, work with class identifiers, and use Quick View. In the next chapter, you'll learn about network settings in the registry.

Chapter 8

Understanding Network Settings

WINDOWS NT IS ALMOST ALWAYS PRESENT in a networked environment, and many networks also exist with Windows 95 clients, so it's important to understand the relationship of the registry to the network environment. When network-related problems arise, much of the troubleshooting is done in the registry. The registry entries for most of the network settings are placed there as a result of the network configuration process you perform with the Network applet in the Control Panel. It's better and safer to make any changes in the Control Panel instead of the registry.

We'll look at the Windows 95 and 98 registries first, and then at Windows NT 4.

Network Settings for Windows 95 and 98

In Windows 95 and 98, the Network configuration has three tabs (see Figure 8-1); the Configuration tab covers hardware (adapters) and services (including resource sharing).

The network settings are transferred to the Windows 95 or 98 registry, and they're stored all over the registry.

Network Services

The information about network device drivers for the network services you've configured exists in HKEY_LOCAL_MACHINE\System\CurrentControlSet\Services\Class\Net. The code that follows is the listing for a computer with an NE2000 compatible adapter that includes the services displayed in Figure 8-1. You can see the interdependencies of keys, where a reference in one subkey creates the need for another subkey.

Information about the installer for the network services that were configured exists in the subkey shown below (along with the icon used in the installation wizard).

```
[HKEY_LOCAL_MACHINE\System\CurrentControlSet\Services\Class\Net]
@="Network adapters"
"Installer"="netdi.dll"
"Icon"="-5"
```

147

The subkeys in the following code contain all the specific configuration information for the network services, with subkeys for each card. The subkey in the first line of code begins the tree that describes one instance of the NIC. An instance of a NIC exists for each type of service linked to that NIC. Even though computers begin numbering at 0000, this registry puts the subkeys for 0001 before those for 0000.

```
[HKEY_LOCAL_MACHINE\System\CurrentControlSet\Services\Class\Net\0001]
"DriverDesc"="NE2000 Compatible"
"DevLoader"="*ndis"
"DeviceVxDs"="ne2000.sys"
"EnumPropPages"="netdi.dll,EnumPropPages"
"InterruptNumber"=hex:04,00,00,00
"IOBaseAddress"=hex:02,00,00,00
"InfPath"="NETNOVEL.INF"
"UseIRQ2"="0"
```

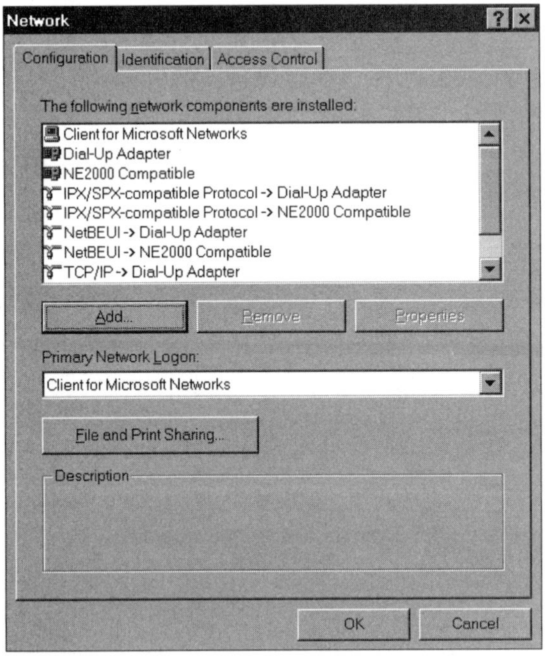

Figure 8-1: All network configurations, including options for sharing, are established in the Windows 95 or 98 Network applet in the Control Panel.

The following subkey begins a tree of information about this instance of the NIC and the Ndi (Network Driver Interface) for the NIC.

```
[HKEY_LOCAL_MACHINE\System\CurrentControlSet\Services\Class\Net\000
 1\Ndi]
"DeviceID"="*PNP80D6"
"InstallInf"=""
"InfSection"="*pnp80d6.ndi"

[HKEY_LOCAL_MACHINE\System\CurrentControlSet\Services\Class\Net\0001
 \Ndi\Interfaces]
"DefUpper"="ndis2,ndis3"
"DefLower"="ethernet"
"UpperRange"="ndis2,ndis3,odi"
"LowerRange"="ethernet"
"Upper"="ndis3,ndis2"
"Lower"="ethernet"

[HKEY_LOCAL_MACHINE\System\CurrentControlSet\Services\Class\Net\0001
 \Ndi\Install]
"ndis3"="ne2000.ndis3"
"ndis2"="ne2000.ndis2"

[HKEY_LOCAL_MACHINE\System\CurrentControlSet\Services\Class\Net\0001
 \Ndi\params]

[HKEY_LOCAL_MACHINE\System\CurrentControlSet\Services\Class\Net\0001
 \Ndi\params\InterruptNumber]
"resc"=hex:04,00,00,00
"ParamDesc"="Interrupt Level"
"flag"=hex:60,00,00,00

[HKEY_LOCAL_MACHINE\System\CurrentControlSet\Services\Class\Net\0001
 \Ndi\params\IOBaseAddress]
"resc"=hex:02,00,00,00
"ParamDesc"="I/O Base Address"
"flag"=hex:20,00,00,00

[HKEY_LOCAL_MACHINE\System\CurrentControlSet\Services\Class\Net\0001
 \Ndi\params\Interrupt]
"resc"=hex:04,00,00,00
"ParamDesc"="Interrupt Level"
"flag"=hex:10,00,00,00

[HKEY_LOCAL_MACHINE\System\CurrentControlSet\Services\Class\Net\0001
 \Ndi\params\IOBase]
"resc"=hex:02,00,00,00
"ParamDesc"="I/O Base Address"
"flag"=hex:10,00,00,00
```

The next set of subkeys holds information about NDIS (Network Driver Interface Specification). All drivers for network adapters and network services conform to the NDIS specification (which was developed by Microsoft and 3COM a number of years ago).

```
[HKEY_LOCAL_MACHINE\System\CurrentControlSet\Services\Class\Net\0001
 \NDIS]
"LogDriverName"="NE2000"
"MajorNdisVersion"=hex:03
"MinorNdisVersion"=hex:0a

[HKEY_LOCAL_MACHINE\System\CurrentControlSet\Services\Class\Net\0001
 \NDIS\NDIS2]
"DriverName"="MS2000$"
"FileName"="ne2000.dos"

[HKEY_LOCAL_MACHINE\System\CurrentControlSet\Services\Class\Net\0001
 \NDIS\ODI]
"DriverName"="NE2000"
"FileName"="ne2000.com"
```

The following subkeys are the beginning of the information tree about the 0000 instance of the NIC (which, in this case, is where the NIC is linked to Dial-Up Networking).

```
[HKEY_LOCAL_MACHINE\System\CurrentControlSet\Services\Class\Net\0000]
"DriverDesc"="Dial-Up Adapter"
"AdapterName"="MS$PPP"
"InfPath"="netppp.inf"
"DevLoader"="*ndis"
"EnumPropPages"="netdi.dll,EnumPropPages"
"DeviceVxDs"="pppmac.vxd"
"SLOWNET"=hex:01
"REDIRSESSIONTIMEOUT"=hex:f0
"Logging"="0"
"IPXHeaderCompression"="1"

[HKEY_LOCAL_MACHINE\System\CurrentControlSet\Services\Class\Net\0000
 \Ndi]
"DeviceID"="*PNP8387"
"CardType"="FORCEENUM"
"HelpText"="The Dial-Up Adapter lets your computer connect to PPP,
 RAS and Netware Connect dial up servers using a modem or cable."
"InstallInf"=""
"InfSection"="PPPMAC.ndi"

[HKEY_LOCAL_MACHINE\System\CurrentControlSet\Services\Class\Net\0000
 \Ndi\params]
```

```
[HKEY_LOCAL_MACHINE\System\CurrentControlSet\Services\Class\Net\0000
 \Ndi\params\Logging]
"ParamDesc"="Record a log file"
"default"="0"
"type"="enum"
@="0"

[HKEY_LOCAL_MACHINE\System\CurrentControlSet\Services\Class\Net\0000
 \Ndi\params\Logging\enum]
"0"="No"
"1"="Yes"

[HKEY_LOCAL_MACHINE\System\CurrentControlSet\Services\Class\Net\0000
 \Ndi\params\IPXHeaderCompression]
"ParamDesc"="Use IPX header compression"
"default"="1"
"type"="enum"
@="1"

[HKEY_LOCAL_MACHINE\System\CurrentControlSet\Services\Class\Net\0000
 \Ndi\params\IPXHeaderCompression\enum]
"0"="No"
"1"="Yes"

[HKEY_LOCAL_MACHINE\System\CurrentControlSet\Services\Class\Net\0000
 \Ndi\Interfaces]
"DefUpper"="ndis3"
"DefLower"="vcomm"
"UpperRange"="ndis3"
"LowerRange"="vcomm"
"Upper"="ndis3"
"Lower"="vcomm"

[HKEY_LOCAL_MACHINE\System\CurrentControlSet\Services\Class\Net\0000
 \Ndi\Install]
@="PPPMAC.Install"
```

VxD Devices

VxD devices are virtual machine devices that operate at Ring 0, so they perform low-level services (they are virtualized as part of the operating system instead of as external devices). Virtual devices are fast and efficient because they bypass all the protected mode safety checks and manage memory extremely well.

Devices that aren't virtualized are called real mode devices, and they're usually loaded in CONFIG.SYS or AUTOEXEC.BAT.

The network settings discussed in this section are services that use these powerful virtual drivers. The specific settings for the services name the virtual driver, and they are kept in the registry. The subkeys exist only if you've installed the service.

The .vxd drivers themselves are found in your Windows 95 or 98 system in *\%SystemRoot%*System.

Understanding Ring 0

The operating system operates at several levels, or modes. The mode with the most privileges is Ring 0, which is also known as Kernel Mode. The name Ring 0 comes from the concept in which modes are visualized as a group of concentric circles around the CPU (picture those models of the solar system we all made in junior high school, especially the planets with rings of moons). The innermost circle is known as Ring 0, and any functions that are permitted to operate in Ring 0 are closer to the CPU and have more direct access to the CPU functions. These are what we call low-level services.

Software applications do not have access to Kernel Mode; instead, they run in User Mode. In User Mode, applications don't have direct access to any functions, and must request services from the operating system. This, of course, is slower than grabbing whatever you need without having to ask the operating system.

Depending on the operating system or how you want to describe the various levels of access to the CPU's features, you can define operating systems as having three Ring levels or two Ring levels. For Windows 95, Windows 98, and Windows NT, we usually discuss only two Ring levels, which are translated as Kernel Mode and User Mode. As another example, however, OS/2 has three clearly defined Rings; some operating system functions are at Ring 0, others are at Ring 1, and applications operate at Ring 3.

A Primer on Protocols

The protocols in the registry dumps that follow this section may just look like names to you. Protocols actually provide the communication pipes that enable computers to communicate with one another. Let's take a moment to explain the protocols that ship with Windows NT 4.

DATA LINK CONTROL (DLC)

DLC is not generally used for direct computer-to-computer communication. It is used when a computer needs to communicate with a DLC device. The two most common DLC devices found in corporate networks are IBM mainframes and certain HP printers (those with their own built-in network devices).

If you use a gateway software service to an IBM mainframe, you only need the DLC protocol on the gateway. However, if you've installed 3270 terminal emulation in workstations in order to reach a mainframe directly, you have to configure the DLC protocol. Incidentally, you can use 5250 emulation and DLC to connect to an IBM AS/400 (finding AS/400 machines on networks is becoming more common these days).

DLC requires an ethernet or token ring interface.

Virtual Devices

Virtual devices are the operating system's method of inventing a fake device in place of a real device. For example, you have a real monitor attached to your computer. In a multitasking operating system, what do you do when two programs (or more) want to use those devices? Imagine that one software program, perhaps your Dial-Up Networking connection, is working in the background and displaying messages in its software window. In the foreground, you're busy using a word processing program to write a letter to Mom. The reason both programs are capable of displaying characters in their respective software windows is that each of them has a virtual monitor. When the software program tells the operating system, "Hey, I want to display a message to the user," the program receives a virtual monitor. The software thinks it's writing to your physical monitor. In fact, your word processor also thinks it's writing to your physical monitor, but it too is sending its display to a virtual monitor. Then, the operating system decides which output to a virtual monitor gets sent to the real monitor. This is all necessary to support multitasking. For multitasking to work, no program can grab a real device because that would prohibit any other program from getting to that device. A multitasking operating system can create as many virtual devices as it needs to support all the requests from software.

Incidentally, even memory works this way. Windows 95 and 98 create as much virtual memory as they need to support the requirements of all the software programs running simultaneously. The software thinks it is sending data to RAM, but the operating system is busy swapping data between RAM and the hard drive (the holding area for data in virtual memory).

The device the operating system uses to create these fictional hardware devices is called a driver. The software that thinks it is sending data to a monitor is actually sending data to a driver.

Real mode devices are the actual devices. DOS is unable to use a virtual device because programs written for DOS don't ask the operating system for anything—they just grab what they need. A DOS word processor just grabs the monitor; nothing in the program code considers asking the operating system's permission for it. Of course, you can't blame the DOS programmers for that rudeness —DOS isn't a multitasking operating system.

NETBEUI

NetBEUI stands for NetBIOS Extended User Interface (NetBIOS is a programming interface that uses NetBEUI for transport—NetBIOS is NOT a protocol). This protocol, which IBM developed several years ago, was designed for small networks. It was adopted by Microsoft as the standard protocol for NT. It continues to be a fast, efficient protocol for networks that are cabled together.

However, as networks become larger and workstations are no longer directly connected by cable (there's no way to do that when you open a branch office in another city), NetBEUI becomes less efficient. Although you could continue to use this protocol by configuring a WAN, the performance of NetBEUI over WAN lines is impossibly awful. Also, you can't route NetBEUI, so there is no chance to improve WAN performance by building routers and gateways.

NetBEUI is self-configuring — there are no user-induced tweaking functions.

NETWORK DDE

Network Dynamic Data Exchange is the network version of DDE (which has been a part of Windows since Windows 2.0). It is used to connect to shares on connected machines (the connection can be of any type: cable, phone, satellite, whatever). The shares have to be created specifically for use via NetDDE, and share names used for this purpose are considered reserved names — you can't use NetDDE share names for other share types. The format for these NetDDE share names is *Name_of_Server*\ndde$.

NetDDE is used by applications — it's not something you install and configure for computer-to-computer communication. Windows Chat is one application that makes use of this protocol; another such application is the Clipbook Viewer (which enables you to share clipboard data around a network). Windows NT ships with an application named DDESHARE.EXE, which applications can use to exchange data via NetDDE.

NWLINK (IPX/SPX)

Novell invented IPX/SPX, and NWLink is Microsoft's version of this protocol. It is a "Microsoft-ized" version of the protocol (not really 100 percent compatible, but good enough for accessing NetWare servers for file and print services), and does not, by itself, enable users to log in to a NetWare network. To do that, you must also run one of the Microsoft redirectors: either Client Services for Netware for Windows NT workstation or Gateway Services for NetWare for Windows NT Server.

TCP/IP

Today, Transmission Control Protocol/Internet Protocol is the standard for connectivity over telephone lines, and is growing in its popularity as a protocol for computers that are directly connected. It handles both connection types equally well.

The advantages of TCP/IP are that it can be routed from anywhere to anywhere, it provides incredibly easy connection to the Internet, it can issue an address during boot (making it easy to identify and find computers via IP addresses), and it can run on all kinds of computers (from PCs to mainframes).

STREAMS

Windows NT also supports the Unix-based Streams protocol. It is used primarily for transferring data when a system is changed from Unix to NT, because its performance level is fairly poor. It takes a great deal of overhead to run Streams (because it is designed to exchange data over multiple channels simultaneously, which is not usually available in standard network topology).

SERVER MESSAGE BLOCKS (SMB)

This is another protocol used by Windows NT that you don't install and configure. NT uses this protocol to communicate between computers and redirector software. The message blocks use a variety of message types to complete their work:

◆ Session Control messages, which set up or close a redirector connection to a remote resource.

◆ File messages, which give access to files on a server.

◆ Printer messages, which manipulate and manage print queues.

◆ Message messages, which are used to pass information between applications and remote computers.

The VDX Drivers in the Registry

Now that you understand the protocols, let's look at the registry information about those protocols and the drivers that control them.

IPX/SPX

If you're using IPX/SPX to connect to a NetWare server, information about drivers is stored in HKEY_LOCAL_MACHINE\System\CurrentControlSet\Services\VxD\ NWLink (see Figure 8-2).

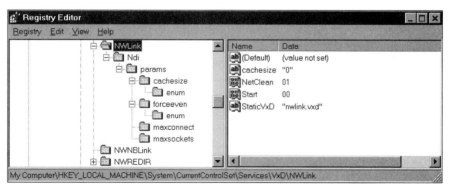

Figure 8-2: NetWare protocol configuration information is stored in its own set of subkeys.

The \Ndi subkey is where the Network Driver Interface (NDI) device driver exists. This is a network specification that enables NICs to work independently of the protocol used on the network.

Subkeys under \Ndi hold the settings for the NDI driver installed through the Network applet in the Control Panel. You can match those subkeys against the properties of the IPX/SPX listing.

The subkeys are:

◆ \params, which contains specific parameters (described in this list).

◆ \params\cachesize, which is the size of the cache used with source routing (the data displays the number of entries, not bytes). You choose this via a drop-down list in the Control Panel, and the default is Off.

◆ \params\cachesize\enum, which holds the contents of the drop-down list for \params\cachesize.

◆ \params\forceeven, which enables users who are connecting to Ethernet 802.3 to frame type force packets of even length.

◆ \params\forceeven\enum, which holds the Control Panel choices for the forceeven option (in this case, the choices are Yes and No).

◆ \params\maxconnect, which defines the maximum number of connections that can be created with IPX.

◆ \params\maxsockets, which specifies the maximum number of IPX sockets that the driver can create.

NETBEUI

Registry settings for NetBEUI, which is used with Microsoft Networks, are found in HKEY_LOCAL_MACHINE\System\CurrentControlSet\Services\VxD\NETBEUI (see Figure 8-3). The key, which mirrors the properties for this service, contains the current settings for ncbs (network control blocks) and the maximum sessions.

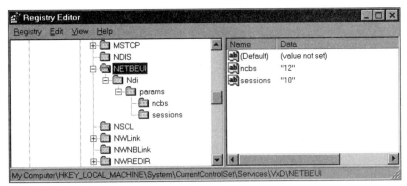

Figure 8-3: The specific settings for NetBEUI configuration are stored in the registry.

Like IPX/SPX, NetBEUI has a subkey \Ndi, which enables NICS to work independently of the current protocol and under the subkey \params. The subkeys under \Ndi\params are:

- \params\ncbs, which stores the network control blocks information (the maximum number of NetBIOS commands the driver can use).

- \params\sessions, which is the maximum number of remote computers the protocol redirector can support.

NWREDIR

The NWREDIR key defines the network redirector for Microsoft's client for NetWare. This enables the user to open, read, write, and delete files, and also contains the specifications for sending jobs to network printers.

As with the two keys discussed previously, NWREDIR also contains an \Ndi subkey, which has subkeys for params. In this case, let's look at an actual registry for a Windows 95 machine, instead of listing the subkeys (just to break the monotony). Notice again that where choices appear in the Control Panel, data also appears in the subkey, and below that, an \enum subkey lists the available choices.

```
[HKEY_LOCAL_MACHINE\System\CurrentControlSet\Services\VxD\NWREDIR]
"FirstNetworkDrive"=hex:06
"PreferredTree"=""
"DefaultContext"=""
"NeighborhoodContext"=""
"SearchMode"=hex:00
"Start"=hex:00
"NetClean"=hex:01
"PreserveCase"="1"


[HKEY_LOCAL_MACHINE\System\CurrentControlSet\Services\VxD\NWREDIR\Nd
 i]


[HKEY_LOCAL_MACHINE\System\CurrentControlSet\Services\VxD\NWREDIR\Nd
 i\params]


[HKEY_LOCAL_MACHINE\System\CurrentControlSet\Services\VxD\NWREDIR\Nd
 i\params\PreserveCase]
"ParamDesc"="Preserve Case"
"default"="1"
"type"="enum"
@="1"


[HKEY_LOCAL_MACHINE\System\CurrentControlSet\Services\VxD\NWREDIR\Nd
 i\params\PreserveCase\enum]
"0"="No"
"1"="Yes"


[HKEY_LOCAL_MACHINE\System\CurrentControlSet\Services\VxD\NWREDIR\Se
 rviceProvider]
```

```
"Class"=hex:08,00,00,00
"ProviderPath"="sapnsp.dll"

[HKEY_LOCAL_MACHINE\System\CurrentControlSet\Services\VxD\NWREDIR\Pa
  rameters]

[HKEY_LOCAL_MACHINE\System\CurrentControlSet\Services\VxD\NWREDIR\Pa
  rameters\Winsock]
"HelperDllName"="sapnsp.dll"
```

VNETSUP

In Windows 95 and 98, file and printer sharing is established in the Network applet in the Control Panel. VNETSUP is the name of the service that provides sharing, and it's treated like a network service by the operating system.

Once again, we find an \Ndi key with \params subkeys that define the Ndi driver (see Figure 8-4).

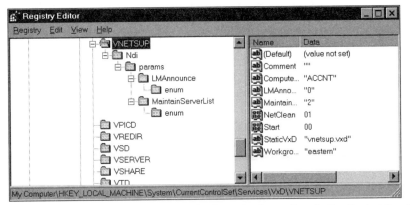

Figure 8-4: When you configure file and printer sharing options in the Control Panel, the specifications are sent to the registry.

The key and its subkeys store information about the computer, its workgroup (in this case, the workgroup "eastern" is an NT domain), and the way file and print services are shared. As with other network registry items, the \Ndi\params subkeys store the configuration options made by the user, and the \enums subkey stores the options the user sees.

```
[HKEY_LOCAL_MACHINE\System\CurrentControlSet\Services\VxD\VNETSUP]
"ComputerName"="ACCNT"
"Workgroup"="eastern"
"Comment"=""
"StaticVxD"="vnetsup.vxd"
```

```
"Start"=hex:00
"NetClean"=hex:01
"MaintainServerList"="2"
"LMAnnounce"="0"

[HKEY_LOCAL_MACHINE\System\CurrentControlSet\Services\VxD\VNETSUP\
  Ndi]

[HKEY_LOCAL_MACHINE\System\CurrentControlSet\Services\VxD\VNETSUP\
  Ndi\params]

[HKEY_LOCAL_MACHINE\System\CurrentControlSet\Services\VxD\VNETSUP\
  Ndi\params\MaintainServerList]
"default"="2"
"ParamDesc"="Browse Master"
"type"="enum"
@="2"

[HKEY_LOCAL_MACHINE\System\CurrentControlSet\Services\VxD\VNETSUP\
  Ndi\params\MaintainServerList\enum]
"2"="Automatic"
"1"="Enabled"
"0"="Disabled"

[HKEY_LOCAL_MACHINE\System\CurrentControlSet\Services\VxD\VNETSUP\
  Ndi\params\LMAnnounce]
"default"="0"
"ParamDesc"="LM Announce"
"type"="enum"
@="0"

[HKEY_LOCAL_MACHINE\System\CurrentControlSet\Services\VxD\VNETSUP\
  Ndi\params\LMAnnounce\enum]
"1"="Yes"
"0"="No"
```

More Network Settings

Remember when I said that the network settings were stored all over the registry? Well, take a quick look at HKEY_LOCAL_MACHINE\Enum\Network. You'll find the configuration details for protocols and bindings.

These subkeys hold settings that are generated by bus enumerators, and the existence of a subkey depends on the network and services you've chosen during your network configuration process. A typical Windows 95 machine's registry is presented below. Note that each instance of a service is numbered (0001, 0002, and so on). The following listing contains the top subkey for each service. If you look at a Windows 95 or 98 computer registry and drill down below these subkeys, you may find more numbered instances than you'd expect (one of the computers on my network has numbered instances running to 0011). That's because each time you open the Network applet in the Control Panel to make any changes or tweak settings, a new subkey is written to the registry.

```
[HKEY_LOCAL_MACHINE\Enum\Network]
[HKEY_LOCAL_MACHINE\Enum\Network\NETBEUI]

[HKEY_LOCAL_MACHINE\Enum\Network\VREDIR]

[HKEY_LOCAL_MACHINE\Enum\Network\NWREDIR]

[HKEY_LOCAL_MACHINE\Enum\Network\VSERVER]

[HKEY_LOCAL_MACHINE\Enum\Network\NWLINK]

[HKEY_LOCAL_MACHINE\Enum\Network\MSTCP]
```

Real Mode Device Drivers

If you're using any real mode drivers, they're registered in HKEY_LOCAL_ MACHINE\Software. There's a subkey for each company, and under that appears the product and then the driver version.

Adapter Settings

The hardware settings exist in one of two places, depending on whether your NIC is Plug and Play (PnP)-compatible.

For PnP NICs, look in HKEY_LOCAL_MACHINE\Enum\ISAPnP.

For non-PnP NICs, look in HKEY_LOCAL_MACHINE\Enum\Root (see Figure 8-5).

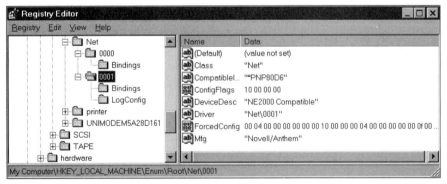

Figure 8-5: The NIC in this machine is not Plug and Play–compatible, so the registry keeps its information in the \Enum\Root subkey.

Windows NT 4 Network Registry Settings

Most of the time, the basic network settings for your Windows NT 4 system are set at installation. However, I've noticed that most of the installation problems I've encountered with NT 4 occurred when there was a problem with the installation steps related to the computer's NIC. In those cases, I've installed NT 4 by telling the operating system there was no NIC in the system (okay, I lied), and then by installing all the network components and options after the operating system itself was installed and running.

Network Settings in Control Panel

Network settings are user-configured in the Networks applet in the Control Panel. The dialog box for NT 4 differs from that in Windows 95 or 98. Let's take a brief look at the tabs for the dialog box, and then at the parts of the registry that contain the configuration information displayed in the tabs:

- ◆ The Identification tab displays the computer's name and workgroup/domain.

- ◆ The Services tab lists the installed services for this computer (see Figure 8-6). A description appears for the selected service.

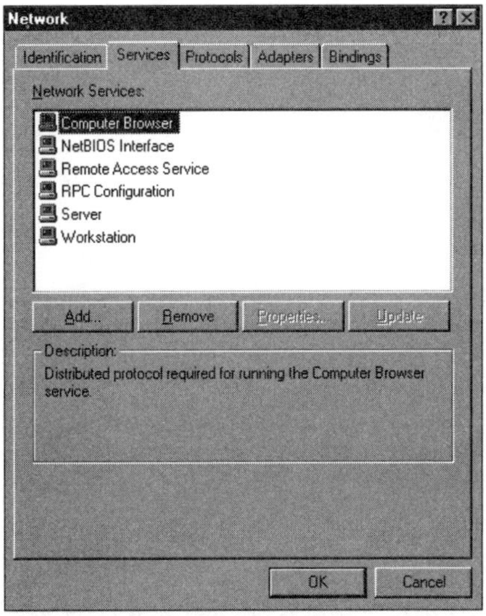

Figure 8-6: The installed services are listed and described in the Services tab of the Network applet in the Control Panel.

♦ The Protocols tab lists the installed services (this particular computer has NetBEUI and TCP/IP installed). You can view and change the properties for some services.

♦ The NIC configuration is in the Adapters tab. You can view and change the IRQ and I/O settings.

♦ The Bindings tab displays the network bindings installed by the operating system. You can enable, disable, and change the order of the bindings.

As you add to and configure your network, subkeys are added to your registry.

Adapter Subkeys

The subkeys that are added for your adapter appear in several places.

The entry for the NIC driver is found in `HKEY_LOCAL_MACHINE\Software\`
`CompanyName\Product\Version`, where:

♦ `CompanyName` is the name of the company that produced the driver (frequently Microsoft).

♦ `Product` is the name of the adapter.

♦ `Version` is the driver version (usually Current).

Figure 8-7, for example, shows the registry entry for `HKEY_LOCAL_MACHINE\`
`Software\Microsoft\NE2000\CurrentVersion`.

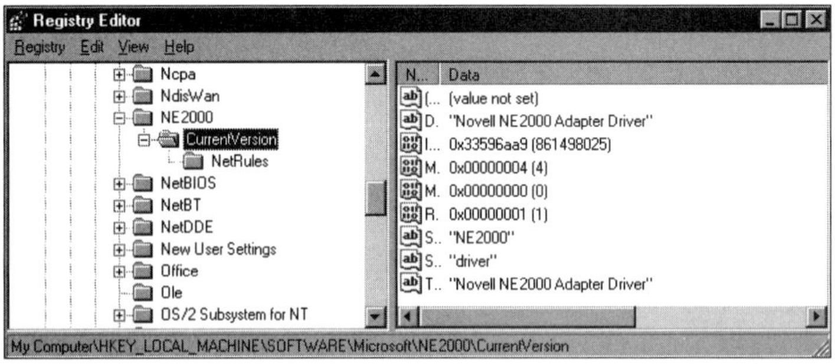

Figure 8-7: The registry entry shows the driver for the popular NE2000 card
from Microsoft.

In `HKEY_LOCAL_MACHINE\Software\Microsoft\WindowsNT\CurrentVersion\`
`NetworkCards` you'll find an entry for each combination of an adapter and a service. This means that the installation of a NIC results in a number of subkeys. For example, in the registry information that follows, you'll see entries for all the services connected to an NE2000 NIC. (Note that the numbering system starts with 1, not the usual 0).

Additionally, each service component key has a subkey named NetRules, which contains information about that component and its relationship with the rest of the network settings.

```
[HKEY_LOCAL_MACHINE\SOFTWARE\Microsoft\Windows
 NT\CurrentVersion\NetworkCards\1]
"ServiceName"="NE20001"
"Manufacturer"="Microsoft"
"Title"="[1] Novell NE2000 Adapter"
"Description"="Novell NE2000 Adapter"
"ProductName"="NE2000"
"OperationsSupport"=dword:00000086
"InstallDate"=dword:33596aa9

[HKEY_LOCAL_MACHINE\SOFTWARE\Microsoft\Windows
 NT\CurrentVersion\NetworkCards\1\NetRules]
"InfName"="oemnadn2.inf"
"type"="ne2000 ne2000Adapter"
"bindform"="\"NE20001\" yes yes container"
"class"=hex(7):6e,65,32,30,30,30,41,64,61,70,74,65,72,20,62,61,73,69
 ,63,00,00
"InfOption"="NE2000"

[HKEY_LOCAL_MACHINE\SOFTWARE\Microsoft\Windows
 NT\CurrentVersion\NetworkCards\2]
"ServiceName"="NdisWan2"
"Manufacturer"="Microsoft"
"Title"="[2] Remote Access WAN Wrapper"
"Description"="Windows NT Remote Access WAN Wrapper"
"ProductName"="NdisWan"
"InstallDate"=dword:3359d808
"Hidden"=dword:00000001

[HKEY_LOCAL_MACHINE\SOFTWARE\Microsoft\Windows
 NT\CurrentVersion\NetworkCards\2\NetRules]
"InfName"="OEMNSVRA.INF"
"type"="ndisWanBH ndisWanAdapterBH"
"bindform"="\"NdisWan2\" yes yes container"
"class"=hex(7):6e,64,69,73,57,61,6e,41,64,61,70,74,65,72,42,48,20,62
 ,61,73,69,\
  63,00,00
"InfOption"="NDISWAN"

[HKEY_LOCAL_MACHINE\SOFTWARE\Microsoft\Windows
 NT\CurrentVersion\NetworkCards\3]
"ServiceName"="AsyncMac3"
"Manufacturer"="Microsoft"
"Title"="[3] Remote Access Mac"
"Description"="Windows NT Remote Access AsyMac Adapter Driver"
"ProductName"="AsyncMac"
"InstallDate"=dword:3359d808
"Hidden"=dword:00000001
```

```
[HKEY_LOCAL_MACHINE\SOFTWARE\Microsoft\Windows
 NT\CurrentVersion\NetworkCards\3\NetRules]
"InfName"="OEMNSVRA.INF"
"type"="rasAsyMac rasAsyMacAdapter"
"bindform"="\"AsyncMac3\" yes yes container"
"class"=hex(7):72,61,73,41,73,79,4d,61,63,41,64,61,70,74,65,72,20,62
,61,73,69,\
  63,00,00
"InfOption"="RASASYMAC"

[HKEY_LOCAL_MACHINE\SOFTWARE\Microsoft\Windows
 NT\CurrentVersion\NetworkCards\4]
"ServiceName"="NdisWan4"
"Manufacturer"="Microsoft"
"Title"="[4] Remote Access WAN Wrapper"
"Description"="Windows NT Remote Access WAN Wrapper"
"InstallDate"=dword:3359d808
"Hidden"=dword:00000001
"ProductName"="NdisWanDialout"

[HKEY_LOCAL_MACHINE\SOFTWARE\Microsoft\Windows
 NT\CurrentVersion\NetworkCards\4\NetRules]
"InfName"="OEMNSVRA.INF"
"type"="ndiswandialout ndisWanAdapterDialOut"
"bindform"="\"NdisWan4\" yes yes container"
"class"=hex(7):6e,64,69,73,57,61,6e,41,64,61,70,74,65,72,44,69,61,6c
,4f,75,74,\
  20,62,61,73,69,63,00,00
"block"=hex(7):69,70,78,54,72,61,6e,73,70,6f,72,74,20,6e,64,69,73,57
,61,6e,41,\
  64,61,70,74,65,72,44,69,61,6c,4f,75,74,00,00
"InfOption"="NDISWAN"

[HKEY_LOCAL_MACHINE\SOFTWARE\Microsoft\Windows
 NT\CurrentVersion\NetworkCards\5]
"ServiceName"="NdisWan5"
"Manufacturer"="Microsoft"
"Title"="[5] Remote Access WAN Wrapper"
"Description"="Windows NT Remote Access WAN Wrapper"
"InstallDate"=dword:3359d808
"Hidden"=dword:00000001
"ProductName"="NdisWanDialoutIp"

[HKEY_LOCAL_MACHINE\SOFTWARE\Microsoft\Windows
 NT\CurrentVersion\NetworkCards\5\NetRules]
"InfName"="OEMNSVRA.INF"
"type"="ndiswandialoutIP ndisWanAdapterDialOutIP"
"bindform"="\"NdisWan5\" yes yes container"
"class"=hex(7):6e,64,69,73,57,61,6e,41,64,61,70,74,65,72,44,69,61,6c
,4f,75,74,\
  49,50,20,62,61,73,69,63,00,00
```

```
"block"=hex(7):69,70,78,54,72,61,6e,73,70,6f,72,74,20,6e,64,69,73,57
,61,6e,41,\
64,61,70,74,65,72,44,69,61,6c,4f,75,74,49,50,00,6e,62,66,54,72,61,6
e,73,70,\
6f,72,74,20,6e,64,69,73,57,61,6e,41,64,61,70,74,65,72,44,69,61,6c,4
f,75,74,\
49,50,00,00
"InfOption"="NDISWAN"
```

Another key that holds information about your network adapter is
`HKEY_LOCAL_MACHINE\System\CurrentControlSet\Services\`*name_of_nic*`.` One
of the subkeys of interest is `Parameters`, which holds the settings (see Figure 8-8).

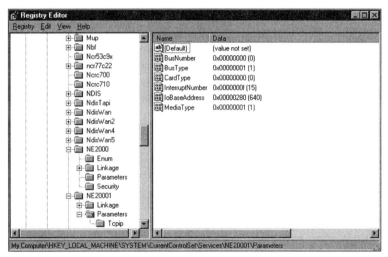

Figure 8-8: The configuration for the network adapter is in the
`Parameters` subkey.

The data items in Figure 8-8 represent the following information:

◆ BusNumber is the number of bus types in your computer, starting with 0 (so
if you have both ISA and EISA, two bus types, the data entry would be 1).

◆ BusType is the type of bus that contains your adapter, where 0=MIPS,
1=ISA, 2=EISA, 3=MCS, 4=TcChannel.

◆ CardType is the type of card used, where 0=standard type for a
desktop computer.

◆ InterruptNumber and IoBaseAddress are self-explanatory.

◆ MediaType is the network type, where 1=Ethernet, 2=IBM Token Ring,
3=ArcNet, 4=FDDI, 5=Apple LocalTalk.

Network Components

The registration of service components is placed in HKEY_LOCAL_MACHINE\System\ CurrentControlSet\Services. A subkey for your adapter appears there. Figure 8-9 shows the NE2000 adapter in a computer that has TCP/IP installed, so a separate subkey exists for the TCP/IP connection to the adapter.

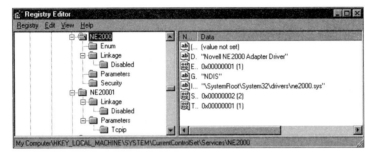

Figure 8-9: The NIC configuration and driver information exists in its own subkey.

Subkeys appear for other network services you've installed, as shown in Figure 8-10.

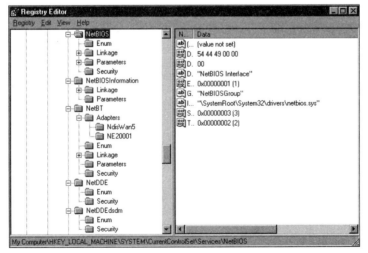

Figure 8-10: HKEY_LOCAL_MACHINE\System\CurrentControlSet\ Services has subkeys for all the network components you've installed.

Binding Information

It's beyond the scope of this book to go into the whole subject of bindings, but if you're familiar with them, this section presents an overview of their registry presence. To oversimplify, the relationships between the various network software files are called bindings, and the operating system checks all those network software files to make sure the relationships are established properly. The following items are checked:

◆ The complete set of network components, and the specific type of each component.

◆ The possible bindings that could occur among the components.

◆ The appropriate way to communicate binding information to each component.

As an example of communicating binding information, if you've installed TCP/IP and then installed or reconfigured an adapter, you'll be asked to configure an IP address that can be passed to the adapter.

During startup, `HKEY_LOCAL_MACHINE\System\CurrentControlSet\Services` is checked, and each network service that's found is examined to see if it contains binding information. If it does, a `Linkage` subkey is created, and its data entry describes the binding information.

Bindings work with rules called *usability requirements*; these rules state that the binding must terminate at an adapter, or at some logical endpoint (such as a software component that takes up the interconnection chores).

As an example, following is the `Linkage` subkey for `Nbf`. The Bind and Export data entries are based on the definitions found in the NetRules subkey for the network component.

```
[HKEY_LOCAL_MACHINE\SYSTEM\CurrentControlSet\Services\Nbf\Linkage]
"Bind"  "\Device\NE20001"
        "\Device\NdisWan4"
"Export"\Device\NE20001"
        "\Device\Nbf_NdisWan4"
"Route" "NE2000"
        "NE20001"
        "NdisWan4"
```

Other Network Information

A number of other network registry items exist that you should know about, so I'll cover them briefly in this section.

SERVER SERVICES

Server information is stored in subkeys under `HKEY_LOCAL_MACHINE\System\CurrentControlSet\Services\LanmanServer`, as seen in Figure 8-11.

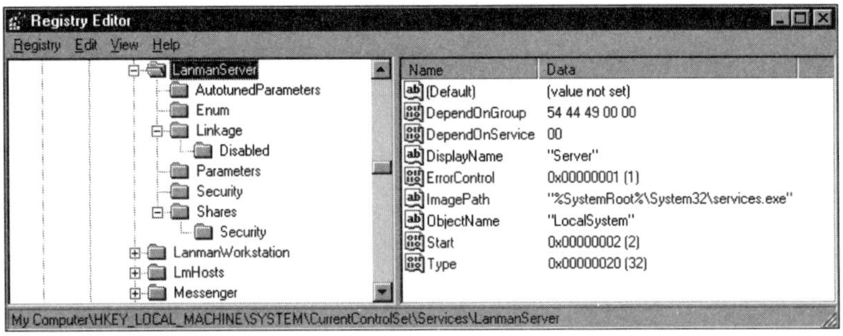

Figure 8-11: Settings for Server services are stored in the registry.

The server information in Figure 8-11 is from a workstation with three shares configured, and Figure 8-12 displays the data for the `Shares` subkey. Additionally, I've opened the data for one share so you can see the detailed information, including the path.

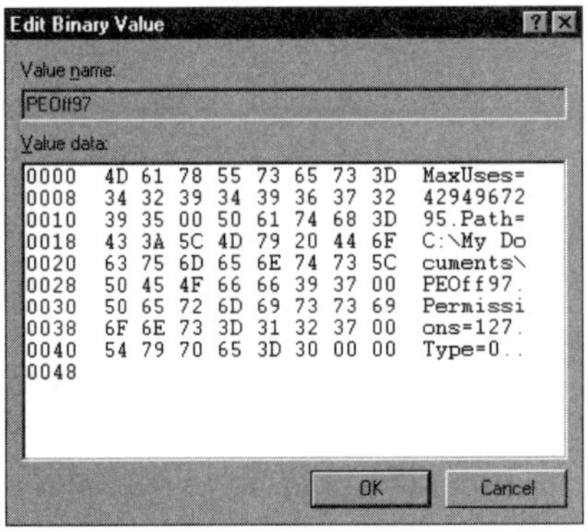

Figure 8-12: A workstation is a server when its shared resources are accessed.

REMOTE ACCESS SERVICE

When you install Remote Access Service (RAS), quite a few entries are added to the registry, but the primary key is `HKEY_LOCAL_MACHINE\System\CurrentControlSet\Services\RemoteAccess` (see Figure 8-13). Also of interest are the parameters (see Figure 8-14).

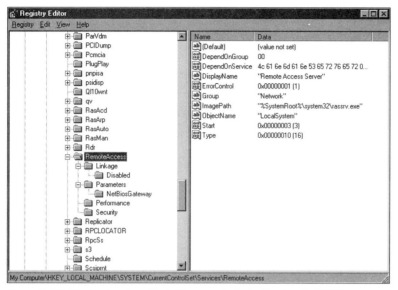

Figure 8-13: The basic values for RAS are part of the Services in HKEY_
LOCAL_MACHINE.

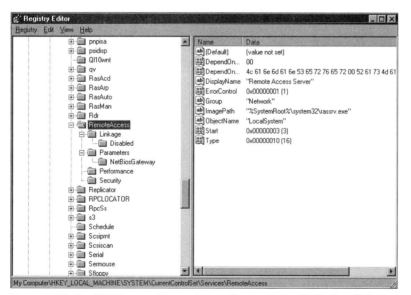

Figure 8-14: The RAS Parameters subkey reflects your configuration choices.

TCP/IP

When you install TCP/IP protocol, a number of keys in `HKEY_LOCAL_MACHINE\System\CurrentControlSet\Services` are created or affected:

♦ `\DHCP\Parameters`

♦ `\WinSock\Parameters`

♦ `\NetBt\Parameters`

♦ `\`*`Adapter`*`\Parameters\Tcpip`

♦ `\Tcpip`

The `\Tcpip` key, of course, contains a number of subkeys, as shown in Figure 8-15.

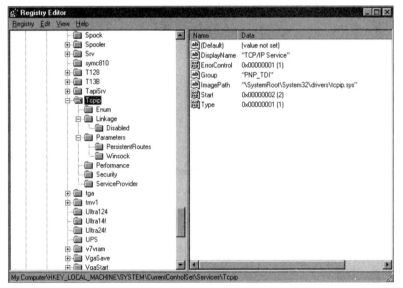

Figure 8-15: The data values in the subkeys reflect your TCP/IP setup.

Depending on the other services you've installed, you may find additional TCP/IP references (for example, ftp parameters).

Summary

This chapter covered network settings in the Windows 95, 98, and NT 4 registries. In the next chapter, you'll learn how to secure the Windows NT 4 registry.

Chapter 9

Securing the Registry

IF YOU WORK EXCLUSIVELY with Windows 95 and 98, skip this chapter; you cannot secure the Windows 95 and 98 registries. Just like the rest of the security issues for those operating systems, security is nonexistent.

Okay, maybe not nonexistent – there are a couple of safeguards you can design. First, delete REGEDIT.EXE from all the Windows 95 and 98 workstations.

From your server or your own administrator's workstation, create a system for backing up the registry files to your computer or a server. Then, you can replace the registry if the user messes up. A batch file should do it:

copy \\UNC*Directory**User*.* *YourComputer**DirectoryForThatUser*

Make sure shares are created for the directories you need to access on the remote computers, and also remember you'll have to change the attributes to find and copy the files if you're using the command line.

So, for all of you who manage Windows NT 4 workstations, let's talk about security for the registry.

Controlling User Access

Every organization has at least one user who knows enough to be dangerous. And then you have those curious folks who look at an executable file in Explorer and think, "I wonder what that does." That thought is frequently followed by a double-click on the filename. When the file happens to be REGEDIT.EXE or REGEDT32.EXE – uh-oh.

The best way to keep a user from messing up the registry is to keep the user away from it. If you installed NTFS, you can set permissions to do this, both on the registry editors and on the hive files in the user's profile folder.

Unfortunately, because of the need to run legacy applications, most NT 4 workstations are FAT, not NTFS, so you'll have to devise an alternative plan.

Changing the ACL

Windows NT maintains an Access Control List (ACL) for the registry, and you can use that to secure registry keys. The ACL is a database that maintains information about permissions for accessing the registry. You can access the ACL with REGEDT32. Launch it and follow these steps:

1. Select the key for which you want to change the ACL.

2. Choose Security → Permissions from the menu bar to open the Registry Key Permissions dialog box (see Figure 9-1).

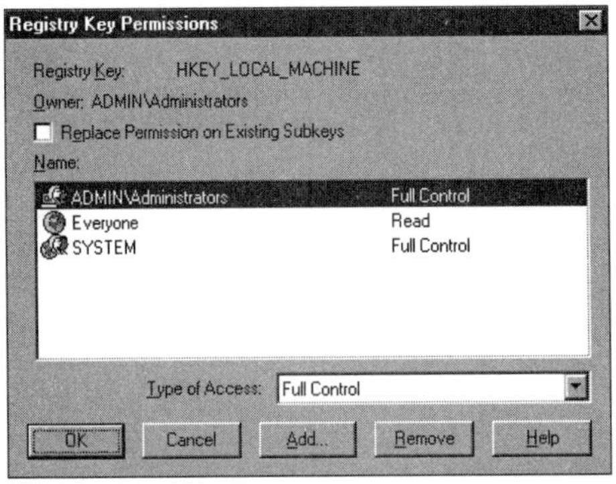

Figure 9-1: Set permissions for registry keys the same way you set file permissions in NTFS.

3. Select Replace Permission on Existing Subkeys to reset all the permissions for this key.

4. To delete a user or group, select it and choose Remove.

5. To add a user or group, choose Add to bring up the Add Users and Groups dialog box (see Figure 9-2).

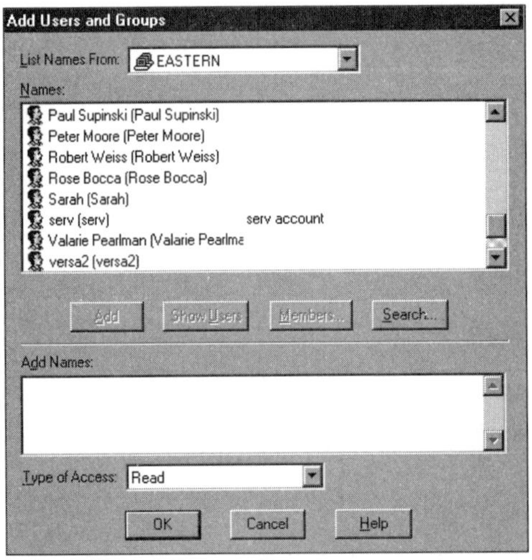

Figure 9-2: Add users or groups who have permission to access this registry key.

6. Select a group from the List Names From box (in this case, the list comes from the domain) and then choose Show Users if you want to add users instead of groups.

7. Select the user or group you want and choose Add (or just double-click).

8. Specify a Type of Access for this user or group using the following guidelines:

   ■ Full Control: The user can read, change, and delete the key.

   ■ Read: The user can only view the key.

9. Repeat the process for each user or group to which you want to give permissions. Then choose OK, and choose OK again on the Registry Key Permissions dialog box to complete the process.

TIP You can make changes to the ACL at any level of the registry; you do not have to work with the top keys.

Setting Special Access Rights

Another access type exists, called Special Access, which is not available in the Add Users and Groups dialog box. You can only assign it to a user or group from the Registry Key Permissions dialog box. This means you have to assign Full Control or Read to a user when you first add him or her, and then select the user in the Registry Key Permissions dialog box and change the access by choosing Special Access from the Type of Access list box.

Special Access means you can configure very specific permissions for a user. When you select this access type, the Special Access dialog box appears (see Figure 9-3).

The following permissions are available in the Special Access dialog box (the permissions begin at the key level for which you are granting permissions):

♦ Query Value: the user can read a value entry.

♦ Set Value: the user can read and modify a value entry.

♦ Create Subkey: the user can create a new subkey.

♦ Enumerate Subkey: the user can expand and read the subkeys.

♦ Notify: the user can audit notification events for a key.

- ◆ Create Link: the user can create a symbolic link from a key.

- ◆ Delete: the user can delete a key.

- ◆ Write DAC: the user can modify a key's permissions.

- ◆ Write Owner: the user can gain ownership of a key.

- ◆ Read Control: the user can read a key's security information.

If you set permissions for a user to have Special Access and you want to make changes, first select that user; the Type of Access box displays Special Access. If you click the down arrow next to the Type of Access list box, you see two instances of Special Access. One is the selected user's permissions, and the other (the real Special Access choice, which has an ellipsis after its name) opens the Special Access dialog box that enables you to change the permissions.

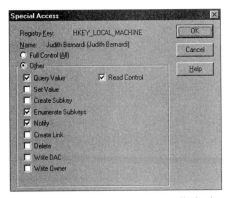

Figure 9-3: Specify very exact, very limited permissions for a user who needs special access.

 Do not mess around with the Full Control permissions for the System, because the operating system and the applications need to have full rights to the registry.

Securing Specific Keys for Safety

According to Microsoft, some keys pose a danger to the system if a user inappropriately manipulates them. To make your registry secure, make sure that the group named Everyone has only certain permissions for these important keys. The permissions are:

◆ Query Value

◆ Notify

◆ Enumerate Subkeys

◆ Read Control

The keys that are considered important for securing the registry are:

◆ `HKEY_LOCAL_MACHINE\Software\Microsoft\RPC` (and all subkeys)

◆ The following subkeys under `HKEY_LOCAL_MACHINE\Software\`
  `Microsoft\WindowsNT\CurrentVersion`:

  ```
  \ProfileList
  \AeDebug
  \Compatibility
  \Drivers
  \Embedding
  \Fonts
  \FontSubstitutes
  \GRE_Initialize
  \MCI
  \MCI Extensions
  ```

◆ `\Port` (and all subkeys)

◆ `\WOW` (and all subkeys)

◆ `HKEY_CLASSES_ROOT` (and all subkeys)

Auditing Registry Access

It's a good idea to audit access to the registry, not just to see which users are accessing it or trying to make changes, but also because it's a good method of troubleshooting any problems that occur in applications.

Setting up auditing is a two-step process: you first must turn on the auditing function for the computer, and then you establish the auditing procedures for the registry.

Enabling Auditing for the Computer

To turn on the auditing function for an NT 4 workstation or server, follow these steps (you must have administrator rights):

1. Open User Manager (or User Manager for Domains if you're on the server).

2. Choose Policies → Audit from the menu bar to display the Audit Policy dialog box (see Figure 9-4).

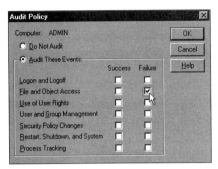

Figure 9-4: You must enable auditing for
this computer before you can configure
auditing procedures for the registry.

3. Select Audit These Events to turn on the audit choices.

4. Place a check mark under Failure for the File and Object Access event.

5. Choose OK and then close User Manager.

You can select additional audits, but choosing Failure for the File and Object
Access event is the basic, minimum requirement for auditing the registry. Selecting
additional auditing will make the audit log awfully large, so unless you have a
reason to track other events, you should avoid other auditing choices.

Setting Up Registry Auditing

To set up auditing in the registry, open REGEDT32, select the key you want to audit,
and then follow these steps:

1. Choose Security → Auditing from the menu bar to open the Registry Key
   Auditing dialog box (see Figure 9-5).

2. Select Audit Permission on Existing Subkeys if you want to extend
   auditing throughout the tree of this key.

3. Click Add to begin adding users and groups.

4. In the Add Users and Groups dialog box, select the users and groups you
   want to audit by double-clicking them. Choose OK when you've finished
   to return to the Registry Key Auditing dialog box.

5. For each user in the Name list box, select the events you want to audit.

6. Choose OK when you've finished establishing auditing options. If you
   selected Audit Permission on Existing Subkeys, you're asked to confirm
   that selection.

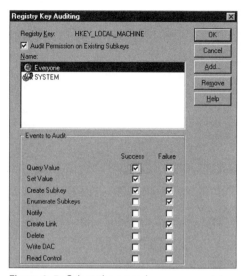

Figure 9-5: Select the procedures you want to audit, and choose whether you want to monitor success, failure, or both.

Selecting Audit Permission on Existing Subkeys can be a bit of a strain on resources. If you find things slowing down, deselect the option or reduce the number of audited events.

Viewing the Audit Log

To check up on audited events, you need to open the Event Viewer (on the Start menu, in the Administrative Tools section of Programs). When the Event Viewer appears, choose Log → Security. All audited events are listed on the log (see Figure 9-6).

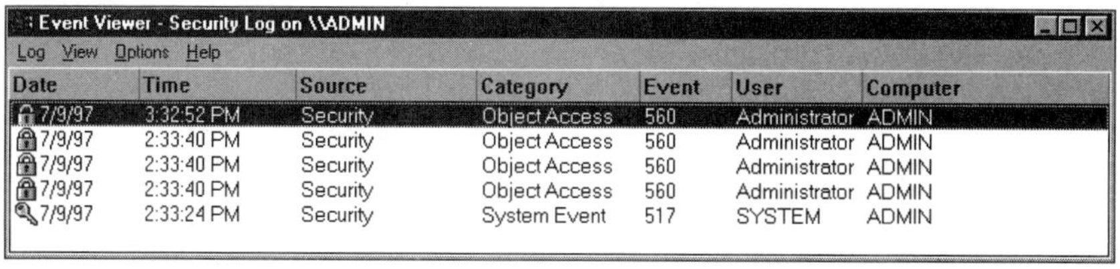

Date	Time	Source	Category	Event	User	Computer
7/9/97	3:32:52 PM	Security	Object Access	560	Administrator	ADMIN
7/9/97	2:33:40 PM	Security	Object Access	560	Administrator	ADMIN
7/9/97	2:33:40 PM	Security	Object Access	560	Administrator	ADMIN
7/9/97	2:33:40 PM	Security	Object Access	560	Administrator	ADMIN
7/9/97	2:33:24 PM	Security	System Event	517	SYSTEM	ADMIN

Figure 9-6: The security Log displays all audited events.

Double-click an event to see the details (see Figure 9-7). You can use the Next and Previous buttons to move through the list of events.

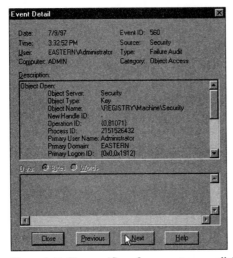

Figure 9-7: The specifics of an event are available in the Event Detail dialog box.

You can drag your mouse over any part of the Event Detail dialog box to select the text. Then, right-click to copy the text if you want to keep notes about that event (paste it wherever you're keeping your notes). If you place your insertion point anywhere in the Description box, you can right-click and choose Select All to capture the entire description.

Setting Registry Key Ownership

Although there's rarely an important reason to do so, it is possible to change the ownership of a registry key. Some rare occasion may arise that makes it necessary for a logged-on user (with administrator permissions) to take ownership of a key.

To take ownership, select the key in question and choose Security → Owner. When the Owner dialog box appears (see Figure 9-8), click Take Ownership. To exit without changing owners, click Close.

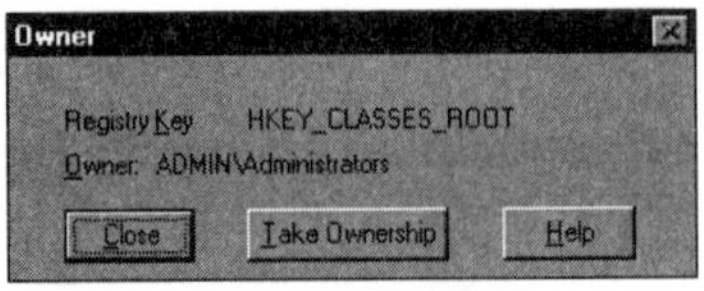

Figure 9-8: If you need to protect a key, take ownership of it.

Securing Remote Access

It's possible to edit a registry from another, connected computer. In fact, for administrators, this is a pretty handy device (see Chapter 11 for information about editing registries on other computers).

For the target computer, this capability may create a problem, so procedures are available to prevent unauthorized users from accessing a computer's registry from a remote computer.

When a remote user tries to connect to the Windows NT registry, the operating system looks for a special subkey:

```
HKEY_LOCAL_MACHINE\System\CurrentControlSet\Control\SecurePipe
  Servers\winreg
```

◆ If the \winreg subkey doesn't exist, any user can access the registry and manipulate it to the limits set by the ACL.

◆ If the \winreg subkey exists, the ACL for it determines whether the user can access and manipulate the registry.

This means that in order to secure your Windows NT workstation, you need to create the \winreg subkey and then configure the ACL for it.

 It's only necessary to create the \winreg subkey in Windows NT Workstation; it is created in NT Server by default (and administrators have Full Control permissions).

To create the \winreg subkey and configure permissions, you must open REGEDT32, go to HKEY_LOCAL_MACHINE\System\CurrentControlSet\Control\ SecurePipeServers, and then follow these steps:

1. Select the SecurePipeServers key and choose Edit → Add Key.

2. Add the key winreg.

3. Select the key and choose Security → Permissions.

4. Configure the permissions for remote users.

Hereafter, only remote users with appropriate permissions will be able to access this registry.

Summary

The registry is useful and dangerous at the same time, a combination that requires careful attention to how it is used and who uses it. Making the registry as secure as possible means you can get the productivity you need from using it, without worrying about inadvertent access that may render workstations unusable.

Chapter 10

Solving Common Problems

DESPITE YOUR BEST INTENTIONS, things can go wrong—sometimes minor, annoying things, and sometimes major, work-stopping things. This chapter looks at some of the common problems you may encounter with your computer, and their solutions. You can use the registry to solve most of the problems mentioned in this chapter.

Troubleshooting Windows 95/98

We'll start with some of the common problems that occur with Windows 95 and Windows 98 workstations.

Safe Mode Startup Doesn't Work

If Windows 95 or Windows 98 does not start in Safe Mode, you need to troubleshoot the following items:

◆ The computer may be infected with a virus. Boot to MS-DOS with a floppy disk and run a DOS-based virus detection program to eliminate the virus.

◆ The computer's CMOS settings may be incorrect. Use the appropriate keystrokes during bootup to enter the CMOS setup program.

◆ There may be a hardware conflict, such as a conflict in PCI BIOS settings, redundant COM ports (for example, two serial ports set as COM1 or an internal modem set for a COM port that exists as a physical port), or an IRQ conflict.

If everything is fine, you probably have a failing computer (RAM, motherboard, or other hardware problems), and the problem is unrelated to Windows 95/98.

Roaming Profiles Fail for Windows 95/98

Occasionally, you may find that roaming Windows 95/98 users don't get their configured desktops; instead, the default user configuration is loaded, even though the user logged on with the user name connected to the roaming profile.

If this occurs, it's probably because the user was validated by a BDC instead of the PDC. (Perhaps you're using a BDC for load balancing, or perhaps the PDC is down and the BDC has taken over logons).

Windows 95/98 clients can only receive roaming profiles from a PDC. This is a bug, and the only workaround I can think of is to continue to update the default user profile for any machines with which this user may come in contact, so that the default profile is acceptable to the roaming user.

Windows 95/98 Logon Scripts Are Ignored

If your Windows 95/98 workstations log on to a PDC with a centralized logon script (usually a Winlogon batch file), sometimes the script file isn't processed. This is because the client is accessing the logon script file while another Windows 95/98 client is doing the same thing. The first client to access the script file takes exclusive use (the file is being read in "exclusive mode"), and any other user trying read the file is denied access while it's in use. This is a known bug, and you'll have to tell your Windows 95/98 users to wait a minute or two and then log on again.

Recovering TrueType Fonts in Windows 95

If your Windows 95 installation was an upgrade from Windows 3.1x, you may have some problems with your TrueType Fonts. (At the time of writing, there is no upgrade path from Windows 3.1x to Windows 98.) You may not see your TrueType fonts in the Fonts folder, even if you add a new font. Or, you may see an error message during font installation indicating that the font is installed already, along with a rejoinder that you should remove the old version.

To fix the fonts key in your registry, follow these steps:

1. Run REGEDIT and move to `HKEY_LOCAL_MACHINE_Software\Microsoft\Windows\CurrentVersion`.

2. You probably won't see a subkey named `Fonts`. Add one.

3. Open Explorer and create a temporary folder.

4. Move (do not copy) all the fonts from `C:\%Windows95SystemRoot%\Fonts` into the temporary folder.

5. Select the now empty fonts directory in Explorer.

6. Choose File → Install New Font from the Explorer menu bar.

7. When the Add Fonts dialog box appears (see Figure 10-1), select the temporary folder as the source.

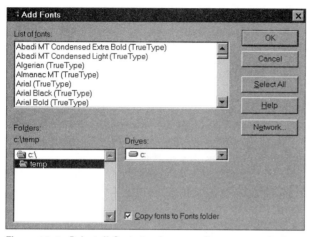

Figure 10-1: Reinstall fonts to clean up after an upgrade from Windows 3.1x.

8. Select all the fonts in the folder and choose OK.

9. Make sure you select the Copy fonts to Font folder option.

10. Close REGEDIT and Explorer.

You can now remove the fonts from the temporary file.

Stopping Repeated Printer Detection in Windows 95

If you have one of those printers (usually an HP4L or HP DeskJet660C) that Windows 95 detects every time the operating system starts, you're probably getting incredibly annoyed by now. That Plug and Play message telling you that "Windows has found new hardware and is installing the software for it" is getting really old, and the delay while the installation takes place is getting even older.

To stop this, fix the registry key by deleting HKEY_LOCAL_MACHINE\Enum\ Lptenum. The next time you start the computer you'll see the message again, but this time it will replace the key you deleted with the correct data, and the semiautomatic detection shouldn't occur again.

Disabling Routing in Windows 95

If you upgraded to Windows 95 from Windows for Workgroups, and you see this error message when Windows 95 starts: "Windows protection error. You need to restart your computer" — you've probably already figured out that you can ignore the error. It's there because in WFW you probably had IP routing enabled, which is a common configuration setting for that operating system. Windows 95, however, doesn't need IP routing and doesn't support it. Nonetheless, the routing setting was copied to the registry during installation of Windows 95, and remains there to annoy you. To get rid of it, you have to get rid of the registry subkey that causes the problem, which is `HKEY_LOCAL_MACHINE\System\CurrentControlSet\Services\VxD\MSTCP`.

For some reason, removing this key on some systems causes even stranger behavior, especially during operating system startup and dial-up networking access. In fact, network access could be shut down. If this happens, put the key back and live with the spurious error message. This means you should export the key (which has subkeys if you've configured dial-up networking) so you can import it back into the registry in case of problems.

The technical editor for this book reported the same symptom during system startup, and it turned out to have nothing to do with IP routing. Instead, it was Norton's SYMEVENT that caused the problem (the tech editor determined that it was a bug in Norton's program .dll files).

Troubleshooting Windows NT 4

Let's look at some of the commonly reported problems with Windows NT; in this case, we'll cover both server and workstation problems.

User Manager Does Not Print Reports

The User Manager tools (both User Manager and User Manager for Domains) have no way of providing a printed list of users. (The Help files don't even contain the word *print*). A printed list of users for your domain can be useful in many ways, but when you need it you'll have to complete the task outside of User Manager.

Just open a command session on the domain controller and type **net user>file-name**. (Substitute your own filename, of course.) The file that's produced is a list of domain users. I usually add the extension .txt so I can double-click this file in Explorer and it opens in the associated software (usually Notepad).

You can also perform this task from your NT workstation, but the command is **net user/domain>filename**. Do not substitute the name of your domain – the actual word *domain* is used in this command.

To produce a list of users for an individual workstation, use the command **net user>filename** in a command session on that workstation.

Windows 95/98 Clients Not Listed in Server Manager

When you open Server Manager on your Windows NT network server, you may find that the Windows 95/98 computers on your network do not show up in the computer list. The solution is very simple: you just have to change the view. Open the View menu and deselect Show Domain Members Only.

This happens because Windows 95/98 computers are not members of the domain in the same way that Windows NT computers are. (Notice that the Identification tab of the Network applet in the Control Panel for a Windows 95/98 machine does not have a field for the domain name. Instead, you just enter the domain name in the Workgroup field.) Windows 95 clients can access the domain shares and resources only because an administrator has added the logged-on user name to the domain's user list.

Windows 95/98 computers log on to a domain, but Windows NT computers join a domain (they log on to the local workstation). The difference is the location in which the client gets authenticated by the SAM. A SAM exists on the NT client computer, but not on the Windows 95/98 client; therefore, the Windows 95/98 client must go through a logon process to be authenticated.

The Show Domain Members Only view turns off browser enumeration, and Windows 95/98 computers only show up when the browser has assembled and displayed the list.

Synchronizing Domain Controllers Manually

The domain's user database is constantly replicated from the PDC to all the BDCs on the domain. This replication process is also called *synchronization*, and it's automatic. You can, however, synchronize manually if you have to; you usually want to do this if one or more BDCs were down and need to catch up.

To perform this task, go to the command line and enter **net accounts /sync** in a command prompt window, using these guidelines:

◆ To synchronize all the BDCs with the PDC, use the command on the PDC.

◆ To synchronize one BDC with the PDC, use the command on that BDC.

Do Not Use Server Manager for Manual Synchronization

The menu items (and the help files) in Server Manager say that you can be at the PDC and select a BDC, and then synchronize it using Computer, Synchronize With Domain Controller from the menu bar. If you do this, it appears to work because you see messages indicating that synchronization is taking place. However, the synchronization is probably a partial replication. This used to work in previous versions of NT, but NT 4 changed the way manual synchronization works. Now, the only guarantee you have of a complete synchronization is to use the command line. As of this writing, Microsoft has not repaired the flaw.

Controlling Selection Time on Dual-Boot Computers

Windows NT 4 computers that dual boot (usually with Windows 95) have a built-in limit for the time given to users to decide which operating system to boot. The default duration of time for decision-making is thirty seconds, after which Windows NT 4 boots.

Some users complain about this timing; apparently, it doesn't give them enough time to run to the coffee machine or sneak out for a smoke. Or, perhaps some users are just terribly slow at making decisions. Whatever the reason, you can accommodate these users by enabling them to take as long as they need to decide.

You change the timing for dual-boot decisions by making a change to the file BOOT.INI. This file resides on the root directory of the computer and has Hidden and Read-Only attributes.

The contents of BOOT.INI vary depending on the configuration of the computer. Following are the contents of the file for a computer that dual boots between NT 4 and Windows 95:

```
[boot loader]
timeout=30
default=multi(0)disk(0)rdisk(0)partition(1)\WINNT
[operating systems]
multi(0)disk(0)rdisk(0)partition(1)\WINNT="Windows NT Workstation
  Version 4.00"
multi(0)disk(0)rdisk(0)partition(1)\WINNT="Windows NT Workstation
  Version 4.00 [VGA mode]" basevideo /sos
C:\="Microsoft Windows"
```

When this computer boots, the user sees a message about the choices:

```
Please select the operating system to start:
Microsoft Windows NT Workstation Version 4.00
Microsoft Windows NT Workstation Version 4.00 [VGA Mode]
Microsoft Windows
```

A countdown of seconds begins, and when it reaches 0, the default operating system boots (in this case, Windows NT Workstation 4).

To change the decision-making time to "forever," follow these steps:

1. Right-click BOOT.INI in Explorer and change the attributes to deselect Read Only.

2. Double-click the file to open it in Notepad.

3. Make the following change: **timeout = 1**

4. Choose File → Save and then choose File → Exit.

5. Right-click the file in Explorer and reset the attributes.

The next time this computer boots, the countdown message will not appear, and the user will have an infinite amount of time to make a decision.

You can use the same technique to force a decision and prevent the user from choosing any operating system except Windows NT. Change the timeout value to 0 to make the computer boot into the default operating system immediately.

Unlocking a Locked-out User

When a user is locked out because he or she has exceeded the allowed number of bad password attempts, there are a couple of things you can do.

You can tell the user to wait for the lockout duration you've specified in User Manager for Domains to elapse, and also to be more careful about typing.

If the user has completely forgotten the password, you can assign a new one in User Manager for Domains.

You can unlock the workstation by following these steps:

1. Open User Manager for Domains.

2. Double-click the user entry.

3. The Account Locked Out field should be active and checked, instead of showing its normal, grayed-out status. Deselect the check box.

 This action only unlocks the workstation for this particular lockout instance — it does not change the configuration for this option, and more bad passwords will result in more lockouts.

Stopping Error Messages About Deleted Shared Folders

If you delete a folder that is shared without first removing the share, Windows NT gets annoyed and reports an error in the Event Viewer. This is because the share itself is registered, as if it were unconnected to the folder. The share remains in the registry because you didn't specifically remove the share. You need to remove the share manually to prevent the error message in the Event Viewer. Follow these steps:

1. In either registry editor, move to `HKEY_LOCAL_MACHINE\System\CurrentControlSet\Services\LanmanServer\Shares`.

2. Find the subkey of the share for which you deleted the folder.

3. Reboot.

Controlling Autoexec.bat Processing

When you installed NT 4, it parsed the environment settings in your Autoexec.bat file (if one existed) and wrote the settings to the registry. Most of the time, this doesn't cause any problems, and the data made available to NT 4 could have included path statements, device settings, and application settings.

But sometimes, these settings cause problems – things happen during bootup that don't make sense, or error messages flash in your face (which are annoying, even if you can safely ignore them). Usually, this occurs because your Autoexec.bat file contained settings for legacy devices or applications.

To make sure that none of these settings are used during bootup, you can instruct the registry not to load them by following these steps:

1. In either registry editor, move to `HKEY_CURRENT_USER\Software\Microsoft\WindowsNT\CurrentVersion\WinLogon`.

2. Add a new value named ParseAutoexec.

3. Choose REG_SZ as the data type and enter a value of 0 for the data.

4. Reboot.

Forcing Password Protected Screen Savers in NT

Some workstations should never be left unsecured. When a user in the accounting department leaves the room, you certainly don't want any passerby to open software or look at onscreen data, especially if the user works on the payroll. In fact, the entire accounting department should be forced to use screen savers that are password protected.

To do this without counting on user cooperation, you need to accomplish two things: force the use of the secured screen saver, and remove the capability of the user to change your settings.

To force a secured screen saver operation, open either registry editor and go to `HKEY_CURRENT_USER\Control Panel\Desktop`. As shown in Figure 10-2, you'll see a number of items relating to screen savers.

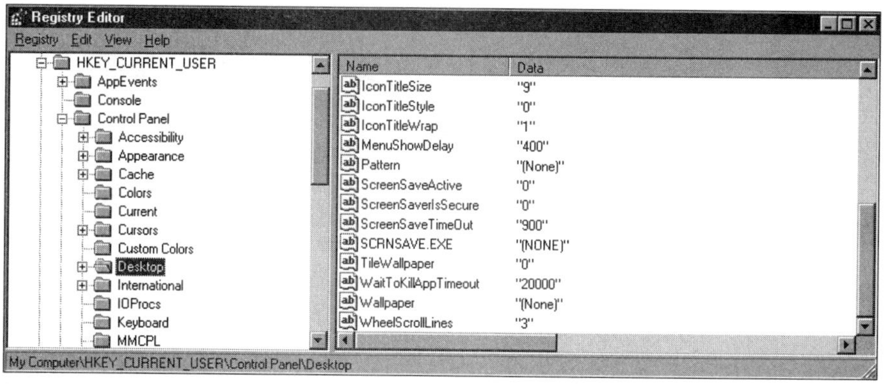

Figure 10-2: The data items for screen savers are all in the same subkey.

Make the following changes:

◆ Change the data value of ScreenSaveActive to 1.

◆ Change the data value of ScreenSaverIsSecure to 1.

◆ Change the value of SCRNSAVE.EXE to the filename of the screen saver you want to use.

◆ Change the value of ScreenSaveTimeOut to the number of seconds you want to elapse before the screen saver is launched.

The next time the user logs on, these settings are in effect. After the elapsed time expires, the screen saver is launched. When a mouse click or a key press removes the screen saver, a message appears telling the user that the computer has been locked and can be unlocked only by the user (the current logged-on user name is displayed) or by an administrator.

Pressing Ctrl+Alt+Del displays the logon dialog box, and as soon as the user enters the right password, the computer is unlocked.

Now, make sure the user can't change these settings. The best way to do that is to remove the Screen Saver tab from the Display Properties dialog box, using these steps (I've included instructions for both registry editors):

1. In either registry editor, go to HKEY_CURRENT_USER\Software\Microsoft\
   Windows\CurrentVersion\Policies. You have to add a new subkey under this key (the new subkey is named System), so make sure the Policies subkey is selected.

2. In REGEDT32, choose Edit → Add Key from the menu bar to display the Add Key dialog box. Name the key System and enter REG_DWORD as the class.

3. In REGEDIT, right-click a blank spot in the right pane and choose New →
   Key to create a new item in the left pane. Enter `System` as the subkey
   name, replacing the default name New Key #1.

4. Add the data item you need to this new subkey in REGEDT32, by selecting
   the subkey and choosing Edit → Add Value from the menu bar. When the
   Add Value dialog box appears, enter the name **NoDispScrSavPage**, which
   is a REG_DWORD data type.

5. To add the new value item using REGEDIT, select the new subkey and
   right-click in the right pane. Choose New → REG_DWORD. Then, enter
   NoDispScrSavPage to replace the default name that appears.

6. Open the new data item and enter a data value of 1.

You have a new registry subkey named `HKEY_CURRENT_USER\Software\`
`Microsoft\Windows\CurrentVersion\Policies\System` and its data item prevents the user from changing settings for the Screen Saver.

Cleaning Out Deleted NIC Settings

It's common to remove a network adapter from the Network applet in the Control
Panel after you've upgraded to a new NIC. And sometimes, you remove and then
reinstall an NIC to overcome a setup problem. After completing either of these procedures, you're likely to run into some strange behavior, error messages, or other
annoying problems. That's because Windows NT doesn't always remove the settings for the deleted NIC from the registry. You can perform this task manually,
however, by following these steps:

1. Use either registry editor to move to `HKEY_LOCAL_MACHINE\Software\`
   `Microsoft\WindowsNT\CurrentVersion\NetworkCards\X`, where X is
   the card number for the NIC you want to delete.

2. Select the card number subkey and press Delete. If subkeys appear under
   the card number subkey, delete them first.

3. Reboot.

Before taking these steps, select the card number subkey and read the description
to make sure you've chosen the appropriate NIC (see Figure 10-3).

Problems with Multiple NICs

Configuring a server for multiple network interface cards for use on the same network segment is often a good idea for productivity. If you install NetBEUI, however, it binds itself to all the NICs in the machine (NetBEUI is self-configuring). The
real problem is that only one NIC in a PC can use NetBIOS. Because NetBEUI is
linked to NetBIOS, this causes problems. The operating system actually sees the

NICs as two machines, not two NICs. And, those two machines have the same name, which is a no-no. As a result, system services will not start, and an error message is generated during startup of the operating system.

The solution is to configure multiple NICs by manually disabling the NetBEUI bindings to all but one NIC. Although you could do this in the registry, so many subkeys exist in which bindings are tracked that it's easier to do this from the Network applet in the Control Panel. Open the Bindings tab and expand the NetBIOS interface, and then expand the NetBEUI protocol. You see the NICs to which the protocol is bound. Select one and choose Disable from the dialog box.

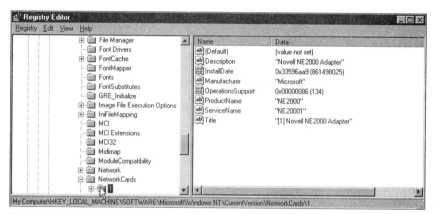

Figure 10-3: Read the description value to make sure you delete the correct subkey.

Other Controls Available Through the System Subkey

Once you've created this new subkey, a few other restrictions use it as a container. In case you'd like to add more controls, the others are listed as follows; in each case, add the data item, and then enter a data value of 1:

DisableTaskManager prevents users from launching Task Manager (neither the taskbar right-click access nor TASKMGR.EXE program file will work).

NoDispCPL prevents users from accessing the Display Properties dialog box.

NoDispAppearancePage prevents users from accessing the Appearance tab of the Display Properties dialog box.

NoDispBackgroundPage prevents users from accessing the Background tab from the Display Properties dialog box.

NoDispSettingsPage prevents users from accessing the Settings tab and Plus tab in the Display Properties dialog box.

Cleaning Out TCP/IP Settings

If you remove TCP/IP Settings and then try to reinstall TCP/IP, you may find you can't because Windows NT 4 keeps giving you the error message, "The Registry Subkey Already Exists."

This occurs because the deletion process wasn't complete and the registry wasn't cleaned out properly when you deleted TCP/IP.

Here are the subkeys to delete (they may not all exist in your registry, depending on your installation choices):

```
HKEY-LOCAL_MACHINE\Software\Microsoft\DhcpMibAgent
HKEY-LOCAL_MACHINE\Software\Microsoft\DhcpServer
HKEY-LOCAL_MACHINE\Software\Microsoft\Wins
HKEY-LOCAL_MACHINE\Software\Microsoft\WinsMibAgent
HKEY-LOCAL_MACHINE\Software\Microsoft\SimpTcp
HKEY-LOCAL_MACHINE\Software\Microsoft\FTPSVC
HKEY-LOCAL_MACHINE\Software\Microsoft\LPDSVE
HKEY-LOCAL_MACHINE\Software\Microsoft\TcpPring
HKEY-LOCAL_MACHINE\Software\Microsoft\RFC1156Agent
HKEY-LOCAL_MACHINE\Software\Microsoft\SNMP
HKEY-LOCAL_MACHINE\Software\Microsoft\NetBT
HKEY-LOCAL_MACHINE\Software\Microsoft\Tcpip
HKEY-LOCAL_MACHINE\Software\Microsoft\TcpipCU
HKEY-LOCAL_MACHINE\System\CCS\Services\DhcpServer
HKEY-LOCAL_MACHINE\System\CCS\Services\Wins
HKEY-LOCAL_MACHINE\System\CCS\Services\SimpTcp
HKEY-LOCAL_MACHINE\System\CCS\Services\FTPSVC
HKEY-LOCAL_MACHINE\System\CCS\Services\LPDSVC
HKEY-LOCAL_MACHINE\System\CCS\Services\SNMP
HKEY-LOCAL_MACHINE\System\CCS\Services\DHCP
HKEY-LOCAL_MACHINE\System\CCS\Services\Services\Lmhosts
HKEY-LOCAL_MACHINE\System\CCS\Services\NetBt
HKEY-LOCAL_MACHINE\System\CCS\Services\NetDrivern\Parameters\Tcpip
```

(where NetDrivern=the number for the NIC).

General Troubleshooting for All Computers

Some of the problems you encounter occur across all operating systems: Windows 95, Windows 98, and Windows NT 4. In this section, I discuss some issues that have identical solutions for all systems.

Speeding Up Network Logon

Sometimes, logons seem to take forever—not just the boot process of the operating system (which *does* take forever), but also the processes involved after you enter a logon name and password. One of the time-consuming events during logon is the reconnection of network computers and shares. When you establish mappings and specify that the connection be reestablished during logon, that process takes some time.

You can configure Windows 95, Windows 98, and Windows NT 4 so that the network connections aren't restored during logon. Instead, they are restored when the user needs to access the connection. Use the registry to change this logon procedure in this manner:

1. Go to `HKEY_LOCAL_MACHINE\System\CurrentControlSet\Control\ NetworkProvider`.

2. Add a new REG_WORD item named RestoreConnection.

3. Set the value to 0.

Briefcase Turns into a Folder

I don't know how it happens, but I see it frequently: the desktop Briefcase suddenly looks and acts like a folder. No special commands exist for updating the contents on the shortcut menu or the folder menu. Actually, I suspect user interference, but I've never figured out just what the users do to cause this. Regardless of the cause, here's the fix:

1. Open the registry editor and go to `HKEY_LOCAL_MACHINE\Software\ Classes\Briefcase\CLSID`.

2. Edit the data value so it reads `{85BBD920-42A0-1069-A2E4- 08002B30309D}`. (If the value isn't there, create this String Value item and use this data value.)

3. Move to the DefaultIcon key for the Briefcase (it's the next subkey) and enter the following data:

   - For Windows NT 4: %SystemRoot%\system32\syncui.dll

   - For Windows 95 and Windows 98: %SystemRoot%\system\syncui.dll

The next system startup should produce the correct Briefcase icon and behavior.

Mandatory Profiles Fail

Users may encounter problems when mandatory profiles are enabled on your network.

If a user logs on and then sees the error message, "The operating system was unable to load your profile. Please contact your Network Administrator," it means that one of two things has probably happened:

- ◆ The server has gone down.

- ◆ The user was not given Read privileges in the subfolder that contains the profile.

If the problem is the server, you're probably already working to restart it. If the server is running, however, check the permissions for the share you created for the subfolder. Be sure that Read permissions are granted to the Everyone group. Additionally, check the root directory of the server to make sure that Read permissions are granted for this user, because without that, all subdirectories will lack Read permissions for the user.

Sometimes, if the problem is permissions, the user receives the error message, "You do not have permission to access your central profile located at \\server\ share\username.man. The operating system is attempting to log you on with your local profile."

 A missing server or insufficient privileges can also result in a desktop with no taskbar and no desktop icons after the logon process is complete. This usually happens without any error message, so it can be confusing.

Summary

This chapter showed you how to use the registry to solve many common problems with your computer. In the next chapter, we'll turn to remote registry administration.

Chapter 11

Remote Administration

ONE OF THE REAL ADVANTAGES available to system administrators who work with Windows 95, 98, and Windows NT 4 clients is the capability to administer those computers without having to sit in front of them. You can just sit in front of your own computer, at your own desk, and do what needs to be done. "What needs to be done" could be anything from fixing a problem to setting a policy that restricts the user of the remote computer. You can administer a computer remotely using standard administrative tools or by accessing the registry directly.

Preparing Windows 95 and 98 Workstations

Unlike Windows NT 4, which is automatically configured for remote administration, including remote administration of the registry, Windows 95 and 98 need to be prepared to accept your remote access. This is a two-step process: you start by establishing the proper configuration for the workstation to make sure it accepts remote administration, and then you install the remote registry service to administer the registry remotely.

Okay, when I said you could administer the workstations from your own desk instead of having to walk all over the building to administer client workstations, I overstated the case for Windows 95 and 98. You need to be in front of the target computers to configure them for remote administration, and *then* you can work on them from your own Windows NT computer.

Setting Up Remote Administration

To establish a Windows 95 or 98 client workstation so it can be administered remotely, follow these steps on the target workstation:

1. Open the Network applet in the Control Panel (or right-click Network Neighborhood and choose Properties) to open the Network properties dialog box.

2. Click File and Print Sharing (see Figure 11-1) and select both the file sharing and print sharing options. Click OK.

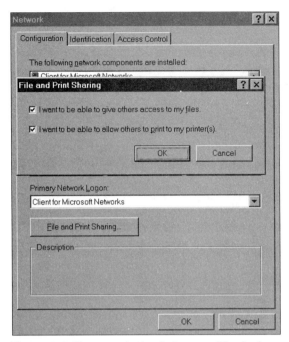

Figure 11-1: The computer has to be accessible via shares to permit remote administration.

3. Move to the Access Control tab and enable User-level security (see Figure 11-2).

TIP

Technically, in order to access and administer a computer remotely, you can use either user-level security or share-level security. The only rule is that both the computers involved in the remote administration process need to have the same type of security invoked. To open and change the registry, however, the security type must be user-level. This means you could administer Windows 95 and 98 computers remotely, but you could not make registry changes as part of that administration. Also, as an added incentive for choosing user-level security, it's actually more secure because anyone with the password for the share could get into a Windows 95 or 98 computer protected with share-level security. In many offices, I've seen the password for a computer's shared resource written on a piece of paper and taped to at least half the monitors in the organization. Incidentally, to enable user-level security, you must have a server-based network, because the server (either NT Server or NetWare) provides the security.

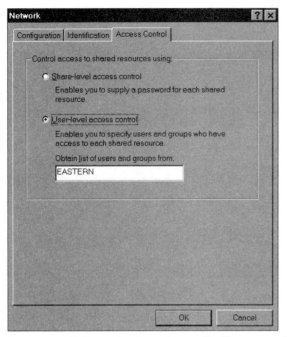

Figure 11-2: Pick user-level security to edit this computer's
registry from a remote computer.

4. Select the user(s) who should have access to the computer.

5. Click OK. Then, click OK again to close the dialog box, and reboot (you'll
   see a message telling you to reboot to have this change take effect).

That takes care of the first phase of preparing the Windows 95 or 98 workstation.
In the next phase, you enable remote administration as a service. Follow these steps:

1. Open the Passwords applet in the Control Panel and move to the Remote
   Administration tab (see Figure 11-3).

2. Select Enable Remote Administration of this server.

3. Choose Add to bring up the Choose Administrators dialog box (see
   Figure 11-4).

4. Select a name from the left column and click Add to move it to the
   list of administrators for this computer. Repeat this step until you have
   added all the people or groups to which you want to grant remote
   administrative permissions.

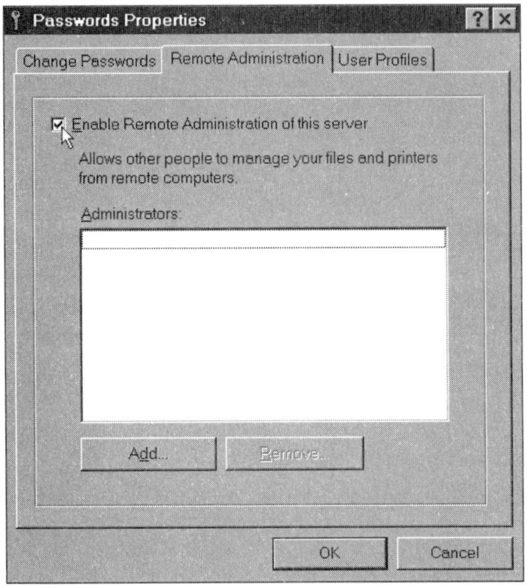

Figure 11-3: You need to specifically enable remote administration of a computer and name the users who can access it.

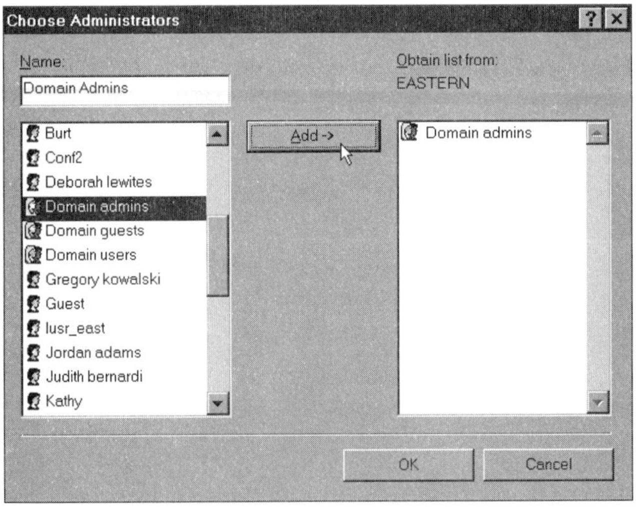

Figure 11-4: Add the individual(s) or group(s) who should have remote administration permissions for this computer.

When you establish user-level security, Windows 95 and 98 automatically enable remote administration and put the Domain Administrators group in the list of administrators with permissions.

5. Click OK, and then click OK again to close the dialog box.

If you enabled share-level security, the dialog box in Figure 11-3 looks different, and permits only the entry of the password for the shared resource. Everyone who needs or wants to access the computer must know that password.

At this point, the Windows 95 or 98 workstation is set up to accept remote administration (it's a good idea to restart the computer before attempting to administer it from a remote location). You can access files and shares and make changes, but you cannot access the registry. Now, you must establish remote registry service to include access to the registry in your remote administration.

Setting Up Remote Registry Service

Setting up the remote registry service is the last step in preparing for remote registry administration for Windows 95 and 98 machines. The following checklist is important:

♦ Both computers must have remote administration enabled and user-level security in place.

♦ There must be a security provider, which means a server that enforces security (and of course, both computers must log on to that server). NT 4 Server and NetWare are both security providers (you cannot administer a registry remotely on a Windows 95 or 98 peer-to-peer network).

♦ You must have the Windows 95 or 98 CD-ROM available on both computers.

Once you're ready, follow these steps to install the remote registry service on both the administrator's Windows 95 or 98 computer and the target computer:

1. Open the Network Properties dialog box (from the Control Panel, or by right-clicking Network Neighborhood and choosing Properties). The dialog box opens with the Configuration tab in the foreground, displaying a list of network components for this computer (see Figure 11-5).

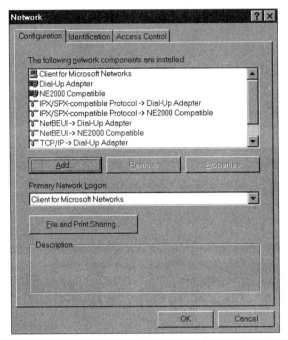

Figure 11-5: You need to add remote registry services to the existing services.

2. Choose Add to begin the process of adding a new service.

3. When the Select Network Component Type dialog box appears, choose Service, and then click Add.

4. The Select Network Service Dialog box appears, displaying a list of available Windows 95 or 98 services (none of which fit the bill). Choose Have Disk to install the remote registry service, which isn't part of the normal Windows 95 or 98 network components.

5. In the Install From Disk dialog box, enter the path to the remote registry service files on your Windows 95 or 98 CD: **d:\Admin\Nettools\ RemotReg**, where d: is the drive letter for your CD-ROM. Then, click OK.

6. Choose Microsoft Remote Registry and click OK.

7. When you return to the Network Properties dialog box, click OK. The files are transferred. Then, Windows needs to transfer some system files and will ask you to insert the Windows 95 or 98 CD-ROM (see Figure 11-6). Click OK and enter the path to the operating system files: **d:\win95** or **d:\win98,** where d:\ is your CD-ROM drive.

8. Restart the operating system.

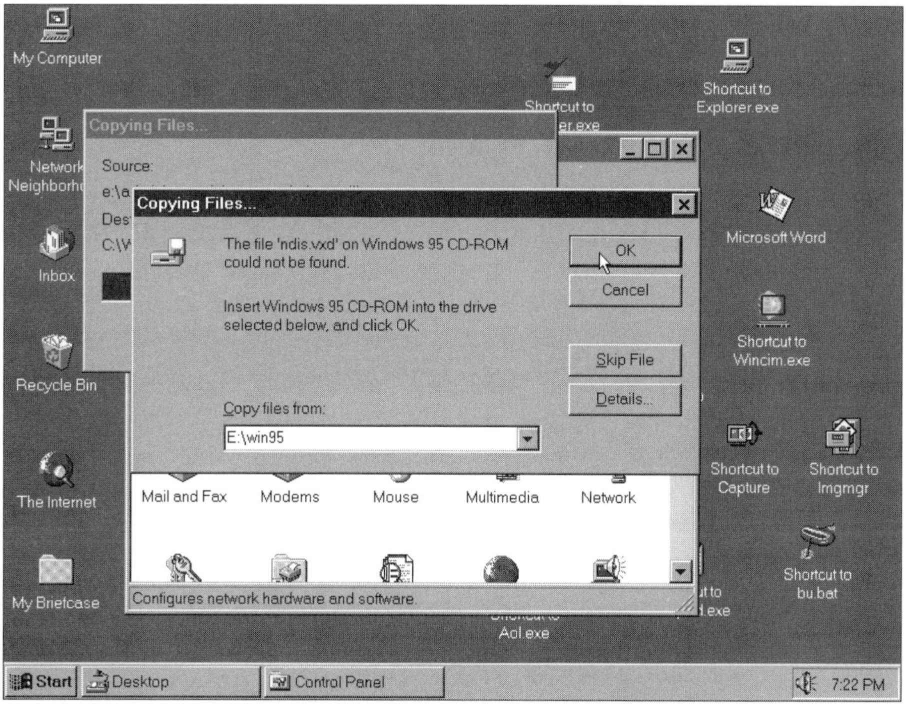

Figure 11-6: This isn't really an error — Windows just doesn't realize you're already using the original CD-ROM.

TIP
The reason for the instructions in Step 7 is that Windows 95 and 98 don't realize they will be transferring the files from the original Windows 95 or 98 CD for remote registry services. When these programs need files from the operating system, they instruct you to place the Windows 95 or 98 CD-ROM into the drive. To set things right, you simply need to point to the correct path for the regular operating system files (d:\win95 or d:\win98). Windows thinks you've placed the original Windows CD-ROM in the drive and continues along cheerfully, transferring the needed system files to your hard drive.

Repeat this entire process for each Windows 95 or 98 computer you want to administer remotely, and for your own Windows 95 or 98 computer.

Using Administrative Tools on Remote Windows 95 and 98 Machines

You can administer another Windows 95 or 98 computer from your own Windows 95 or 98 computer, which is a nifty way to perform some basic diagnostic and troubleshooting tasks. Someone must be logged on to the remote machine for you to administer it remotely.

The most straightforward way to administer a remote Windows 95 or 98 machine is to use the tools available via Network Neighborhood:

1. Open Network Neighborhood and right-click the Windows 95 or 98 computer you want to administer.

2. Choose Properties from the shortcut menu.

3. Move to the Tools tab and select the tool you want to use (see Figure 11-7).

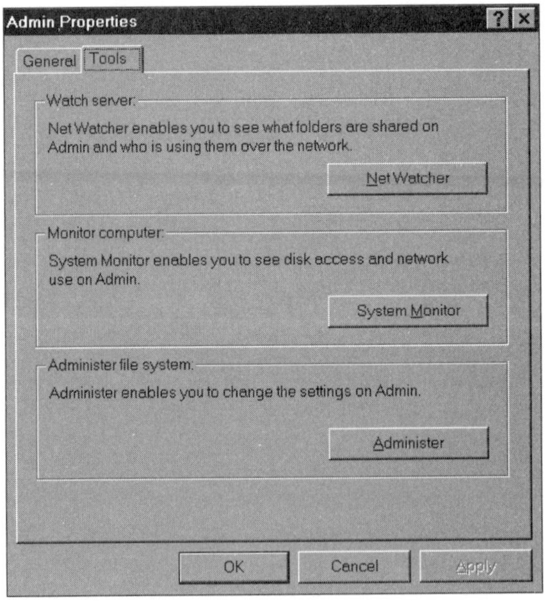

Figure 11-7: From the comfort of my own workstation, I can administer the computer named Admin.

If you have enabled remote administration on both machines, but haven't installed remote registry services, you cannot access System Monitor in the Tools dialog box.

To use the tools in the Properties dialog box for a remote computer, you need to have installed those tools as part of your operating system setup.

Instead of using Network Neighborhood, you can access the tools through the Start menu (Programs → Accessories → System Tools) and use the menu options on the software menu bar to connect to a remote computer.

Net Watcher

You can use Net Watcher to see who is connected to the remote computer (see Figure 11-8). You can also determine which files are open, and you can disconnect a user.

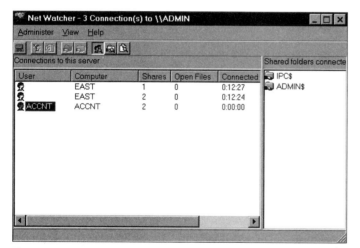

Figure 11-8: Net Watcher even displays the Administrative Shares, which are hidden from all other system tools.

Some of the functions you may find useful in Net Watcher include the following:

◆ Disconnecting users, which means you can stop a user from accessing a shared resource. If you're doing this because you want to get users off the computer so you can perform a maintenance task, be sure to notify the user so they don't lose data. If you want to disconnect a user because that user shouldn't be there, the rudeness of an instant disconnection is acceptable.

- Closing files, which means you can shut down any file that is open. If a user is accessing a file, this can be annoying (if not dangerous), but most of the time you'll use this function to close files that users inadvertently left open.

- Adding folder shares, which enables you to create a share for a folder that is currently not a shared resource. You'll have to configure the share, of course, which means naming it and setting permissions.

- Changing properties of shared folders, which means you can change the permissions (or even the name, but that's not a normal occurrence).

System Monitor

Use this tool to observe the performance of the remote computer (see Figure 11-9). You can add new variables to watch, if you wish.

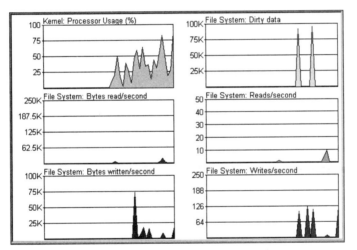

Figure 11-9: Monitoring system performance is a good way to start troubleshooting.

Incidentally, you can use multiple instances of System Monitor to keep an eye on multiple computers.

Administering Remote Registries in Windows NT 4

You can administer any Windows NT computer from any other Windows NT computer, as long as you have the appropriate permissions level. It doesn't matter whether you're working on Windows NT Server or Workstation, or whether the target computer is running Windows NT Server or Workstation. The registries of Server and Workstation are the same—although, of course, the data entries are different.

Before you attempt to reach out and touch another registry, make sure a user is logged on to the remote computer.

To administer a remote registry, use REGEDT32.EXE. Start the program from the Run command on the Start menu. When the editor window opens, you see the keys for your local machine (see Figure 11-10).

Loading the Remote Registry

To access a remote computer, choose Registry → Select Computer from the menu bar, and choose the remote computer you want to work on by selecting its icon or entering its UNC. The remote computer's registry is loaded in your software window (see Figure 11-11).

Notice that when you use REGEDT32.EXE, only two keys are loaded for the remote computer: HKEY_LOCAL_MACHINE and HKEY_USERS. This is because all other keys are derivatives of these two main keys, so there's no point in loading all the keys you'd see if you were working locally. When you make changes to either of these keys, any aliases are changed at the same time.

Removing Keys from the Editor Window

It's a bit crowded in the registry editor, with four local keys and two remote keys, so you should get rid of any windows you don't need.

To remove the local keys (windows), select any one of them, and then choose Registry → Close from the menu bar. All the local keys disappear, and only the remote keys remain in the editor window. If you're a neatness freak, use the Window menu item to arrange them.

If you just want to get rid of one or two keys, you have to minimize them. You can't close individual windows—it's all or nothing.

TIP

Sometimes, you may want to make changes to the remote registry that match configuration options you've selected for the local registry. In that case, it's probably a good idea not to close the local keys, so you can examine them.

Editing the Remote Registry

You can edit the remote registry as though you were editing the local registry (see Figure 11-12).

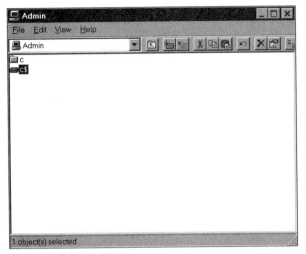

Figure 11-10: The REGEDT32 editor window opens with a display of the keys for the local machine.

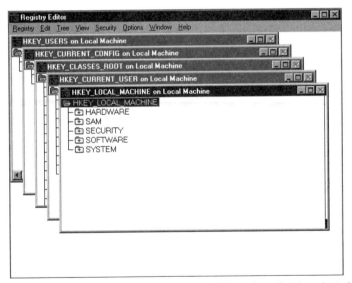

Figure 11-11: The registry editor has loaded the registry for the selected remote computer.

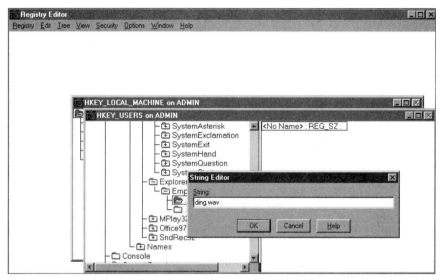

Figure 11-12: Adding or changing app events is usually safe — and the changes take place immediately.

When you've completed the changes, choose Close from the Registry menu. The following reminders are important to bear in mind:

♦ You have to double-click a key to expand it in REGEDT32 — clicking the plus sign doesn't work.

♦ Registry changes you make may be immediate, or they may be delayed until the local user reboots, depending on which specific key you change (and whether it is read during boot or when it's needed by an application).

♦ Auto Refresh is unavailable when you are working with a remote registry.

♦ There's no Undo button, so be careful.

Using Administrative Tools on Remote NT Machines

You can use a number of Windows NT tools on remote NT machines, which makes it much easier to administer and troubleshoot a network from the comfort of your own workstation.

Many of the tools described in this section enable you to select a computer via the Select Computer dialog box, which shows all the connected computers, regardless of the operating system running on those computers. If you try to select a computer running Windows 95 or 98, you'll see an error message telling you that you can only administer NT computers. When you use your NT tools, you can only administer an NT computer from your NT workstation or server.

Windows NT Diagnostics

You can use your Windows NT Diagnostics program (in the Administrative Tools section of the Programs menu) on any connected Windows NT computer. You cannot make any changes on the remote computer, but you can view the statistics. Follow these steps:

1. Open the software, and then choose File → Select Computer from the menu bar.

2. In the Select Computer dialog box (see Figure 11-13), enter the UNC for the computer you want to work on, or double-click its object. Then, click OK.

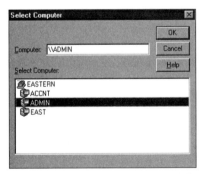

Figure 11-13: Choose the Windows NT computer you want to work on.

3. The title bar for Windows NT Diagnostics changes to indicate the remote computer, and you can view the remote computer's statistics (see Figure 11-14).

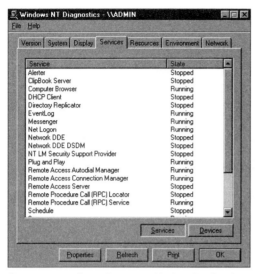

Figure 11-14: Sometimes, troubleshooting involves finding out which services are running and which have stopped.

Event Viewer

You can use your local Event Viewer to look at the Event Log of a connected computer:

1. Launch Event Viewer and choose Select Computer from the Log menu.

2. From the Select Computer dialog box, choose the computer you want to view.

3. The title bar of Event Viewer displays the name of the connected computer.

4. Use the Log menu to select the specific log you need.

5. Double-click any entry to see the details (see Figure 11-15).

6. You have the entire feature set of Event Viewer available to you, and you can clear the log of the remote computer if you wish.

Performance Monitor

To use Performance Monitor to measure activity on a connected computer, choose Edit → Add to Chart (or click the Add Counter icon on the toolbar). When the Add to Chart dialog box opens, you can replace the local computer with the UNC for the computer you want to administer remotely (see Figure 11-16).

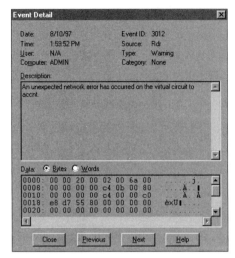

Figure 11-15: The user on Accnt shut down,
which disconnected the user on Admin; this is
annoying, because the printers are attached
to Accnt.

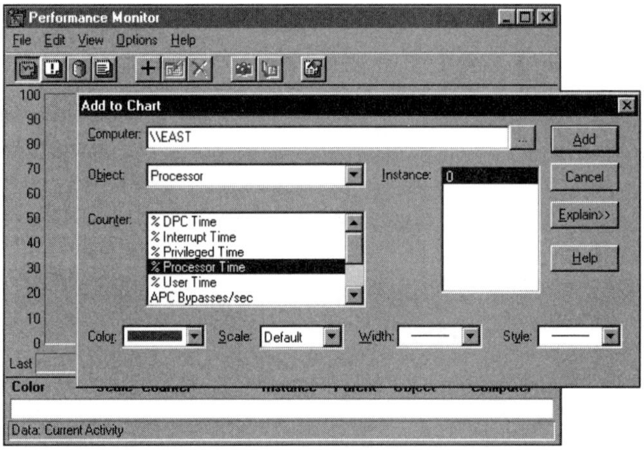

Figure 11-16: When you need to track processes for troubleshooting,
use Performance Monitor.

Summary

In this chapter, you learned about remote registry administration. The next chapter
covers how to use the Policy Editor.

Chapter 12

Using the Policy Editors

Windows 95, Windows 98, and Windows NT 4 have Policy Editors — programs you can use to set policies for your own and other computers. Policies are controls you can set to determine what the users of a controlled computer can do. The policy editors set these controls by changing the registry, eliminating the need for you to make changes directly into the registry. For example, you can use policy settings to:

◆ Restrict application functions

◆ Configure desktop settings

◆ Configure network settings

◆ Restrict access to Control Panel applets

The Windows NT 4 Policy Editor is installed as part of the Windows NT Server operating system and is accessed through the Start menu (Programs → Administrative Tools). Policy Editor is not automatically installed on Windows NT 4 Workstation.

The Windows 95 and 98 Policy Editors are not installed automatically as part of the operating system, but they are included on the CD-ROM for both operating systems. If you installed Windows 95 or 98 from floppy disks, head for `http://www.microsoft.com` to download the Policy Editor.

Differences Between Policy Editors

The registry for a Windows 95 or 98 computer is not the same as the registry for a Windows NT 4 computer. Much of the registry information is stored differently, although the data for the current user (`HKEY_CURRENT_USER`) is stored as files on both systems. In Windows 95 and 98, the file is in the `Win95SystemRoot` or `Win98SystemRoot` directory and is named USER.DAT. In Windows NT 4, the data is in a file named NTUSER.DAT, and is also stored in the `WinNTSystemRoot` directory.

Understanding Policy Files

When you create policies with the Policy Editor, the policies are saved as a file with the extension .POL. Those files are placed on a server. Windows 95 and 98 and

Windows NT 4 workstations look for .POL files during the logon process. If one is found, it is downloaded and the policies in the file are established by changing the registry.

By default, the following search for .POL files is made (but you can change the default search patterns):

♦ On NT networks, the user's home directory (in the `Netlogon` folder) on the server is searched (the default is to search the PDC regardless of the logon server).

♦ On NetWare networks, the user's mail directory on the server is searched.

♦ On peer-to-peer networks, the `%WindowsSystemRoot%` directory is searched.

Distributing .POL files is a much safer way to make registry changes than hacking the registry directly. The Policy Editors use plain English to describe the policies and then change the registry in multiple locations if the policy settings require that action.

Understanding Policy Templates

The scope and default settings of the configuration settings presented in the Policy Editor are established by an administration file that is a template (administration files have the extension .ADM).

The administration file provided with the Policy Editor for Windows 95 and 98 is ADMIN.ADM, and Windows NT 4 comes with WINDOWS.ADM, WINNT.ADM and COMMON.ADM.

More settings are available for configuration than are presented by the supplied templates, and you can obtain third-party templates or create your own. In fact, sometimes it is desirable to load a template that provides fewer settings for change. When you want to use a different template you must load it by choosing Options → Template (in Windows 95 and 98) or Options → Policy Template in Windows NT 4. A dialog box opens so you can select the new template.

 You must close all active policy files before attempting to load a new template.

See the section "Creating Templates" at the end of this chapter for more details about .ADM files.

Installing the Windows 95 and Windows 98 Policy Editor

To install the Policy Editor on a Windows 95 or 98 computer, place the Windows 95 or 98 CD-ROM into your CD-ROM drive and follow these steps:

1. Open Add/Remove Programs in the Control Panel and move to the Windows Setup tab.

2. Choose Have Disk and enter the path **d:\admin\apptools\poledit** where d: is the drive letter for your CD-ROM.

3. Click OK. In the Have Disk dialog box, select both options (Figure 12-1).

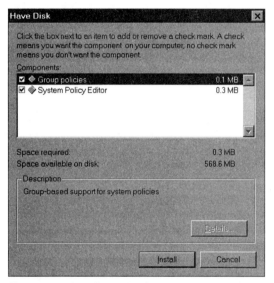

Figure 12-1: Install support for group policies as well as the Policy Editor to set policies for other Windows 95 or 98 computers.

4. Choose Install. The files are transferred and the Start menu is updated.

You can launch the Policy Editor from the Start menu (Programs → Accessories → System Tools → System Policy Editor).

Using the Windows 95 and 98 Policy Editor

You can use the System Policy Editor to configure settings for specific computers. These settings can prevent users from changing hardware and environment settings, which ensures that Windows 95 or 98 starts and runs in an expected manner.

To use the Policy Editor, you should already have enabled Remote Administration on the Windows 95 or 98 computers you want to manipulate, and the remote registry services must be running on both your computer and the remote computers (see Chapter 11 for information about these features).

You can accomplish these tasks in the Windows 95 and 98 System Policy Editor in one of two ways: Registry mode or Policy File mode.

Using the Registry mode, as you create policies, you are changing the registry of the local or remote computer. Use this mode when you are changing only one computer.

With the Policy File mode, the editing of the registry is indirect. Changes take place after the policy is downloaded when the user logs on. The user must be logging on to a network server. Use this mode to change multiple computers.

Using Registry Mode

To use the Policy Editor in Registry mode, follow these steps:

1. Choose File → Connect from the menu bar.

2. When the Connect dialog box opens (see Figure 12-2), enter the name of the remote computer you want to work on (use the UNC).

Figure 12-2: Enter the name of a Windows 95 or 98 computer; you cannot use the Windows 95 or 98 Policy Editor on a computer running another operating system.

3. The title bar of the Policy Editor changes to reflect the computer to which you are connected (see Figure 12-3). The User and Computer icons in the editor window are connected to that computer.

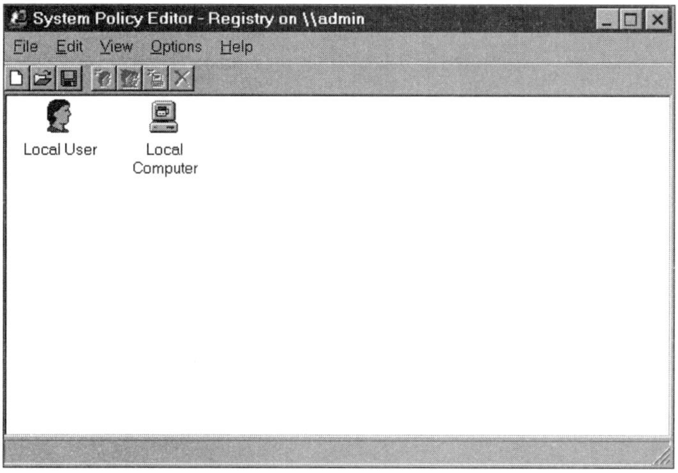

System Policy Editor - Registry on \\admin

File Edit View Options Help

Local User   Local
              Computer

Figure 12-3: Notice that the title bar indicates the name of the remote computer and registry mode.

Now you can begin to create policies. As you do, the computer's registry changes immediately to reflect the policies you're creating. You can make changes either to User settings or to Computer settings.

TIP In the interest of speaking to administrators, I structured the preceding instructions to access a remote computer. You can, of course, skip the Connect step and use the Policy Editor in Registry mode to work on the computer in front of which you're sitting. To do so, choose File → Open Registry after you launch the Policy Editor. The local registry will accept all the changes you make.

If you want to work in Policy File mode, skip the preceding steps and dive right into creating policies – then you'll send those policy files to all the computers you want to change.

SETTING COMPUTER POLICIES

To set policies for computers, double-click the computer icon in the Policy Editor window. The Local Computer Properties dialog box appears (see Figure 12-4).

You can set policies for Network settings and System settings. Expand the appropriate icon, and then continue to expand the settings to find the specific configuration you want to alter. Some of the settings require additional information, and selecting them opens a window for adding that data. For example, if you want to add a logon banner, selecting that option opens a window so you can enter the text (see Figure 12-5).

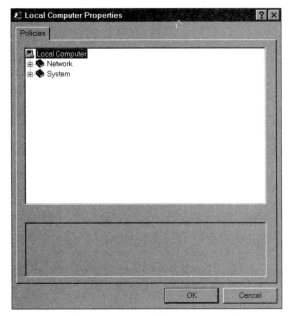

Figure 12-4: Set computer policies to change those
configuration settings stored in the machine-related
sections of the registry.

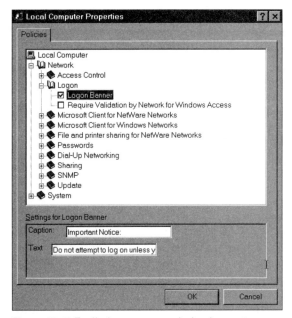

Figure 12-5: To display a message during logon, turn on
the function and then create the message.

Move through the choices to make your selections. When you're finished, choose OK to write the information to the registry (or choose Cancel if you change your mind).

SETTING USER POLICIES

Double-click the User icon to configure user policies for the computer (see Figure 12-6).

Figure 12-6: You can establish configuration settings and limit access with User Policies.

Some of the controls you can impose for users include the following:

♦ The Control Panel options enable you to restrict access to certain items in the Control Panel.

♦ The Desktop section enables you to specify configuration options (such as wallpaper).

♦ Use the Network choices to enable or disable sharing.

♦ The choices under Shell are for enabling or disabling the user's capability to create custom folders (such as folders on the Start menu) and also to impose restrictions on access to certain functions (see Figure 12-7).

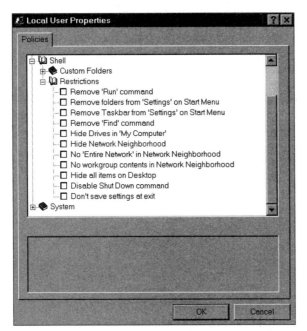

Figure 12-7: Sometimes it's safer to keep users away from certain features and functions.

◆ The System choices include restrictions on using the command prompt, and restricting the user's capability to access registry editing tools.

Move through the choices to make your selections. When you're finished, choose OK to write the information to the registry (or choose Cancel if you change your mind).

Using Policy File Mode

To use the Policy Editor for creating files you can later download to computers in order to apply the new policies, follow these steps:

1. Launch the Policy Editor.

2. Choose File → New from the menu bar to create a new policy. Icons representing a Default User and a Default Computer appear in the window (see Figure 12-8).

If you already have policies in place, you can choose File → Open to call up those policy files and edit them.

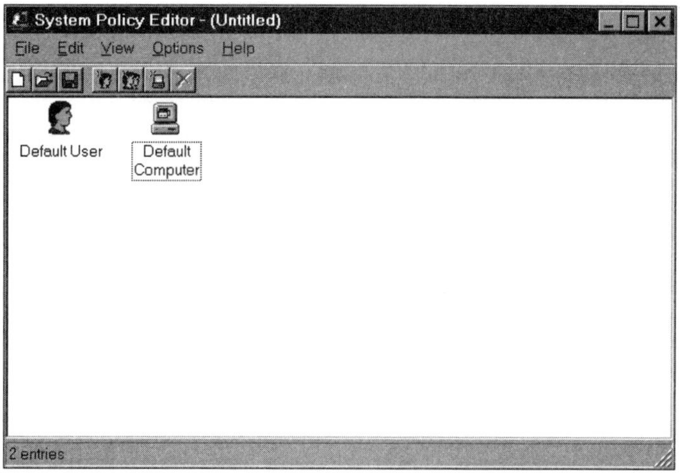

Figure 12-8: The icons represent the users and computers that will receive the policy changes.

UNDERSTANDING THE OPTIONS

The options available for policies (which are changes to the target computer's registry, but the changes aren't made in real time — they're sent to the affected computers later) are similar to those available when you use Policy Editor in Registry mode. When you work in file mode, however, each option can be set to one of three states: checked, cleared, or grayed. Each time you click an option's check box, the display cycles through the three states. This is different from clicking a standard check box, which only sets an option on or off.

Checked policies mean that the policy will be implemented. The registry on the target computer will be changed to implement the policy, unless the policy was already implemented on that computer.

Cleared policies mean that the policy will not be implemented. If the target computer is implementing the policy at the time of receiving the policy file, those settings are removed from the registry in order to conform to the new cleared state.

Grayed policies mean that the current setting on the target computer will remain unchanged. Whatever user settings are in place remain in place.

SETTING POLICIES

Double-click the appropriate object (either Default Computer or Default User) to see the available policy categories (see Figure 12-9).

While it is beyond the scope of this book to cover using the Policy Editor in great detail, it's worthwhile to know some of the policies you can set.

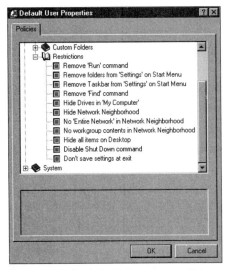

Figure 12-9: By default, these user policies are in the "don't change the target" state.

CONTROL PANEL   Here are some of the options you'll find in the Policy Editor that are connected to Control Panel applets, along with the resulting restrictions.

To restrict access to the Display applet in the Control Panel:

◆ Disable Display Control Panel prevents access to the Display applet.

◆ Hide Background Page prevents access to the Background properties of the Display applet.

◆ Hide Screen Saver Page prevents access to the Screen Saver properties of the Display applet.

◆ Hide Appearance Page prevents access to the Appearance properties of the Display applet.

◆ Hide Settings Page prevents access to the Settings properties of the Display applet.

To restrict access to the Network applet in the Control Panel:

◆ Disable Network Control Panel prevents access to the Network applet.

◆ Hide Identification Page prevents access to the Identification properties of the Network applet.

◆ Hide Access Control Page prevents access to the Access Control (user level and share level) properties of the Network applet.

To restrict access to the Passwords applet in the Control Panel:

◆ Disable Passwords Control Panel prevents access to the Passwords applet.

◆ Hide Change Passwords Page prevents access to the Change Passwords properties of the Passwords applet.

◆ Hide Remote Administration Page prevents access to the Remote Administration properties of the Passwords applet.

◆ Hide User Profiles Page prevents access to the Profiles properties of the Passwords applet.

To restrict access to Printers Settings:

◆ Hide General and Details Pages prevents access to the General and Details properties for the Printers.

◆ Disable Deletion of Printers prevents the user from deleting installed printers.

◆ Disable Addition of Printers prevents the user from installing printers.

To restrict access to the System applet in the Control Panel:

◆ Hide Device Manager Page prevents access to the Device Manager properties in the System applet.

◆ Hide Hardware Profiles Page prevents access to the Hardware Profiles properties in the System applet.

◆ Hide File System Button prevents access to the File System button in the Performance properties in the System applet.

◆ Hide Virtual Memory Button prevents access to the Virtual Memory button in the Performance properties in the System applet.

SHELL SETTINGS   Following are some of the restrictions you can apply to shell access:

◆ Remove 'Run' command prevents access to the Run command on the Start menu.

◆ Remove folders from 'Settings' on Start Menu prevents access to any item listed under Settings on the Start menu.

◆ Remove Taskbar from 'Settings' on Start Menu prevents access to the Taskbar items listed under Settings on the Start menu.

- ◆ Remove 'Find' command prevents access to the items listed under Find on the Start menu.

- ◆ Hide Drives in 'My Computer' prevents access to the contents of My Computer.

- ◆ Hide Network Neighborhood prevents access to the contents of Network Neighborhood.

- ◆ No 'Entire Network' prevents access to the Entire Network icon in Network Neighborhood.

- ◆ Disable Shut Down command prevents access to the Shut Down command on the Start menu.

- ◆ Don't save settings at exit prevents the user from saving any changes to settings.

SYSTEM SETTINGS   You can prevent users from accessing applications at will with these settings:

- ◆ Disable Registry Editing Tools prevents access to Registry Editor.

If you disable access to the Registry Editor (REGEDIT.EXE in Windows 95 and 98), the user can still change the registry by using the Policy Editor. Therefore, make sure the Policy Editor is not installed on any workstation that is the target of your policy file.

- ◆ Only Run Allowed Windows Applications prevents the user from running any Windows-based applications except those that are listed. Choosing this option requires you to establish the list of approved applications.

- ◆ Disable MS-DOS Prompt prevents access to the MS-DOS command prompt.

DISTRIBUTING POLICIES

When you have made your changes and saved them in a policy file, you can distribute that file in a variety of ways. The choices you make depend on the network in place (NetWare or NT). In fact, within both network types you'll find differences in the distribution method depending on the network access services you're using, the way users log on, where they log on, and so on. You can get specific information from the Help files in Policy Editor or the Windows 95 Resource Kit (which is available on the Windows 95 CD-ROM).

Using the Windows NT 4 Policy Editor

More configuration options are available through the Windows NT 4 Policy Editor than are available in the Windows 95 and 98 Policy Editor. Additionally, there's no setup or special steps you have to go through. It's there — just go to your Windows NT server (it's only on server installations) and use it.

You can use the Windows NT 4 Policy Editor to set policies for groups, individuals, or the entire domain. Use the options on the Edit menu to create and specify those entities. You can, for example, assign the policy file to an existing group (from User Manager for Domains) or create a new group.

Sometimes you'll find that you create a series of policy files, one for each group, and then also make policy changes for specific individuals. If the target computer fits multiple definitions, all of the policy files are accepted and processed, but there is a pecking order you should be aware of:

◆ Multiple group policies are downloaded in priority order, with the lowest priority group policy downloaded first.

◆ User policies are downloaded last and replace group policies.

As with the Windows 95 and 98 Policy Editor, you can change configuration in either of two ways: Registry mode or Policy File mode.

Using Registry mode, as you create policies, you are changing the Registry of the local or remote computer. Use this mode when you are changing only one computer.

With Policy File mode, the editing of the registry is indirect. Changes take place after the policy is downloaded, when the computer logs on.

Using Registry Mode

To use the Windows NT 4 Policy Editor in Registry mode, follow these steps:

1. Choose File → Connect from the menu bar.

2. When the Connect dialog box opens, enter the name of the remote computer you want to work on (use the UNC).

3. The Users on Remote Computer dialog box appears and asks you to choose the user account you want to administer (see Figure 12-10).

4. The title bar of the Policy Editor changes to reflect the computer to which you are connected. The User and Computer icons in the editor window are connected to that computer.

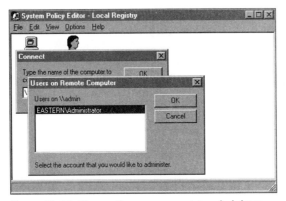

Figure 12-10: Choose the user account to administer —
in most cases only one user is listed.

 The user icon represents HKEY_CURRENT_USER and the Computer icon
represents HKEY_LOCAL_MACHINE.

Now you can begin to create policies. As you do, the computer's registry is
changed immediately to reflect the policies you're creating. You can make changes
either to User settings or to Computer settings.

If you want to work in Policy File mode, you can skip the preceding steps and
dive right into creating policies – then you'll send those policy files to all the
computers you want to change.

Using Policy File Mode

To use the Policy Editor for creating files you can later download to computers in
order to apply the new policies, follow these steps:

1. Launch the Policy Editor.

2. Choose File → New from the menu bar to create a new policy. Icons
    representing a Default User and a Default Computer appear in the window.

If you already have policies in place, you can choose File → Open to call up
those policy files and edit them.

Setting Policies

The method of setting policies in Windows NT 4 Policy Editor is the same as used for the Windows 95 and 98 Policy Editor. Double-click the appropriate icon and start.

Creating Templates

You can create your own templates (.ADM files) and it's not terribly difficult to do so if you use an existing template as a template for your own material. The template files are in `%systemRoot%\inf`.

Template files are ASCII and you can edit and create them with any text editor or word processor (make sure you save the file as text).

Template Formats

Template text follows a certain format (it resembles the format for programming code):

```
Class
   Category
      Policy
         Part
           End Part
        End Policy
     End Category
```

`Class` can be either `MACHINE` or `USER`.
`Category` can be either `SYSTEM` or `NETWORK` and the syntax is:

```
CATEGORY name_of_Category
KEYNAME name_of_key
```

`Policy` is the name of the policy (if the name has spaces, you must use quotation marks) and the syntax is:

```
POLICY name_of_policy
KEYNAME name_of_key
definition statements for the policy
```

`Part` is the definition of the controls you are setting for the policy (part names that have spaces require quotation marks) and the syntax is:

```
PART name type_of_part (and dependent data)
KEYNAME name_of_key
VALUENAME name_of_value
```

Sample ADM File

It might be worth spending a moment looking at an ADM file (this happens to be a section of COMMON.ADM from Windows NT that is under CLASS User):

```
CATEGORY !!Shell
    CATEGORY !!Restrictions
        KEYNAME
 Software\Microsoft\Windows\CurrentVersion\Policies\Explorer
            POLICY !!RemoveRun
            VALUENAME "NoRun"
            END POLICY

            POLICY !!RemoveFolders
            VALUENAME "NoSetFolders"
            END POLICY

            POLICY !!RemoveTaskbar
            VALUENAME "NoSetTaskbar"
            END POLICY

            POLICY !!RemoveFind
            VALUENAME "NoFind"
            END POLICY

            POLICY !!HideDrives
            VALUENAME "NoDrives"
            VALUEON NUMERIC 67108863; low 26 bits on (1 bit per drive)
            END POLICY

            POLICY !!HideNetHood
            VALUENAME "NoNetHood"
            END POLICY

            POLICY !!NoEntireNetwork
            KEYNAME
 Software\Microsoft\Windows\CurrentVersion\Policies\Network
            VALUENAME "NoEntireNetwork"
            END POLICY

            POLICY !!NoWorkgroupContents
            KEYNAME
 Software\Microsoft\Windows\CurrentVersion\Policies\Network
            VALUENAME "NoWorkgroupContents"
            END POLICY

            POLICY !!HideDesktop
            VALUENAME "NoDesktop"
            END POLICY

            POLICY !!DisableClose
            VALUENAME "NoClose"
            END POLICY
```

```
            POLICY !!NoSaveSettings
            VALUENAME "NoSaveSettings"
            END POLICY
      END CATEGORY
END CATEGORY    ; Shell
```

You can create as many templates as you think you'll need. If you delegate administrative work to other administrators, or if your company has multiple locations and multiple administrators at each location, it's a good idea to create templates for small sections of the registry and distribute them. Then, when changes to user configurations are desired, the appropriate templates can be loaded. This eliminates the risk of inadvertent changes to policies.

Summary

In this chapter, you learned how to use the Windows 95, 98, and NT 4 Policy Editors. We covered policy files, policy templates, and how to create your own templates.

Chapter 13

HKEY_CLASSES_ROOT

HKEY_CLASSES_ROOT is the same for Windows 95, Windows 98, and Windows NT 4. This section of the registry is in charge of three important tasks:

◆ Keeping track of the file extensions and their associations with file types. A group of file extension subkeys is devoted to this purpose.

◆ Keeping track of the programs associated with the file types that are registered in the system. A group of class-definition subkeys is devoted to this information.

◆ Keeping track of information about OLE objects and documents. Within the subkey \CLSID are the class identifier subkeys that are devoted to tracking this information.

The fact is that you very probably don't even need this key – it's a duplicate of HKEY_LOCAL_MACHINE\Software\Classes. It's actually even more than a duplicate – it's a hot link, and if you make changes to a key in one, the same change is made to the other instantaneously.

Because the two keys are identical, I've chosen to look at the structure and contents of HKEY_CLASSES_ROOT instead of HKEY_LOCAL_MACHINE\Software\Classes, because it's the first key in the registry, and it requires less typing to type the key name.

The key has two types of subkeys: file extensions and class definitions. All the file extensions are listed first, in alphabetical order. Then, the class definitions are listed in alphabetical order.

The file extension subkeys are the registered file extensions for your computer. Because they're extensions, they start with a period and therefore appear first in the list of subkeys.

The first extension subkey is for an extension represented by an asterisk (*); it contains information about handling default items on the shortcut menu, as well information about handling the properties dialog boxes for all file types – including any that are undefined. The key expands to the subkeys ContextMenuHandlers and PropertySheetHandlers and additional subkeys under those depend on your system configuration. For example, one of my computers has a WinZip subkey under the ContextMenuHandlers key, and the other doesn't (because I haven't installed WinZip on that system yet).

Following the asterisk file extension subkey are subkeys for all file extensions in the system. Almost all of these file extension subkeys also contain information that specifies the file type for the extension. Also, most extensions have a corresponding class definition for each type (you'll find details about class definition subkeys in the next section).

As you browse the list of file extensions, you'll notice that some of the subkeys have a plus sign to the left, indicating additional subkeys below them. That's because, if no class definition exists for an extension, the information that Windows needs in order to handle this extension is found in the file extension subkey itself (and the subkey has a plus sign next to it).

Some extensions have information in both places: in the class definition subkeys (which have information about the extension's link to applications, along with other information) and in the file extension subkey itself. For instance, the extensions .txt, .wav, and others each have a class definition, but also have a plus sign next to their entry in the file extension section of HKEY_CLASSES_ROOT. If a plus sign appears, that means a subkey exists below the extension's subkey named ShellNew, which contains information about creating new files for that extension (you may need to drill down past additional subkeys to get to ShellNew).

While most of the ShellNew subkeys don't contain any specific information about creating files (programmers can import information if they're using the extension in some unique way), some extensions do. For example, shortcuts use the extension .lnk and the ShellNew subkey under the .lnk subkey contains the following command:

```
"RunDLL32AppWizCpl,NewLinkHere %1".
```

The .mdb extension subkey (Microsoft Access Database) has the following command in its ShellNew subkey:

```
"msaccess.exe/NEWDB 1"
```

If you want to add a new file extension to your system, it's best to use the tool available in Explorer or My Computer (choose View → Options, move to the File Type tab and choose New Type). That way, all the information (which may be spread among several subkeys) will be transferred back to the registry automatically.

Class-Definition Subkeys

The second set of alphabetic entries under HKEY_CLASSES_ROOT are the class-definition subkeys. There's no second-level subkey separating the first set of keys (File Extension) and these subkeys. You just go through the first set until you get to the end of the alphabet. After the last extension entry, you see a new alphabetic listing begin and you know you've reached the class-definition subkeys. The other clue is that the first class-definition subkey is the first listing without a period in front of the subkey name. The class-definition subkeys contain information about:

◆ The full name of the file type (the name you see under the Type column when you're working in Explorer)

◆ The path to the associated application

◆ Any commands (switches, parameters) that have to be passed to that application in order to print or open a document

◆ Information about handling embedded objects of this type, which usually includes the application to use and the commands within that application that are supported during OLE processes

◆ The file and the number within that file of the icon used for the file type

◆ Whether or not Quick View can be used for the file type

The number of entries in this section of HKEY_CLASSES_ROOT varies, depending on the software applications you've installed.

TIP If you need to add or change associations, it's best to do that through Explorer or My Computer, which writes information back to all the parts of the registry that store this information.

CLSID Entries

The most complicated part of HKEY_CLASSES_ROOT are the CLSID entries. No special part of the key holds this data — CLSID is merely an entry in the class-definition subkeys portion of the key. However, when you click the plus sign to expand CLSID, the list that appears is overwhelming (see Figure 13-1).

CLSID is the class identifier, and every Windows OLE object has a unique class identifier — which covers an awful lot of ground because it includes file types, .EXE files, .DLL files, and Windows functions.

The keys can't be read by human beings; they are hexadecimal and all follow the same pattern, which consists of five groups of digits with a specific number of digits in each group: 8-4-4-4-12

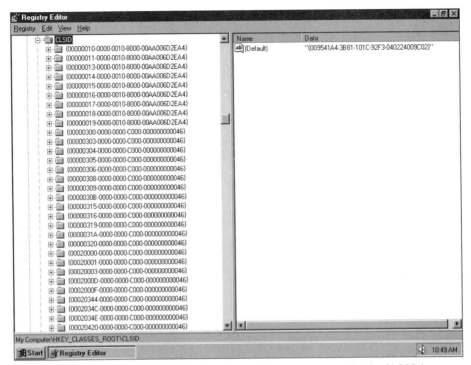

Figure 13-1: Additional layers of subkeys and names you can't read make the CLSID keys rather daunting.

Each subkey in the CLSID branch contains additional subkeys, and some contain more than others. For example, the CLSID key for MS Organization Chart 2.0 has quite a few subkeys, as shown in Figure 13-2. Other CLSID keys have as few as one subkey (the .DLL file used for OLE processes, which is the ImprocServer).

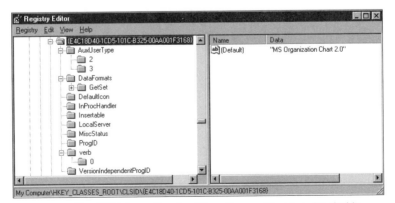

Figure 13-2: The OLE information for this software object is quite sizable.

There is really no reason to alter any information in the `CLSID` keys, and there's not much you could do even if you were in the mood to do some serious registry hacking. The only changes you would ever have to make would be new path statements if you decided to move the critical system .DLL and .EXE files (and I can't think of one valid reason to do that, so I believe it would be an incredibly silly thing to do).

However, you can learn a lot about the way objects are handled in OLE processes by examining the appropriate keys. Here are the important types of data found in the `CLSID` keys:

♦ `ImprocServer`, which is a pointer to the In-Process Server, the .DLL that handles this object.

♦ `ImprocServer32`, for object types that use a 32-bit In-Process Server.

♦ `DefaultIcon`, which specifies the icon attached to the object type.

♦ `ImprocHandler`, which is a pointer to the .DLL file that works as an Object Handler (meaning it works in connection with an .EXE file) to manage objects of this type.

♦ `LocalServer`, which holds the path\filename of a server application that handles objects of this type.

♦ `ProgID`, which is usually the short name for the object type (txtfile, for example).

♦ `Shellex`, which holds additional subkeys, defining the .DLL files and commands used to get to the object's shortcut menu and/or Properties dialog box.

CLSID Reference for Common Objects

Following is a list of some of the common objects you might find in your registry. These are the first-level subkeys under `CLSID`, and most of these subkeys have additional subkeys that contain the information discussed in the previous section. These are presented as a quick reference, so when you see the HEX you can check this list to see which object the key represents:

```
{00000300-0000-0000-C000-000000000046}
"StdOleLink"
```

```
{00000301-0000-0000-C000-000000000046}
"StdMemStm"
```

```
{00000302-0000-0000-C000-000000000046}
"StdMemBytes"

{00000303-0000-0000-C000-000000000046}
"FileMoniker"

{00000304-0000-0000-C000-000000000046}
"ItemMoniker"

{00000305-0000-0000-C000-000000000046}
"AntiMoniker"

{00000306-0000-0000-C000-000000000046}
"PointerMoniker"

{00000308-0000-0000-C000-000000000046}
"PackagerMoniker"

{00000309-0000-0000-C000-000000000046}
"CompositeMoniker"

{0000030A-0000-0000-C000-000000000046}
"DdeCompositeMoniker"

{0000030B-0000-0000-C000-000000000046}
"DfMarshal"

{0000030C-0000-0000-C000-000000000046}
"PSGenObject"

{0000030D-0000-0000-C000-000000000046}
"PSClientSite"

{0000030E-0000-0000-C000-000000000046}
"PSClassObject"

{0000030F-0000-0000-C000-000000000046}
"PSInPlaceActive"

{00000310-0000-0000-C000-000000000046}
"PSInPlaceFrame"

{00000311-0000-0000-C000-000000000046}
"PSDragDrop"

{00000312-0000-0000-C000-000000000046}
"PSBindCtx"

{00000313-0000-0000-C000-000000000046}
"PSEnumerators"

{00000314-0000-0000-C000-000000000046}
"PSStore"
```

{00000315-0000-0000-C000-000000000046}
"Picture (Metafile)"

{00000316-0000-0000-C000-000000000046}
"Picture (Device Independent Bitmap)"

{00000319-0000-0000-C000-000000000046}
"Picture (Enhanced Metafile)"

{00000320-0000-0000-C000-000000000046}
"oleprx32_PSFactory"

{00020000-0000-0000-C000-000000000046}
"Microsoft AVI Files"

{00020001-0000-0000-C000-000000000046}
"AVI Compressed Stream"

{00020003-0000-0000-C000-000000000046}
"Microsoft Waveform Audio Files"

{0002000D-0000-0000-C000-000000000046}
"AVIFile Proxy/Stub"

{0002000F-0000-0000-C000-000000000046}
"ACM Compressed Audio Stream"

{0002001F-0000-0000-C000-000000000046}
"Microsoft AVI Files"

{00020344-0000-0000-C000-000000000046}
"MAPILogonRemote"

{00020420-0000-0000-C000-000000000046}
"PSDispatch"

{00020421-0000-0000-C000-000000000046}
"PSEnumVARIANT"

{00020422-0000-0000-C000-000000000046}
"PSTypeInfo"

{00020423-0000-0000-C000-000000000046}
"PSTypeLib"

{00020424-0000-0000-C000-000000000046}
"PSAutomation"

{00020425-0000-0000-C000-000000000046}
"PSTypeComp"

{00020801-0000-0000-C000-000000000046}
"Microsoft Graph 5.0"

```
{00020810-0000-0000-C000-000000000046}
"Microsoft Excel Worksheet"

{00020812-0000-0000-C000-000000000046}
"Microsoft Excel Application"

{000208EC-0000-0000-C000-000000000046}
"Microsoft Graph 5.0 Application"

{00020900-0000-0000-C000-000000000046}
"Microsoft Word Document"

{00020901-0000-0000-C000-000000000046}
"Microsoft Word Picture"

{00020C01-0000-0000-C000-000000000046}
"Wave Sound"

{00020D05-0000-0000-C000-000000000046}
"InsertedFile"

{00020D09-0000-0000-C000-000000000046}
"InsertedMessage"

{00020D30-0000-0000-C000-000000000046}
"IPM"

{00020D32-0000-0000-C000-000000000046}
"IPM.Document"

{00020D33-0000-0000-C000-000000000046}
"IPM.Resend"

{00020D34-0000-0000-C000-000000000046}
"Report.Any"

{00020D35-0000-0000-C000-000000000046}
"IPM.POST"

{00021290-0000-0000-C000-000000000046}
"Microsoft Clip Gallery"

{000212F0-0000-0000-C000-000000000046}
"Microsoft WordArt 3.0"

{00021302-0000-0000-C000-000000000046}
"MSWorksWin4"

{00021400-0000-0000-C000-000000000046}
"Desktop"

{00021401-0000-0000-C000-000000000046}
"Shortcut"
```

{00021700-0000-0000-C000-000000000046}
"Microsoft Equation 2.0"

{00022601-0000-0000-C000-000000000046}
"Media Clip"

{00022602-0000-0000-C000-000000000046}
"Video Clip"

{00022603-0000-0000-C000-000000000046}
"MIDI Sequence"

{00022613-0000-0000-C000-000000000046}
"Multimedia File Property Sheet"

{00025E15-0000-0000-C000-000000000046}
"DAO.DBEngine"

{00025E19-0000-0000-C000-000000000046}
"DAO.PrivateDBEngine"

{00025E43-0000-0000-C000-000000000046}
"DAO.TableDef"

{00025E4C-0000-0000-C000-000000000046}
"DAO.Field"

{00025E55-0000-0000-C000-000000000046}
"DAO.Index"

{00025E5F-0000-0000-C000-000000000046}
"DAO.Group"

{00025E68-0000-0000-C000-000000000046}
"DAO.User"

{00025E7A-0000-0000-C000-000000000046}
"DAO.QueryDef"

{00025E8B-0000-0000-C000-000000000046}
"DAO.Relation"

{00028B00-0000-0000-C000-000000000046}
"The Microsoft Network"

{00028B02-0000-0000-C000-000000000046}
"Text Conferencing Application"

{00028B05-0000-0000-C000-000000000046}
"Shortcut to The Microsoft Network"

{00028B07-0000-0000-C000-000000000046}
"Main MOS API Object"

```
{00028B0C-0000-0000-C000-000000000046}
"Properties for Shortcuts to The Microsoft Network"

{00028B1E-0000-0000-C000-000000000046}
"Calling Card Icon Handler"

{00028B50-0000-0000-C000-000000000046}
"MSN Attached File"

{00028b79-0000-0000-c000-000000000046}
"MSN StockQuotes"

{0002B400-0000-0000-C000-000000000046}
"Quattro Pro 7 Notebook"

{0002DF01-0000-0000-C000-000000000046}
"Internet Explorer(Ver 1.0)"

{0002E005-0000-0000-C000-000000000046}
"Component Categories Manager"

{00030000-0000-0000-C000-000000000046}
"Microsoft Excel Worksheet"

{00030003-0000-0000-C000-000000000046}
"Microsoft Word 2.0 Document"

{00030006-0000-0000-C000-000000000046}
"Microsoft Graph 3.0"

{00030007-0000-0000-C000-000000000046}
"Microsoft Drawing"

{00030009-0000-0000-C000-000000000046}
"Microsoft WordArt 1.0"

{0003000A-0000-0000-C000-000000000046}
"Paintbrush Picture"

{0003000B-0000-0000-C000-000000000046}
"Equation"

{0003000C-0000-0000-C000-000000000046}
"Package"

{0003000D-0000-0000-C000-000000000046}
"Wave Sound"

{0003000E-0000-0000-C000-000000000046}
"Media Clip"

{00030026-0000-0000-C000-000000000046}
"Microsoft ClipArt Gallery"
```

{00031003-0000-0000-C000-000000000046}
"RFTDCA"

{0003100B-0000-0000-C000-000000000046}
"Lotus 123"

{00031018-0000-0000-C000-000000000046}
"WrdPrfct5x"

{00041943-0000-0000-C000-000000000046}
"Microsoft Organization Chart 2.0"

{0004697E-0000-0000-C000-000000000046}
"WordPerfect Document (6.0)"

{0004A3C8-0000-0000-C000-000000000046}
"Netscape Hypertext Document"

{0006FE01-0000-0000-C000-000000000046}
"WordMail Mail Message"

{0006FE02-0000-0000-C000-000000000046}
"exchng32.exe"

{0006FE04-0000-0000-C000-000000000046}
"File Attachment"

{0006FE05-0000-0000-C000-000000000046}
"Message Attachment"

{016FD9C4-A2DC-101B-BCB0-00AA0042B7CE}
"ImexGrid Property Page"

{02B01C80-E03D-101A-B294-00DD010F2BF9}
"Fax Viewer Document"

{05780C00-9449-11CE-8DAE-00608CBB744B}
"PFViewShell"

{06DD38D3-D187-11CF-A80D-00C04FD74AD8}
"ActiveXPlugin Object"

{0713E8A8-850A-101B-AFC0-4210102A8DA7}
"TreeView Property Page"

{08B0E5C0-4FCB-11CF-AAA5-00401C608500}
"Java(TM) Support for Internet Explorer"

{08B0E5C0-4FCB-11CF-AAA5-00401C608501}
"Control for Java(TM)"

{0BA686AF-F7D3-101A-993E-0000C0EF6F5E}
"THREED FRAME CONTROL"

```
{0BE35202-8F91-11CE-9DE3-00AA004BB851}
"Picture Property Page"

{0BE35203-8F91-11CE-9DE3-00AA004BB851}
"Standard Font"

{1395F281-4326-101B-8B9A-CE293EF38449}
"WordPerfect 6.1 File"

{197F20A0-C37C-11CF-92B1-00AA00B8A733}
"VrmlViewer Object"

{19a5fa20-c662-11ce-9d06-00805f845683}
"Language dependant CB engine"

{1A127A20-C381-11CF-92B1-00AA00B8A733}
"VrmlView General Propery Page Object"

{1A4DA620-6217-11CF-BE62-0080C72EDD2D}
"MarqueeCtl Object"

{1B53F360-9A1B-1069-930C-00AA0030EBC8}
"HyperTerminal Connection Page Ext"

{1C3B4210-F441-11CE-B9EA-00AA006B1A69}
"Microsoft Forms 2.1 DataObject"

{1D00C4C0-8000-11CE-BE61-00608CEA1E6F}
"Thesaurus"

{1D582140-CCCD-11CE-949A-00608CE82FF5}
"PerfectFit Automation Object (Ver 1.0)"

{1F2059A0-1504-11CF-AB99-00C0F00683EB}
"QuoteScan Document"

{20C46560-8491-11CF-960C-0080C7F4EE85}
"Shell Frame Automation Service"

{217FC9C0-3AEA-1069-A2DB-08002B30309D}
"Shell Copy Hook"

{21B22460-3AEA-1069-A2DC-08002B30309D}
"File system attributes"

{21EC2020-3AEA-1069-A2DD-08002B30309D}
"Control Panel"

{2227A280-3AEA-1069-A2DE-08002B30309D}
"Printers"

{22405250-AD50-11CE-AA56-00608C37B6CE}
"PFMarker"
```

{2256FE6B-C42E-11CF-A5D4-00AA00A47DD2}
"OptionObj Object"

{25336920-03F9-11cf-8FD0-00AA00686F13}
"Windows HTML Viewer"

{2542F180-3532-1069-A2CD-00AA0034B50B}
"FONT PROPERTY PAGE"

{2600CD4C-D703-11CD-8C3F-00AA0042B7CE}
"Field List Control"

{275D9D51-5FF5-11CF-A5E1-00AA006BBF16}
"Private Debug Manager for Java(TM)"

{28DD9320-6F69-11ce-8B69-00608CC97D5B}
"WonderWare Engine"

{2E8D0FE0-8B43-11CF-ABBD-00A0C9034926}
"HideCtl Object"

{2F155EE4-C332-11CD-B23C-0000C0058192}
"THREED PANEL PROPERTY PAGE 2"

{336EC2C1-A0D8-11CE-AE3A-02608C8EBFE1}
"PFPRINTER"

{338E9310-7C07-11CE-8CA9-00AA0044BB60}
"Microsoft Forms 2.1 ControlPalette"

{33E3BE41-DF43-11CF-A5D4-00AA00A47DD2}
"MultiListCtl Object"

{3472D900-5A27-11CF-8B11-00AA00C00903}
"ButtonCtl Object"

{3C374A40-BAE4-11CF-BF7D-00AA006946EE}
"Microsoft Url History Service"

{3C448284-633F-101B-A63C-0000C0BB4E92}
"Sheridan Tabbed Dialog Property Page"

{3C4F3BE7-47EB-101B-A3C9-08002B2F49FB}
"Help"

{3D92FF40-5A24-11CF-8B11-00AA00C00903}
"CheckboxCtl Object"

{3DC7A020-0ACD-11CF-A9BB-00AA004AE837}
"The Internet"

{3E6392A0-5E5D-11CE-8C91-00608CEA1751}
"Spell Checker"

{3EA48300-8CF6-101B-84FB-666CCB9BCD32}
"OLE Docfile Property Page"

{3EFB1800-C2A1-11CF-960C-0080C7C2BA87}
"Execute Object for Java(TM)"

{3EFC0B01-F4AA-101A-8932-08002B327C2D}
"File Sharing"

{3F337921-55A0-11CF-BA61-00805F749BD1}
"QFREPOSITORY"

{3F337922-55A0-11CF-BA61-00805F749BD1}
"QFSRLIST"

{3F337923-55A0-11CF-BA61-00805F749BD1}
"PFWORDSTREAM"

{3F337924-55A0-11CF-BA61-00805F749BD1}
"QFRETRIEVE"

{3F337925-55A0-11CF-BA61-00805F749BD1}
"QFINDEXER"

{3F337926-55A0-11CF-BA61-00805F749BD1}
"QFQUERY"

{3FA7DEB3-6438-101B-ACC1-00AA00423326}
"MAPI 1.0 Session (v1.0)"

{402EFE61-1999-101B-99AE-04021C007002}
"Presentations 7 Chart"

{402EFE62-1999-101B-99AE-04021C007002}
"Presentations 7 Show"

{402EFE70-1999-101B-99AE-04021C007002}
"PFQUICKART"

{4319F60A-E9CF-11CE-AE2B-00608CE83CB8}
"PerfectFit Dialog Extender"

{438C0EA0-5731-11CF-9AF8-0020AF73AD51}
"Microsoft Sitemap"

{45172C00-7E89-11CE-8C91-00608CEA1751}
"WTAPI 2.0 User Word List Editor"

{46763EE0-CAB2-11CE-8C20-00AA0051E5D4}
"Obsolete Font"

{46E31370-3F7A-11CE-BED6-00AA00611080}
"Microsoft Forms 2.0 MultiPage"

{474C24A0-BDF6-11CE-949A-00608CE82FF5}
"Presentations for Windows (OLE Auto Ver 1.0)"

{481ED670-9D30-11ce-8F9B-0800091AC64E}
"Netscape Hypertext Document"

{4C599241-6926-101B-9992-00000B65C6F9}
"Microsoft Forms 2.0 Image"

{4d2f086c-6ea3-101b-a18a-00aa00446e07}
"MAPIPSFactory"

{4DB969E0-5979-11CE-82A6-00608CBB7395}
"WTAPI 2.0 Tool Manager"

{5512D110-5CC6-11CF-8D67-00AA00BDCE1D}
"Microsoft Forms 2.0 HTML SUBMIT"

{5512D112-5CC6-11CF-8D67-00AA00BDCE1D}
"Microsoft Forms 2.0 HTML IMAGE"

{5512D114-5CC6-11CF-8D67-00AA00BDCE1D}
"Microsoft Forms 2.0 HTML RESET"

{5512D116-5CC6-11CF-8D67-00AA00BDCE1D}
"Microsoft Forms 2.0 HTML CHECKBOX"

{5512D118-5CC6-11CF-8D67-00AA00BDCE1D}
"Microsoft Forms 2.0 HTML OPTION"

{5512D11A-5CC6-11CF-8D67-00AA00BDCE1D}
"Microsoft Forms 2.0 HTML TEXT"

{5512D11C-5CC6-11CF-8D67-00AA00BDCE1D}
"Microsoft Forms 2.0 HTML Hidden"

{5512D11E-5CC6-11CF-8D67-00AA00BDCE1D}
"Microsoft Forms 2.0 HTML Password"

{5512D122-5CC6-11CF-8D67-00AA00BDCE1D}
"Microsoft Forms 2.0 HTML SELECT"

{5512D124-5CC6-11CF-8D67-00AA00BDCE1D}
"Microsoft Forms 2.0 HTML TextAREA"

{56117100-C0CD-101B-81E2-00AA004AE837}
"Shell Scrap DataHandler"

{5728F10E-27CC-101B-A8EF-00000B65C5F8}
"Microsoft Forms 2.1 SubForm95"

{59099400-57FF-11CE-BD94-0020AF85B590}
"Disk Copy Extension"

```
{59850400-6664-101B-B21C-00AA004BA90B}
"Microsoft Office Binder"

{59850401-6664-101B-B21C-00AA004BA90B}
"Microsoft Office Binder Explode"

{59850403-6664-101B-B21C-00AA004BA90B}
"Microsoft Office Binder Briefcase Reconciler"

{59850404-6664-101B-B21C-00AA004BA90B}
"Microsoft Office Binder Briefcase Notifier"

{5E6AB780-7743-11CF-A12B-00AA004AE837}
"Microsoft Internet Toolbar"

{5F354881-1D7E-101B-A9DE-00AA0033819A}
"Print Sharing"

{6027C2D4-FB28-11CD-8820-08002B2F4F5A}
"Appearance Property Page"

{60403D81-872B-11CF-ACC8-0080C82BE3B6}
"Netscape.Help.1"

{612A8628-0FB3-11CE-8747-524153480004}
"Toolbar Property Page"

{614DD2C0-7B09-101B-9B38-00AA000C4F5D}
"MSNet Pages"

{61D8DE20-CA9A-11CE-9EA5-0080C82BE3B6}
"Netscape Hypertext Document"

{61E218E0-65D3-101B-9F08-061CEAC3D50D}
"ShellFind"

{62823C20-41A3-11CE-9E8B-0020AF039CA3}
"Button Property Page"

{644C1FE0-9035-11CE-8DAE-00608CBB744B}
"PFViewMgr"

{645FF040-5081-101B-9F08-00AA002F954E}
"Recycle Bin"

{648A5600-2C6E-101B-82B6-000000000014}
"Microsoft Comm Control"

{654C2A40-71B6-11CE-A850-444553540000}
"OPWNoLink"

{687738C0-5A24-11CF-8B11-00AA00C00903}
"RadioCtl Object"
```

{6B53FE20-B308-11CE-977B-00AA001F1074}
"PFDATETIME"

{6B7E6393-850A-101B-AFC0-4210102A8DA7}
"StatusBar Property Page"

{6D5140C1-7436-11CE-8034-00AA006009FA}
"PSFactoryBuffer"

{6D78EC20-5AA6-101B-8681-366FBD64CEB9}
"File Sharing Menu Handlers"

{6DA1A220-65D0-101B-A657-9EB70524D8E7}
"Folder Copy Hook"

{6E182020-F460-11CE-9BCD-00AA00608E01}
"Microsoft Forms 2.0 Frame"

{702F98C0-AAF5-11CE-8311-00608C86D1E7}
"PFTOOLBAR"

{73FDDC80-AEA9-101A-98A7-00AA00374959}
"WordPad Document"

{79176FB0-B7F2-11CE-97EF-00AA006D2776}
"Microsoft Forms 2.0 SpinButton"

{79eac9c3-baf9-11ce-8c82-00aa004ba90b}
"Hyperlinking ProxyStub Factory"

{79eac9d0-baf9-11ce-8c82-00aa004ba90b}
"StdHlink"

{79eac9e0-baf9-11ce-8c82-00aa004ba90b}
"URL Moniker"

{79eac9f1-baf9-11ce-8c82-00aa004ba90b}
"UrlMoniker ProxyStub Factory"

{79eac9f2-baf9-11ce-8c82-00aa004ba90b}
"Async BindCtx"

{7AF0E583-499B-11CF-8E76-00805FE414E3}
"PerfectFit Address Book"

{7BA4C740-9E81-11CF-99D3-00AA004AE837}
"Microsoft SendTo Service"

{7BD29E00-76C1-11CF-9DD0-00A0C9034933}
"Internet Cache Folder"

{7CBBABF0-36B9-11CE-BF0D-00AA0044BB60}
"Microsoft Forms 2.1 ControlSelector"

```
{7CF9B5A0-BDF5-11CE-949A-00608CE82FF5}
"WordPerfect.PerfectScript.1"

{7D9E4B80-9EBC-11CF-B512-0080C711D98A}
"P2D"

{812034D2-760F-11CF-9370-00AA00B8BF00}
"Office Compatible 1.0"

{812AE312-8B8E-11CF-93C8-00AA00C08FDF}
"Microsoft HTML Layout Control 1.0"

{85BBD920-42A0-1069-A2E4-08002B30309D}
"Briefcase"

{86747AC0-42A0-1069-A2E6-08002B30309D}
"Shell Moniker"

{86F19A00-42A0-1069-A2E9-08002B30309D}
".PIF file property pages"

{86F19A00-42A0-1069-A2EB-08002B30309D}
".PIF file handler"

{88895560-9AA2-1069-930E-00AA0030EBC8}
"HyperTerminal Icon Ext"

{89292102-4755-11cf-9DC2-00AA006C2B84}
"Internet Mail"

{89FE3FE3-9FF6-101B-B678-04021C007002}
"WordPerfect 6.1"

{8A6443A5-ED5A-11CF-9662-00A0C905428A}
"LicenseMgr 1.0 Object"

{8BD21D10-EC42-11CE-9E0D-00AA006002F3}
"Microsoft Forms 2.0 TextBox"

{8BD21D20-EC42-11CE-9E0D-00AA006002F3}
"Microsoft Forms 2.0 ListBox"

{8BD21D30-EC42-11CE-9E0D-00AA006002F3}
"Microsoft Forms 2.0 ComboBox"

{8BD21D40-EC42-11CE-9E0D-00AA006002F3}
"Microsoft Forms 2.0 CheckBox"

{8BD21D50-EC42-11CE-9E0D-00AA006002F3}
"Microsoft Forms 2.0 OptionButton"

{8BD21D60-EC42-11CE-9E0D-00AA006002F3}
"Microsoft Forms 2.0 ToggleButton"
```

{8E26BFC1-AFD6-11CF-BFFC-00AA003CFDFC}
"Helper Object for Java(TM)"

{8E27C92F-1264-101C-8A2F-040224009C02}
"Calendar Property Page"

{9365CF60-DAC1-11CF-9034-00AA006024BA}
"Java Class (com.ms.applet.BrowserAppletFrame)"

{9508ED80-9129-11CE-BC37-00805F9869E7}
"PerfectFit Moniker"

{9508ED85-9129-11CE-BC37-00805F9869E7}
"PerfectFit Moniker Helper"

{972C4270-11FD-11CE-B841-00AA004CD6D8}
"Microsoft Forms 2.1 Font"

{978C9E23-D4B0-11CE-BF2D-00AA003F40D0}
"Microsoft Forms 2.0 Label"

{984787E0-6289-11CF-ABBD-00A0C9034926}
"ComboCtl Object"

{99180163-DA16-101A-935C-444553540000}
"Reconciliation interface ProxyStub Factory"

{992CFFA0-F557-101A-88EC-00DD010CCC48}
"Dial-Up Networking"

{9b1c0180-a4c7-11ce-81ee-00aa00a71bab}
"MSN Custom Application"

{9E56BE60-C50F-11CF-9A2C-00A0C90A90CE}
"NeverShowExt"=""

{9E804EB0-5984-11CE-82A6-00608CBB7395}
"WTAPI 2.0 Tool Registry"

{9E804EEE-5984-11CE-82A6-00608CBB7395}
"Concept Base Interface"

{9E804EEF-5984-11CE-82A6-00608CBB7395}
"Language Independent CB engine"

{9ED94444-E5E8-101B-B9B5-444553540000}
"TabStrip Property Page"

{A4C4671C-499F-101B-BB78-00AA00383CBB}
"VBA Collection Object"

{A57B9B40-5AA6-101B-8681-366FBD64CEB9}
"Printer Sharing Menu Handlers"

{A7A5F9C0-BDF6-11CE-949A-00608CE82FF5}
"QuattroPro for Windows (OLE Auto Ver 1.0)"

{AAE68660-C718-11CE-8D9B-444553540000}
"WordPerfect 7 Document"

{AC9F2F90-E877-11CE-9F68-00AA00574A4F}
"Microsoft Forms 2.1 FormPackage"

{AFC20920-DA4E-11CE-B943-00AA006887B4}
"Microsoft Forms 2.1 FontNew"

{B16553C0-06DB-101B-85B2-0000C009BE81}
"SpinButton"

{B196B286-BAB4-101A-B69C-00AA00341D07}
"PSFactoryBuffer"

{B3CF0180-AD50-11CE-AA56-00608C37B6CB}
"PFOBJECTCONTEXT"

{B3CF01A0-AD50-11CE-AA56-00608C37B6CD}
"PFHelp"

{B54DCF20-5F9C-101B-AF4E-00AA003F0F07}
"Microsoft Access Database Application"

{B54F3741-5B07-11CF-A4B0-00AA004A55E8}
"VB Script Language"

{B66834C6-2E60-11CE-8748-524153480004}
"Tab Property Page"

{b722bcc4-4e68-101b-a2bc-00aa00404770}
"DocObject ProxyStub Factory"

{B768AEA3-C75D-11CE-BC37-00805F9869E7}
"PerfectFit NameSpace Browser Frame"

{B8D15090-EDD7-11CE-9A8D-00805FF4CA37}
"PerfectFit Natural Language"

{B95057E0-44DB-11CE-A5D1-00608C83BD3F}
"Shell Extensions for WordPerfect"

{BB7DF450-F119-11CD-8465-00AA00425D90}
"Microsoft Access Custom Icon Handler"

{BD84B381-8CA2-1069-AB1D-08000948F534}
"PANOSE Core Mapper"

{BDC217C5-ED16-11CD-956C-0000C04E4C0A}
"Sheridan Tabbed Dialog Control"

{C20D7340-5525-101B-8F15-00AA003E4672}
"Microsoft JET Briefcase Reconciler"

{C62A69F0-16DC-11CE-9E98-00AA00574A4F}
"Microsoft Forms 2.0 Form"

{C917BA20-D238-11CE-A9F8-00608CEA1751}
"Quick Spell Checker"

{C932BA89-4374-101B-A56C-00AA003668DC}
"MaskEd Property Page"

{C9DA6C40-83B1-11CE-81AC-00608CB9F83B}
"Grammatik"

{CA8A9780-280D-11CF-A24D-444553540000}
"Acrobat Control for ActiveX"

{CA8A9784-280D-11CF-A24D-444553540000}
"Acrobat Control Property Page"

{CD949A21-BDC8-11CE-8919-00608C39D066}
"QuickFinder Index Shell Extension"

{CFCDAA03-8BE4-11CF-B84B-0020AFBBCCFA}
"RealAudio(tm) ActiveX Control (32-bit) Object"

{D14E3180-11FD-11CE-B841-00AA004CD6D8}
"Microsoft Forms 2.1 Picture"

{D2029F40-8AB3-11CF-85FB-00401C608501}
"PSFactoryBuffer"

{D3B1DE00-6B94-1069-8754-08002B2BD64F}
"Disk Tools Extension"

{D3E34B21-9D75-101A-8C3D-00AA001A1652}
"Bitmap Image"

{D4A97620-8E8F-11CF-93CD-00AA00C08FDF}
"Microsoft ActiveX Image Control 1.0"

{D5FC9641-FE01-101A-A4F0-04021C009402}
"TextArt 2.0 Document"

{D5FC9641-FE01-101A-A4F0-04021C009403}
"TextArt 7 Document"

{D7053240-CE69-11CD-A777-00DD01143C57}
"Microsoft Forms 2.0 CommandButton"

{DA6781B0-C24A-11CF-B584-00AA00A71D1A}
"ISCtrl Picture"

```
{DBCE2480-C732-101B-BE72-BA78E9AD5B27}
"ICC Profile"

{DDF5A600-B9C0-101A-AF1A-00AA0034B50B}
"COLOR PROPERTY PAGE"

{DF0B3D60-548F-101B-8E65-08002B2BD119}
"PSSupportErrorInfo"

{DF9A1DA0-23C0-101B-B02E-FDFDFDFDFDFD}
"Adobe Acrobat Document"

{DFD181E0-5E2F-11CE-A449-00AA004A803D}
"Microsoft Forms 2.0 ScrollBar"

{e0d79300-84be-11ce-9641-444553540000}
"WinZip"

{E0DC8C80-3486-101B-82B6-000000000014}
"Mscomm Buffers Property Page"

{E328732C-9DC9-11CF-92D0-004095E27A10}
"Netscape.TalkNav.1"

{E4C18D40-1CD5-101C-B325-00AA001F3168}
"MS Organization Chart 2.0"

{E6246810-030F-11CF-8875-00608CF5AB6F}
"Natural Language Interface for Help"

{E67D6A10-4438-11CE-8CE4-0020AF18F905}
"Netscape.Registry.1"

{E7E4BC40-E76A-11CE-A9BB-00AA004AE837}
"Shell DocObject Viewer"

{EA7BAE70-FB3B-11CD-A903-00AA00510EA3}
"Microsoft PowerPoint Presentation"

{EA8A8060-D08B-11CE-AA56-00608C37B6CB}
"PFDESKTOP"

{EAB22AC3-30C1-11CF-A7EB-0000C05BAE0B}
"Microsoft Web Browser Control"

{EAE50EB0-4A62-11CE-BED6-00AA00611080}
"Microsoft Forms 2.0 TabStrip"

{EE230860-5A5F-11CF-8B11-00AA00C00903}
"PasswordCtl Object"

{EF5F7050-385A-11CE-8193-0020AF18F905}
"Netscape.Network.1"
```

{F0F08735-0C36-101B-B086-0020AF07D0F4}
"SCC Quick Viewer"

{F25C14C0-FBCF-101A-A58B-08002B2F4B0B}
"MS Network objects"

{F365CCA0-60E5-101B-A657-9EB70524D8E7}
"Printer Copy Hook"

{F414C260-6AC0-11CF-B6D1-00AA00BBBB58}
"JScript Language"

{F748B5F0-15D0-11CE-BF0D-00AA0044BB60}
"Microsoft Forms 2.1 Toolbox"

{FBF23B40-E3F0-101B-8488-00AA003E56F8}
"Internet Shortcut"

{FBF23B41-E3F0-101B-8488-00AA003E56F8}
"MIME and Internet Property Sheet Hook"

{FBF23B42-E3F0-101B-8488-00AA003E56F8}
"The Internet"

{FC2AC420-6284-11CF-ABBD-00A0C9034926}
"ListCtl Object"

{FC7AF71D-FC74-101A-84ED-08002B2EC713}
"Picture Property Page"

{FF393560-C2A7-11CF-BFF4-444553540000}
"Url History Folder"

Summary

You learned about HKEY_CLASSES_ROOT in this chapter. We covered the different ways in which it keeps track of file extensions, keeps track of programs associated with registered file types, and keeps track of information about OLE objects and documents.

Chapter 14

HKEY_CURRENT_USER

THIS KEY ISN'T REALLY A KEY — it doesn't exist as a distinct entity. It's an alias to the current user's subkey in the key HKEY_USERS (a subkey exists for every user who has a profile). If you make changes to one, you're automatically changing the other.

User Profile Folders

In Windows 95 and 98, the data contained in this key is stored in the current user's profile, in a file named USER.DAT. There's also a backup file with the last saved configuration named USER.DA0. The path to these files is \%Windows95Root%\ Profiles or \%Windows98Root%\Profiles.

In Windows NT 4, user data is kept in \%WindowsNTRoot%\Profiles\ <UserName>\NTUSER.DAT. There is no copy of the last backup, but a log of changes is kept in NTUSER.DAT.LOG.

A folder also exists for each user on the local hard drive, and information about the path for every profile folder on the computer is kept in HKEY_LOCAL_MACHINE.

For Windows 95 or 98, look in HKEY_LOCAL_MACHINE\Software\Microsoft\ Windows\CurrentVersion\ProfileList. A subkey for each profile is easily identified (see Figure 14-1).

In Windows NT 4, the profile paths are kept in HKEY_LOCAL_MACHINE\ Software\Microsoft\WindowsNT\CurrentVersion\ProfileList, but instead of user names, an identification key appears for each user (see Figure 14-2). Select a subkey to see the name in the data panel.

The profile folders on the hard drive represent the configuration options for each user (see Figure 14-3). As you make changes to your system, such as installing software or creating desktop shortcuts, those changes are reflected in your profile folders as well as in the registry.

You can use those folders as a quick way to add items to the Start menu or the SendTo command of your shortcut menus. For example, you can move an application shortcut into the Programs subfolder, and as a result it will appear on your Start menu (and will be launched when you click it). You can do the same thing with desktop shortcuts; in fact, if you look in another user's profile and see desktop shortcuts you'd like to have on your desktop, copy them to the appropriate subfolder in your profile folder.

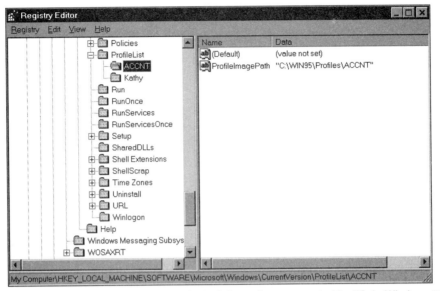

Figure 14-1: Registry keys for profile folder information are easy to identify in Windows 95 and 98.

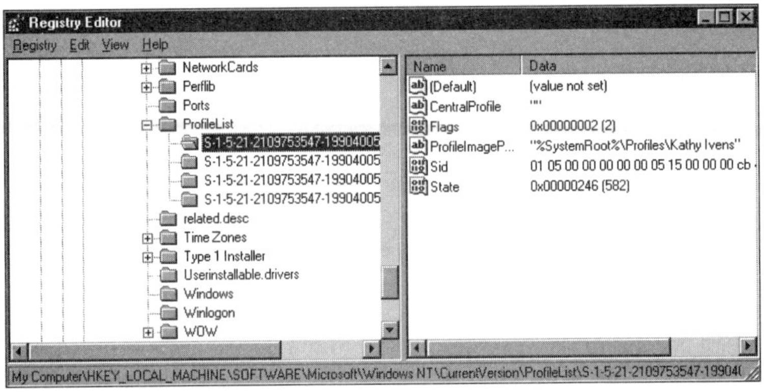

Figure 14-2: Windows NT 4 stores the path information for profile folders in subkeys with names that human beings can't read.

Windows NT Subkeys

The expanded tree for HKEY_CURRENT_USER in Windows NT looks like Figure 14-4.

Several of the subkeys expand further down, and as you drill down you'll find the configuration options this user has set. You'll also find many of the system's default options for a variety of configuration settings.

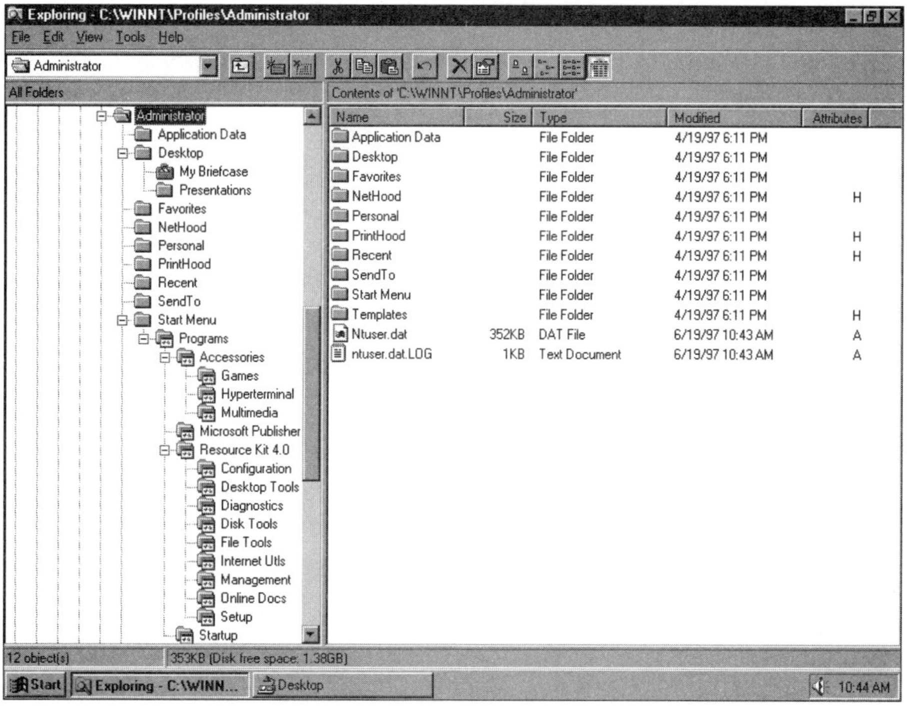

Figure 14-3: The profile tree for Administrator on a Windows NT 4 workstation displays the environment for that user.

AppEvents

The AppEvents subkey contains information about all the sounds associated with events; these sounds come from system events and installed applications that establish their events in the registry.

The EventLabels subkey lists the available sounds and their standard associations.

The Schemes subkey lists the actual sound/event associations. Most of these keys include several subkeys: the default association and the current association, and the specific sounds for Open and Close for application events. For example, the following listing is from the AppEvents export file for an NT User (it's just a section of the original listing, enough to give you an idea of how to read the data). Where a sound association has been configured by this user, you'll see the sound label; otherwise, you'll see quote marks.

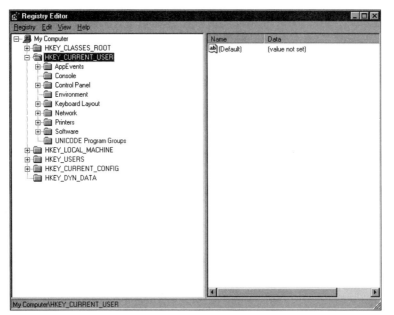

Figure 14-4: The information in this Windows NT registry tree is specific to the current user.

The registry keeps this information in a hierarchical format; for example, there's a subkey for each possible event with a current configuration, and also a separate subkey for the same event's default configuration:

```
[HKEY_CURRENT_USER\AppEvents\Schemes\Apps]

[HKEY_CURRENT_USER\AppEvents\Schemes\Apps\.Default\AppGPFault\
 .Current]
" "

[HKEY_CURRENT_USER\AppEvents\Schemes\Apps\.Default\AppGPFault\
 .Default]
" "

[HKEY_CURRENT_USER\AppEvents\Schemes\Apps\.Default\Close]

[HKEY_CURRENT_USER\AppEvents\Schemes\Apps\.Default\Close\.Current]
" "

[HKEY_CURRENT_USER\AppEvents\Schemes\Apps\.Default\Close\.Default]
" "

[HKEY_CURRENT_USER\AppEvents\Schemes\Apps\.Default\MailBeep]
```

```
[HKEY_CURRENT_USER\AppEvents\Schemes\Apps\.Default\MailBeep\
 .Current]
"ding.wav"

[HKEY_CURRENT_USER\AppEvents\Schemes\Apps\.Default\MailBeep\
 .Default]
"ding.wav"

[HKEY_CURRENT_USER\AppEvents\Schemes\Apps\.Default\Maximize]

[HKEY_CURRENT_USER\AppEvents\Schemes\Apps\.Default\Maximize\
 .Current]
""

[HKEY_CURRENT_USER\AppEvents\Schemes\Apps\.Default\Maximize\
 .Default]
""

[HKEY_CURRENT_USER\AppEvents\Schemes\Apps\.Default\MenuCommand]

[HKEY_CURRENT_USER\AppEvents\Schemes\Apps\.Default\MenuCommand\
 .Current]
""

[HKEY_CURRENT_USER\AppEvents\Schemes\Apps\.Default\MenuCommand\
 .Default]
""

[HKEY_CURRENT_USER\AppEvents\Schemes\Apps\.Default\MenuPopup]

[HKEY_CURRENT_USER\AppEvents\Schemes\Apps\.Default\MenuPopup\
 .Current]
""

[HKEY_CURRENT_USER\AppEvents\Schemes\Apps\.Default\MenuPopup\
 .Default]
""

[HKEY_CURRENT_USER\AppEvents\Schemes\Apps\.Default\Minimize]

[HKEY_CURRENT_USER\AppEvents\Schemes\Apps\.Default\Minimize\
 .Current]
""

[HKEY_CURRENT_USER\AppEvents\Schemes\Apps\.Default\Minimize\
 .Default]
""

[HKEY_CURRENT_USER\AppEvents\Schemes\Apps\.Default\Open]

[HKEY_CURRENT_USER\AppEvents\Schemes\Apps\.Default\Open\.Current]
""
```

```
[HKEY_CURRENT_USER\AppEvents\Schemes\Apps\.Default\Open\.Default]
""

[HKEY_CURRENT_USER\AppEvents\Schemes\Apps\.Default\SystemAsterisk]

[HKEY_CURRENT_USER\AppEvents\Schemes\Apps\.Default\SystemAsterisk\
 .Current]
"chord.wav"

[HKEY_CURRENT_USER\AppEvents\Schemes\Apps\.Default\SystemAsterisk\
 .Default]
"C:\\WINNT\\media\\chord.wav"

[HKEY_CURRENT_USER\AppEvents\Schemes\Apps\.Default\SystemExclamation
 ]

[HKEY_CURRENT_USER\AppEvents\Schemes\Apps\.Default\SystemExclamation
 \.Current]
"chord.wav"

[HKEY_CURRENT_USER\AppEvents\Schemes\Apps\.Default\SystemExclamation
 \.Default]
"C:\\WINNT\\media\\chord.wav"

[HKEY_CURRENT_USER\AppEvents\Schemes\Apps\.Default\SystemExit]

[HKEY_CURRENT_USER\AppEvents\Schemes\Apps\.Default\SystemExit\
 .Current]
"Windows NT Logoff Sound.wav"

[HKEY_CURRENT_USER\AppEvents\Schemes\Apps\.Default\SystemExit\
 .Default]
"C:\\WINNT\\media\\tada.wav"

[HKEY_CURRENT_USER\AppEvents\Schemes\Apps\.Default\SystemHand]

[HKEY_CURRENT_USER\AppEvents\Schemes\Apps\.Default\SystemHand\
 .Current]
"chord.wav"

[HKEY_CURRENT_USER\AppEvents\Schemes\Apps\.Default\SystemHand\
 .Default]
"C:\\WINNT\\media\\chord.wav"

[HKEY_CURRENT_USER\AppEvents\Schemes\Apps\.Default\SystemQuestion]

[HKEY_CURRENT_USER\AppEvents\Schemes\Apps\.Default\SystemQuestion\
 .Current]
"chord.wav"

[HKEY_CURRENT_USER\AppEvents\Schemes\Apps\.Default\SystemQuestion\
 .Default]
"C:\\WINNT\\media\\chord.wav"
```

```
[HKEY_CURRENT_USER\AppEvents\Schemes\Apps\.Default\SystemStart]

[HKEY_CURRENT_USER\AppEvents\Schemes\Apps\.Default\SystemStart\
  .Current]
"Windows NT Logon Sound.wav"

[HKEY_CURRENT_USER\AppEvents\Schemes\Apps\.Default\SystemStart\
  .Default]
"Windows NT Logon Sound.wav"

[HKEY_CURRENT_USER\AppEvents\Schemes\Apps\Explorer]
"Windows Explorer"

[HKEY_CURRENT_USER\AppEvents\Schemes\Apps\Explorer\EmptyRecycleBin]

[HKEY_CURRENT_USER\AppEvents\Schemes\Apps\Explorer\EmptyRecycleBin\
  .Current]
"ding.wav"

[HKEY_CURRENT_USER\AppEvents\Schemes\Apps\Explorer\EmptyRecycleBin\
  .Default]
"C:\\WINNT\\media\\ding.wav"

[HKEY_CURRENT_USER\AppEvents\Schemes\Apps\Office97]
"Microsoft Office"

[HKEY_CURRENT_USER\AppEvents\Schemes\Apps\Office97\Office97-
  Reminder]
"Reminder"

[HKEY_CURRENT_USER\AppEvents\Schemes\Apps\Office97\Office97-
  Reminder\.Current]
"C:\\WINNT\\Media\\Office97\\REMINDER.WAV"

[HKEY_CURRENT_USER\AppEvents\Schemes\Apps\Office97\Office97-
  Reminder\.Default]
"C:\\WINNT\\Media\\Office97\\REMINDER.WAV"
```

Console

Console is the term for a character-based window (the command prompt window or the window for a text-based application). Console entries are set by the user in the Console applet in the Control Panel and then transferred to the registry. The data type is REG_DWORD. The following console properties are configured:

- ◆ **Cursor Size:** You can choose from Small, Medium, and Large (the default is Small).

- ◆ **Command History:** A buffer size is allocated for retaining command history, which you can change (the default is 50). Use the up and down arrows to see the command history for this session in this console window.

◆ **Quick Edit Mode:** Quick Edit Mode means you can bypass the Edit command on the title bar icon of the command window and use the mouse instead.

◆ **Insert Mode:** This determines whether the character entry you perform in a console is Insert or Typeover.

◆ **Display Options:** This value determines whether your console opens full-screen or as a window. RISC-based computers do not support the full-screen mode.

◆ **Fonts:** You can choose the fonts and font sizes for consoles. When you change fonts, the window size changes to accommodate the new font.

◆ **Layout:** The layout is the position of the console on the screen, and the size of the window.

◆ **Screen Colors:** This specifies the color of the background and the text for a console.

You can change these values in the registry, but it's actually quicker and safer to use the Console applet in the Control Panel to perform these tasks.

Control Panel

The configuration actions you perform from the Control Panel are stored in this section of the registry (see Figure 14-5).

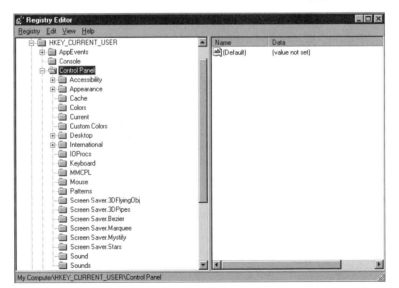

Figure 14-5: Control Panel applets return information to your registry settings when you configure your system.

One of the more interesting subkeys is Desktop, which controls the appearance of your screen background and also determines the position of screen elements (windows and icons). The following listing is fairly typical.

```
[HKEY_CURRENT_USER\Control Panel\Desktop]
"CoolSwitch""1"
"CoolSwitchRows""3"
"CoolSwitchColumns""7"
"CursorBlinkRate""530"
"ScreenSaveTimeOut""900"
"ScreenSaveActive""0"
"SCRNSAVE.EXE""(NONE)"
"ScreenSaverIsSecure""0"
"Pattern""(None)"
"Wallpaper""(None)"
"TileWallpaper""0"
"GridGranularity""0"
"IconSpacing""75"
"IconTitleWrap""1"
"IconTitleFaceName""MS Sans Serif"
"IconTitleSize""9"
"IconTitleStyle""0"
"DragFullWindows""1"
"HungAppTimeout""5000"
"WaitToKillAppTimeout""20000"
"AutoEndTasks""0"
"FontSmoothing""0"
"MenuShowDelay""400"
"DragHeight""2"
"DragWidth""2"
"WheelScrollLines""3"

[HKEY_CURRENT_USER\Control Panel\Desktop\WindowMetrics]
"BorderWidth""1"
```

Incidentally, the CoolSwitch option determines whether or not you can use Alt+Tab to switch between windows.

The Keyboard subkey contains your keyboard settings (see Figure 14-6 for a typical registry entry).

The Mouse subkey contains the value entries for your mouse configuration (see Figure 14-7).

Environment

The Environment subkey holds the variables used by the NT logon and shell (it's similar to the information you used to see in DOS when you typed **SET** at the command line). Because most of the information you used to place in Autoexec.bat to create the environment is now handled by various NT system functions, the data here is usually rather limited (see Figure 14-8).

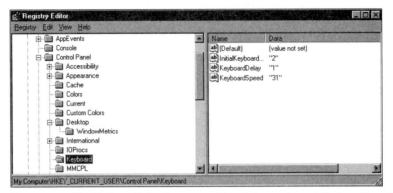

Figure 14-6: The KeyboardDelay is measured in milliseconds, and KeyboardSpeed is measured in characters per second.

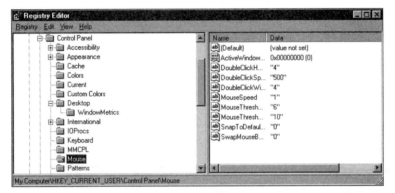

Figure 14-7: Mouse reaction time, along with other settings, are recorded when you configure the mouse.

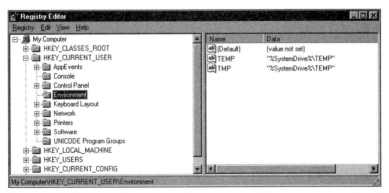

Figure 14-8: User variables, as opposed to system variables, are contained in the Environment subkey.

Settings for this registry key are connected to the System applet in the Control Panel. Two sets of variables exist in an NT 4 system: System Variables and User Variables. The System Variables remain the same regardless of the logged-on user. You can place additional User Variables into your environment by entering a Variable and a Value in the Environment tab of the System Properties dialog box (see Figure 14-9), and then choosing Set. You can also select an existing variable and choose Delete to remove it. Or, if you're comfortable with the registry, you can make the changes there.

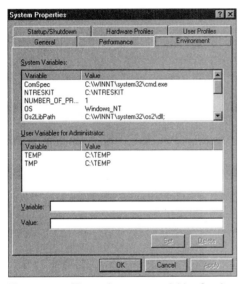

Figure 14-9: The environment variables for the system and the current logged-on user are displayed in the System Properties dialog box as well as in the registry.

Keyboard Layout

This key specifies the primary keyboard layout, and includes two subkeys: Preload, which contains a pointer to the code page for the keyboard layout; and Substitutes, which only has a value if you've installed a substitute. This is not the same information as in the Keyboard subkey under the Control Panel subkey, which is the container for the configuration you set for your keyboard (speed and delay settings).

Network

This key contains a subkey for each currently mapped drive. The drive subkey displays specific information about the connection (see Figure 14-10).

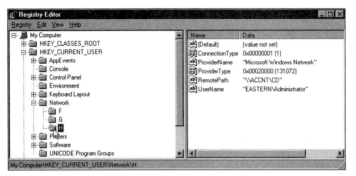

Figure 14-10: This user has mapped the CD on a connected computer named "ACCNT" to drive H.

Printers

Information about installed printers is found in the Printers subkey, which displays the device. There may be subkeys under this key if the printer is not local.

Software

This key holds subkeys for registered system and application software (see Figure 14-11). You can drill down through the subkeys for additional information. Opening the Microsoft subkey will probably produce a very long list.

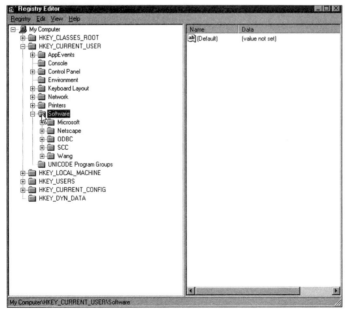

Figure 14-11: Expand any software key to see the installation details.

UNICODE Program Groups

This key contains references to programs that use UNICODE.

Windows 95 and 98 Subkeys

HKEY_CURRENT_USER in the Windows 95 and 98 registry shows some differences from Windows NT 4 when you expand the key (see Figure 14-12).

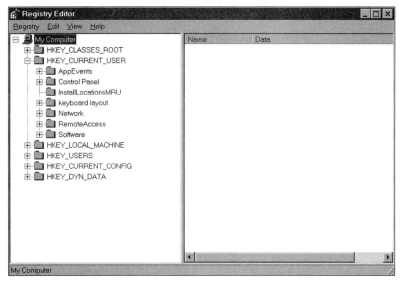

Figure 14-12: The Windows 95 and 98 HKEY_CURRENT_USER key is slightly different from Windows NT 4.

AppEvents

The AppEvents key in Windows 95/98 is identical to the AppEvents key in Windows NT 4.

Control Panel

The Control Panel key in Windows 95 and 98 has fewer subkeys than in Windows NT 4. The Desktop subkey, like that in Windows NT 4, contains the values for the appearance of your desktop:

```
[HKEY_CURRENT_USER\Control Panel\desktop]
CursorBlinkRate
```

```
Wallpaper
TileWallpaper
ScreenSaveLowPowerActive
ScreenSavePowerOffActive

[HKEY_CURRENT_USER\Control Panel\desktop\ResourceLocale]

[HKEY_CURRENT_USER\Control Panel\desktop\WindowMetrics]
IconSpacingFactor
BorderWidth
ScrollWidth
ScrollHeight
CaptionWidth
CaptionHeight
SmCaptionWidth
SmCaptionHeight
MenuWidth
MenuHeight
CaptionFont
SmCaptionFont
MenuFont
StatusFont
MessageFont
IconFont
IconSpacing
IconVerticalSpacing
```

It's probably only sporting of me to point out the fact that I have no idea what the \ResourceLocale subkey is used for. When I checked my own Windows 95 system, I found the data "00000409". Now, in my Windows NT 4 system, that same data appears under \Keyboard Layout\Preload, so I'm guessing that's the code for the standard U.S. keyboard. But I can't prove it and I couldn't find anyone at Microsoft who could answer my question (that doesn't mean there isn't anyone there who can't, it just means I obviously don't know the right people at Microsoft).

InstallLocationsMRU

This key contains the most recently used locations for source files during the installation of software by this user.

Keyboard Layout

This key holds information about the installed keyboard (by the way, that "00000409" data item is here too, under \Preload\1).

Network

This key contains information about network access. Mapped drives that are configured for reconnection at logon are found under the Persistent subkey, and a key exists for each mapped drive. The Recent subkey displays the shares on connected computers that have been accessed by this computer, and also notes the UNC for those shares (see Figure 14-13).

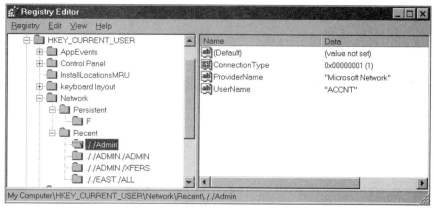

Figure 14-13: Recent network access is displayed in the Network subkey.

RemoteAccess

This key reflects the setup and configuration you've performed in the Dial Up Networking folder in My Computer. Within the subkeys are all the options, dialing configurations, and other Dial-Up Networking features (see Figure 14-14).

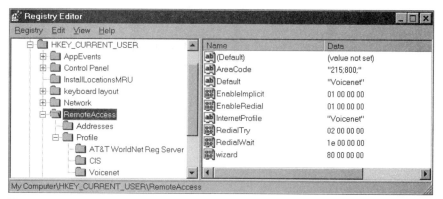

Figure 14-14: The configuration options you install in Dial-Up Networking are transferred to this registry key.

Software

This key holds information about registered system and application software (see Figure 14-15).

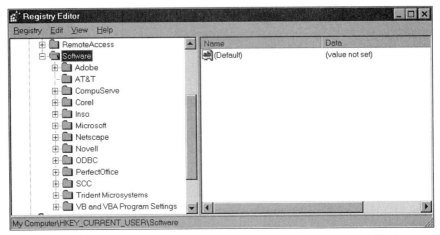

Figure 14-15: The Software subkey contains information about system applications and software installed by this user.

Specific information about the Microsoft environment for the user is contained in the following two subkeys. If you are using Windows 98, replace **Win95** in each subkey with **Win98**.

```
[HKEY_CURRENT_USER\Software\Microsoft\Windows\CurrentVersion\
 Explorer\User Shell Folders]

"Personal"="C:\\My Documents"
"Favorites"="C:\\WIN95\\Favorites"
"Desktop"="C:\\WIN95\\Profiles\\ACCNT\\Desktop"
"Recent"="C:\\WIN95\\Profiles\\ACCNT\\Recent"
"NetHood"="C:\\WIN95\\Profiles\\ACCNT\\NetHood"
"Start Menu"="C:\\WIN95\\Profiles\\ACCNT\\Start Menu"
"Programs"="C:\\WIN95\\Profiles\\ACCNT\\Start Menu\\Programs"
"Startup"="C:\\WIN95\\Profiles\\ACCNT\\Start
 Menu\\Programs\\Startup"

[HKEY_CURRENT_USER\Software\Microsoft\Windows\CurrentVersion\
 Explorer\Shell Folders]

"Desktop"="C:\\WIN95\\Profiles\\ACCNT\\Desktop"
"Programs"="C:\\WIN95\\Profiles\\ACCNT\\Start Menu\\Programs"
"Fonts"="C:\\WIN95\\Fonts"
"Start Menu"="C:\\WIN95\\Profiles\\ACCNT\\Start Menu"
"Templates"="C:\\WIN95\\ShellNew"
"Startup"="C:\\WIN95\\Profiles\\ACCNT\\Start
 Menu\\Programs\\Startup"
"Recent"="C:\\WIN95\\Profiles\\ACCNT\\Recent"
"SendTo"="C:\\WIN95\\SendTo"
"NetHood"="C:\\WIN95\\Profiles\\ACCNT\\NetHood"
"Personal"="C:\\My Documents"
"Favorites"="C:\\WIN95\\Favorites"
```

These subkeys are essentially identical. The first, `User Shell Folders`, contains locations for the important Windows 95 or 98 folders for this user. The second, `Shell Folders`, contains additional information that Windows 95 and 98 use for the Shell: `SendTo`, `Fonts`, and `Templates`.

It's easier to use this alias key to investigate settings or make changes, because it's right there waiting for you when you open a registry editor, and you don't have to find the subkey in `HKEY_USERS`. Remember that what you change here is also changed in `HKEY_USERS\<current user>`, and vice versa.

Summary

This chapter covered `HKEY_CURRENT_USER` and its various subkeys. In the next chapter, we'll investigate `HKEY_LOCAL_MACHINE`.

Chapter 15

HKEY_LOCAL_MACHINE

HKEY_LOCAL_MACHINE is the keeper of the configuration data for a computer. Both hardware and software are tracked in this key, along with other varied information about both entities. For example, not only does this key include specific information about the configuration of your hardware and peripherals, but it also stores all the available choices for making changes (the keyboard language options fill up several pages if you print them out). These are the choices you see as you configure your machine through the Control Panel. This key is enormous.

In principle, this key is pretty much the same for Windows 95, Windows 98, and Windows NT 4, although you'll find some differences as you drill down. The subkeys are a bit different, but in essence, in both operating systems, this is where to find everything you ever wanted to know about a computer — perhaps more than you ever wanted to know.

Windows 95 and 98 Local Machine Settings

When you expand HKEY_LOCAL_MACHINE in Windows 95 and 98, you see the following first-level subkeys:

- ◆ Config
- ◆ Enum
- ◆ Hardware
- ◆ Network
- ◆ Security
- ◆ Software
- ◆ System

The Config Subkey

Config, which exists only for Windows 95 and 98, tracks data relating to all hardware configurations for the computer – it's the "hardware profiles" section of this registry key. It's actually arranged in groups, representing specific hardware profiles. Each profile is numbered starting with 0001, and if you haven't created additional hardware profiles, the 0001 configuration is the only data in this subkey (Figure 15-1).

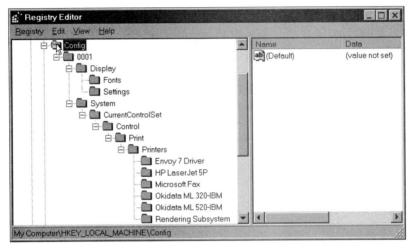

Figure 15-1: The Config subkey expands to display information about the current hardware configuration.

A data dump of this subkey for a computer with a standard configuration, no additional hardware profiles, and three printers looks like this:

```
[HKEY_LOCAL_MACHINE\Config]
[HKEY_LOCAL_MACHINE\Config\0001]
"ProfileFlags"=hex:00,00,00,00
[HKEY_LOCAL_MACHINE\Config\0001\Display]
[HKEY_LOCAL_MACHINE\Config\0001\Display\Settings]
"fonts.fon"="8514sys.fon"
"fixedfon.fon"="8514fix.fon"
"oemfonts.fon"="8514oem.fon"
"DPILogicalX"="120"
"DPILogicalY"="120"
"DPIPhysicalX"="120"
"DPIPhysicalY"="120"
"BitsPerPixel"="8"
"Resolution"="800,600"
[HKEY_LOCAL_MACHINE\Config\0001\Display\Fonts]
```

```
"MS Serif 8,10,12,14,18,24 (8514/a res)"="seriff.fon"
"MS Sans Serif 8,10,12,14,18,24 (8514/a res)"="sseriff.fon"
"Courier 10,12,15 (8514/a res)"="courf.fon"
"Symbol 8,10,12,14,18,24 (8514/a res)"="symbolf.fon"
"Small Fonts (8514/a res)"="smallf.fon"
[HKEY_LOCAL_MACHINE\Config\0001\System]
[HKEY_LOCAL_MACHINE\Config\0001\System\CurrentControlSet]
[HKEY_LOCAL_MACHINE\Config\0001\System\CurrentControlSet\Control]
[HKEY_LOCAL_MACHINE\Config\0001\System\CurrentControlSet\Control\
  Print]
[HKEY_LOCAL_MACHINE\Config\0001\System\CurrentControlSet\Control\
  Print\Printers]
"Default"="HP LaserJet 5P"
[HKEY_LOCAL_MACHINE\Config\0001\System\CurrentControlSet\Control\
  Print\Printers\Okidata ML 320-IBM]
[HKEY_LOCAL_MACHINE\Config\0001\System\CurrentControlSet\Control\
  Print\Printers\Okidata ML 520-IBM]
[HKEY_LOCAL_MACHINE\Config\0001\System\CurrentControlSet\Control\
  Print\Printers\Envoy 7 Driver]
@=""
[HKEY_LOCAL_MACHINE\Config\0001\System\CurrentControlSet\Control\
  Print\Printers\Microsoft Fax]
[HKEY_LOCAL_MACHINE\Config\0001\System\CurrentControlSet\Control\
  Print\Printers\Rendering Subsystem]
[HKEY_LOCAL_MACHINE\Config\0001\System\CurrentControlSet\Control\
  Print\Printers\HP LaserJet 5P]
```

If you haven't created additional hardware profiles, the \Config subkey is identical to the registry key HKEY_CURRENT_CONFIG. If you have created hardware profiles, the profile number that is currently loaded is identical to HKEY_CURRENT_CONFIG.

The Enum Subkey

This is another subkey you only find in Windows 95 and 98. Within this subkey is all the information about every device on the computer, whether or not that device is in use.

The Enum subkey has a series of subkeys representing hardware classes. The number of subkeys varies depending on the hardware in the computer. For example, Figure 15-2 is the expanded Enum subkey for an ISA computer, while Figure 15-3 is the expanded Enum subkey for a computer with ESDI and PCI hardware.

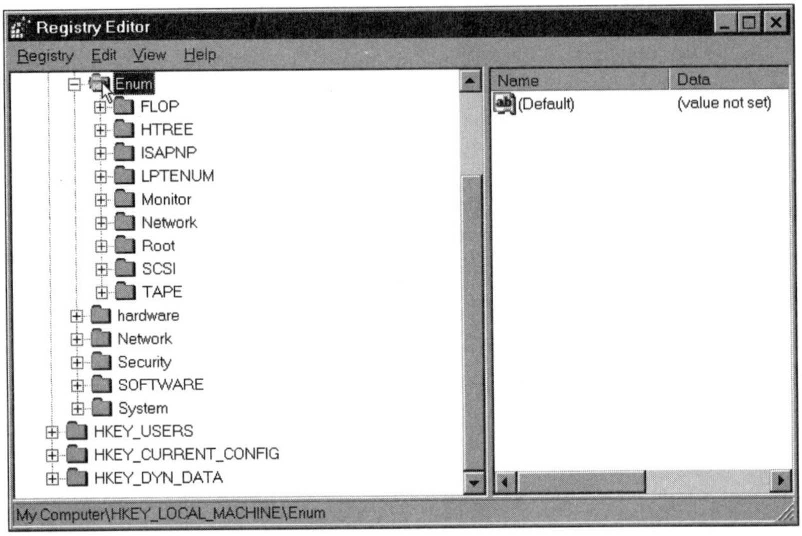

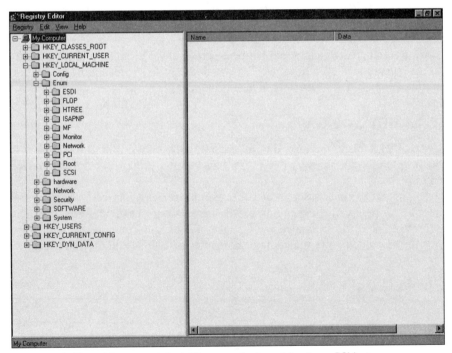

Figure 15-2: Glancing at the subkeys tells you that this computer is ISA only and has a Plug and Play printer attached.

Figure 15-3: The subkeys reveal that this computer has at least one PCI bus.

Following is a list of subkeys you might find under Enum, along with some of the data contained in subkeys for classes in a typical computer:

◆ BIOS, which holds information about devices on a system with a Plug and Play BIOS.

◆ EISA, which has an entry and data for every EISA device that is installed in the computer.

◆ ESDI, which has subkeys for each ESDI drive that's been installed in the computer. For example:

```
[HKEY_LOCAL_MACHINE\Enum\ESDI\GENERIC_IDE__DISK_TYPE46_\MF&CH
  ILD0000&PCI&VEN_8086&DEV_1230&BUS_00&DEV_07&FUNC_0100]
"RevisionLevel"="      "
"ProductId"="IDE   DISK TYPE46"
"Manufacturer"="GENERIC "
"DeviceType"=hex:00
"Int13"=hex:01
"CurrentDriveLetterAssignment"="C"
"HardwareID"="GENERIC_IDE__DISK_TYPE46_,GenDisk,ESDI\\GENERIC
  _IDE__DISK_TYPE46_"
"Class"="DiskDrive"
"Driver"="DiskDrive\\0001"
"Mfg"="(Standard disk drives)"
"DeviceDesc"="GENERIC IDE   DISK TYPE46"
```

◆ FLOP, which has the information about diskette drives. For instance:

```
[HKEY_LOCAL_MACHINE\Enum\FLOP\GENERIC_NEC__FLOPPY_DISK_\ROOT&
  *PNP0700&000000]
"RevisionLevel"="      "
"ProductId"="NEC  FLOPPY DISK"
"Manufacturer"="GENERIC "
"DeviceType"=hex
"Int13"=hex
"Removable"=hex
"CurrentDriveLetterAssignment"="A"
```

◆ ISAPNP, which has information on ISA or EISA Plug and Play devices. For example:

```
[HKEY_LOCAL_MACHINE\Enum\ISAPNP]
[HKEY_LOCAL_MACHINE\Enum\ISAPNP\READDATAPORT]
[HKEY_LOCAL_MACHINE\Enum\ISAPNP\READDATAPORT\0]
"HardwareID"="ISAPNP\\READDATAPORT"
"Class"="System"
"Driver"="System\\0008"
"Mfg"="(Standard system devices)"
"DeviceDesc"="IO read data port for ISA Plug and Play
  enumerator"
```

◆ LPTENUM, which contains a subkey for each Plug and Play printer attached to this computer. For instance:

```
[HKEY_LOCAL_MACHINE\Enum\LPTENUM]
[HKEY_LOCAL_MACHINE\Enum\LPTENUM\HEWLETT-PACKARDHP_LA1EE3]
[HKEY_LOCAL_MACHINE\Enum\LPTENUM\HEWLETT-
  PACKARDHP_LA1EE3\ROOT&*PNP0400&0000]
"Model"="HP LaserJet 6P"
"Manufacturer"="Hewlett-Packard"
"DeviceDesc"="Hewlett-Packard LaserJet 6P Printer"
"Class"="PRINTER"
"HardwareID"="LPTENUM\\HEWLETT-PACKARDHP_LA1EE3"
```

◆ MF, which has information about any multifunction boards in the computer. For example:

```
[HKEY_LOCAL_MACHINE\Enum\MF\CHILD0000\PCI&VEN_8086&DEV_1230&B
  US_00&DEV_07&FUNC_01]
"HardwareID"="MF\\GOODPRIMARY,MF\\CHILD0000"
"Class"="hdc"
"Driver"="hdc\\0003"
"IDENoSerialize"=hex:01
"Mfg"="(Standard hard disk drivers)"
"DeviceDesc"="Primary IDE controller (dual fifo)"
"ConfigFlags"=hex:00,00,00,00
[HKEY_LOCAL_MACHINE\Enum\MF\CHILD0000\ROOT&OPTO930MEDIA&0000]
"HardwareID"="MF\\OPTO930_Dev0"
"Class"="OPTO930MEDIA"
"Driver"="OPTO930MEDIA\\0001"
"Mfg"="OPTi Inc."
"DeviceDesc"="OPTi 930 Sound/OPL3 Device"
```

◆ Monitor, which has a subkey for every monitor that's been installed. A subkey named Default_Monitor has additional subkeys to link a specific monitor to a specific hardware profile. If the system does not contain multiple hardware profiles, the Default_Monitor subkey remains, but contains no data.

◆ Network, which has data about the network to which the computer is attached. This subkey does not have information about the network hardware, however; instead, it holds descriptions of the network protocols and bindings. For example:

```
[HKEY_LOCAL_MACHINE\Enum\Network]
[HKEY_LOCAL_MACHINE\Enum\Network\NETBEUI]
[HKEY_LOCAL_MACHINE\Enum\Network\NETBEUI\0001]
"Class"="NetTrans"
"Driver"="NetTrans\\0003"
"MasterCopy"="Enum\\Network\\NETBEUI\\0001"
"DeviceDesc"="NetBEUI"
"CompatibleIDs"="NETBEUI"
"Mfg"="Microsoft"
"ConfigFlags"=hex
```

```
[HKEY_LOCAL_MACHINE\Enum\Network\NETBEUI\0001\Bindings]
"VREDIR\\0005"=""
"VSERVER\\0011"=""
```

◆ PCI, which has a subkey for every PCI device in the computer. For instance:

```
[HKEY_LOCAL_MACHINE\Enum\PCI\VEN_1013&DEV_00A0]
[HKEY_LOCAL_MACHINE\Enum\PCI\VEN_1013&DEV_00A0\BUS_00&DEV_09&
    FUNC_00]
"DeviceDesc"="Cirrus Logic 5436 PCI"
"HWRevision"="045"
"CompatibleIDs"="PCI\\CC_0300"
"HardwareID"="PCI\\VEN_1013&DEV_00A0&REV_2D,PCI\\VEN_1013&DEV
    _00A0"
"Class"="Display"
"Driver"="Display\\0001"
"Mfg"="Cirrus Logic"
"ConfigFlags"=hex:00,00,00,00
[HKEY_LOCAL_MACHINE\Enum\PCI\VEN_1013&DEV_00A0\BUS_00&DEV_09&
    FUNC_00\LogConfig]
"0000"=hex:
[HKEY_LOCAL_MACHINE\Enum\PCI\VEN_9004&DEV_6178]
[HKEY_LOCAL_MACHINE\Enum\PCI\VEN_9004&DEV_6178\BUS_00&DEV_0A&
    FUNC_00]
"DeviceDesc"="Adaptec AHA-2940AU PCI SCSI Controller"
"HWRevision"="001"
"CompatibleIDs"="PCI\\CC_0100"
"HardwareID"="PCI\\VEN_9004&DEV_6178&REV_01,PCI\\VEN_9004&DEV
    _6178"
"Class"="SCSIAdapter"
"Driver"="SCSIAdapter\\0000"
"Mfg"="Adaptec"
"ConfigFlags"=hex:00,00,00,00
"ForcedConfig"=hex:
```

◆ Root, which is the parent container for any subkeys that are formed to hold information about legacy devices. The subkeys are all named PNP0000, where a hexadecimal number is substituted for 0000.

◆ SCSI, which has a subkey for every SCSI device attached to the computer. For instance (if a computer has a hard drive, a CD-ROM, and an Iomega jaz drive attached to the SCSI controller):

```
[HKEY_LOCAL_MACHINE\Enum\SCSI\QUANTUM_XP32150_____8\ROOT&
    *ADP1540&000000]
"SCSITargetID"="0"
"SCSILUN"="0"
"RevisionLevel"="81HB"
"ProductId"="XP32150            "
"Manufacturer"="Quantum "
"DeviceType"=hex
"Int13"=hex
"CurrentDriveLetterAssignment"="C"
"HardwareID"="QUANTUM_XP32150_____8,GenDisk,SCSI\\QUANTUM
```

```
_XP32150_____8"
"Class"="DiskDrive"
"Driver"="DiskDrive\\0001"
"Mfg"="(Standard disk drives)"
"DeviceDesc"="Quantum XP32150        "
"ConfigFlags"=hex
[HKEY_LOCAL_MACHINE\Enum\SCSI\CHINON__CD-ROM_CDS-535__Q]
[HKEY_LOCAL_MACHINE\Enum\SCSI\CHINON__CD-ROM_CDS-
   535__Q\ROOT&*ADP1540&000030]
"AutoInsertNotification"=hex:01
"UserDriveLetterAssignment"="EE"
"SCSITargetID"="3"
"SCSILUN"="0"
"RevisionLevel"="Q20 "
"ProductId"="CD-ROM CDS-535    "
"Manufacturer"="CHINON    "
"DeviceType"=hex:05
"Removable"=hex:01
"CurrentDriveLetterAssignment"="E"
"HardwareID"="CHINON__CD-ROM_CDS-
   535__Q,GenCD,SCSI\\CHINON__CD-ROM_CDS-535__Q"
"Class"="CDROM"
"Driver"="CDROM\\0000"
"Mfg"="(Standard CD-ROM device)"
"DeviceDesc"="CHINON CD-ROM CDS-535   "
"ConfigFlags"=hex
[HKEY_LOCAL_MACHINE\Enum\SCSI\CONNER__CTMS__3200_____7]
[HKEY_LOCAL_MACHINE\Enum\SCSI\CONNER__CTMS__3200_____7\ROOT&
   *ADP1540&000040]
"SCSITargetID"="4"
"SCSILUN"="0"
"RevisionLevel"="7.10"
"ProductId"="CTMS  3200        "
"Manufacturer"="CONNER  "
"DeviceType"=hex:01
"CurrentDriveLetterAssignment"=""
"HardwareID"="GenTape"
"Class"="Tape"
"DeviceDesc"="CONNER CTMS  3200       "
"ConfigFlags"=hex
"Driver"="Tape\\0000"
"Mfg"="CONNER   "
"HWRevision"="7.10"
[HKEY_LOCAL_MACHINE\Enum\SCSI\IOMEGA__JAZ_1GB_____H]
[HKEY_LOCAL_MACHINE\Enum\SCSI\IOMEGA__JAZ_1GB_____H\ROOT&
   *ADP1540&000040]
"SCSITargetID"="4"
"SCSILUN"="0"
"RevisionLevel"="H.72"
"ProductId"="jaz 1GB          "
"Manufacturer"="iomega   "
"DeviceType"=hex:00
"Removable"=hex:01
"CurrentDriveLetterAssignment"="D"
```

```
"HardwareID"="IOMEGA__JAZ_1GB_____H,GenDisk,SCSI\\IOMEGA_
   _JAZ_1GB_____H"
"Class"="DiskDrive"
"Driver"="DiskDrive\\0002"
"Mfg"="(Standard disk drives)"
"DeviceDesc"="iomega jaz 1GB              "
"ConfigFlags"=hex
```

The `Enum` subkey is connected to the Windows 95 or 98 Device Manager, which you can examine (and configure) by opening the System applet in the Control Panel (see Figure 15-4). This is where you should make your configuration changes, or remove hardware, because it's much safer than performing this task in the registry.

Figure 15-4: The hardware devices are listed, along with their properties, in the Device Manager tab of the Systems Properties dialog box.

The Hardware Subkey

Windows 95 and 98 don't really use this subkey for much (see Figure 15-5). In fact, exporting the registry key produces almost no useful information, as seen here:

```
[HKEY_LOCAL_MACHINE\hardware]
[HKEY_LOCAL_MACHINE\hardware\devicemap]
[HKEY_LOCAL_MACHINE\hardware\devicemap\serialcomm]
"COM1"="COM1"
"COM2"="COM2"
[HKEY_LOCAL_MACHINE\hardware\DESCRIPTION]
```

```
[HKEY_LOCAL_MACHINE\hardware\DESCRIPTION\System]
[HKEY_LOCAL_MACHINE\hardware\DESCRIPTION\System\FloatingPointProcess
  or]
[HKEY_LOCAL_MACHINE\hardware\DESCRIPTION\System\FloatingPointProcess
  or\0]
```

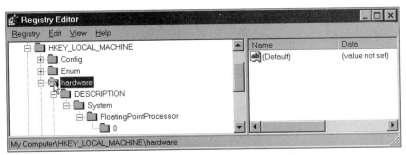

Figure 15-5: Expanding the hardware subkey produces a short tree.

The Network Subkey

This is another subkey exclusive to Windows 95 and 98. The information in the subkey and its tree are specific to the current session. When the user logs on to the computer, the details about the current network connection are stored here (see Figure 15-6).

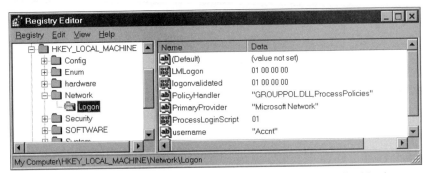

Figure 15-6: Data concerning the current network connection is contained in the HKEY_LOCAL_MACHINE\Network key.

Incidentally, the logon name "Accnt" can indicate either the name used for the current logon, or the last logon name if the current user pressed the Esc key during the logon process. The logonvalidated data entry indicates whether or not the user logs on to a domain server, which validates the logon. In this case, there is a domain server.

The Security Subkey

Windows 95 and 98 use this key to keep information about the security invoked (there really isn't much security in Windows 95 or 98), and about the provider of that security. For instance, here is the information for a computer in which the security provider is an NT domain:

```
[HKEY_LOCAL_MACHINE\Security\Provider]
"Platform_Type"=hex:02,00,00,00
"Address_Book"="msab32.dll"
"Container"="EASTERN"
"Address_Server"="EAST"
```

The platform is NT Server, the domain name is Eastern, and the PDC (Primary Domain Controller) is the server named East.

Shares and network connections are also tracked as other connected computers access them. For example, a computer named Admin, also in the domain named Eastern, accesses this computer's printer:

```
[HKEY_LOCAL_MACHINE\Security\Access\PRINT\HP LaserJet 5P]
"*"=hex:b7,80
"EASTERN\\ADMIN"=hex:b7,00
```

The SOFTWARE Subkey

This key has several functions. First, it holds information about the software installed in the computer. The expanded keys for software follow a pattern of \CompanyName\ProductName\Version (see Figure 15-7).

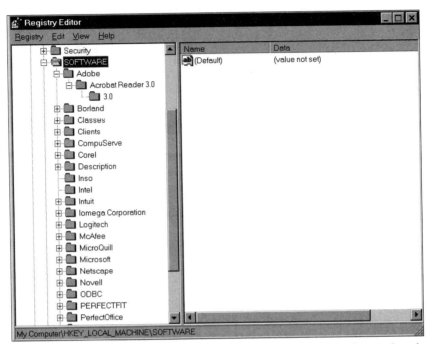

Figure 15-7: The expanded subkeys for Adobe display the company, product, and version.

You'll also find some Windows-specific subkeys in the SOFTWARE subkey:

◆ Classes, which maintains the file associations, stores information for shortcut menus, and so on. The subkey is also aliased as HKEY_CLASSES_ROOT, which I discuss in Chapter 13.

◆ Microsoft, which holds information about Microsoft programs, including Windows 95 or 98. Check the subkey \Windows\CurrentVersion for information about the operating system (see Figure 15-8).

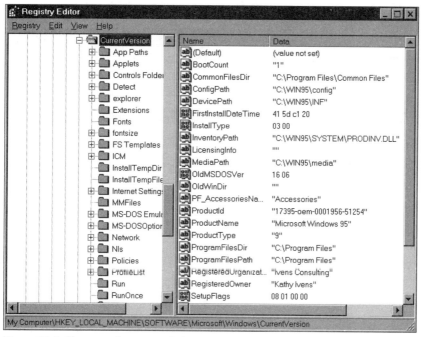

Figure 15-8: The operating system is just another Microsoft program to this registry key.

The System Subkey

In Windows 95 and 98, this subkey has one subkey named `CurrentControlSet`, which in turn has two subkeys (see Figure 15-9).

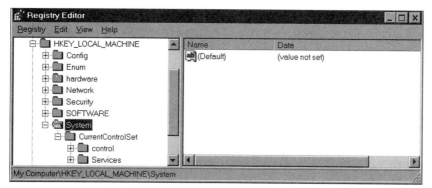

Figure 15-9: The configuration data for this computer's startup is found in the `System` subkey.

The two subkeys under `CurrentControlSet` contain the specific information Windows needs to boot and run.

`Control` has a number of subkeys (some of which have additional subkeys) that provide information about the parameters used to start the operating system (see Figure 15-10).

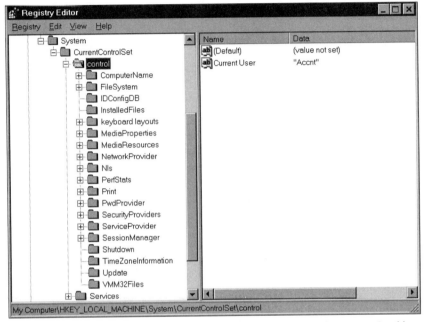

Figure 15-10: The settings needed to start Windows are found in the `Control` subkey.

Here is some of the information found in subkeys under this subkey, which may not be obvious from the subkey names that follow:

◆ `IDConfigDB`, the list of hardware profiles.

◆ `keyboard layouts`, the .DLL files for every available keyboard language.

◆ `MediaResources`, the driver information for all available multimedia devices.

◆ `Nls`, the language used for this computer (there are .nls files for every language available).

◆ `PerfStats`, which are the items the System Monitor is able to track.

◆ Update, which exists if Windows 95 or 98 is an update from a previous version of Windows.

◆ VMM32Files, which is a display of all .vxd files (virtual device drivers) which make up VMM32.VXD.

Services (see Figure 15-11) provides information about device drivers and system services Windows 95 or 98 has to load, along with configuration information about those items.

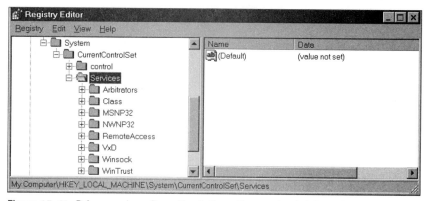

Figure 15-11: Drivers and configuration information are loaded from the Services subkey during the startup of the operating system.

Drilling down through the Services subkey, you find additional subkeys. Some of the subkeys might include:

◆ Arbitrators, which track resources and determine which resources are free (see Figure 15-12).

◆ MSNP32, which holds the configuration data for a Microsoft network.

◆ NWNP32, which holds the configuration information for a NetWare network.

◆ VxD, which contains information about the configuration for the virtual drivers in the Windows 95 or 98 system.

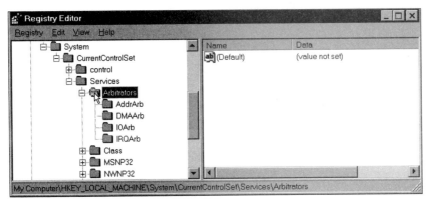

Figure 15-12: Arbitrators know which IRQ, DMA and I/O settings are available.

Windows NT 4 Local Machine Settings

Expanding the HKEY_LOCAL_MACHINE key in Windows NT produces a different set of first-level subkeys (see Figure 15-13):

◆ HARDWARE

◆ SAM

◆ SECURITY

◆ SOFTWARE

◆ SYSTEM

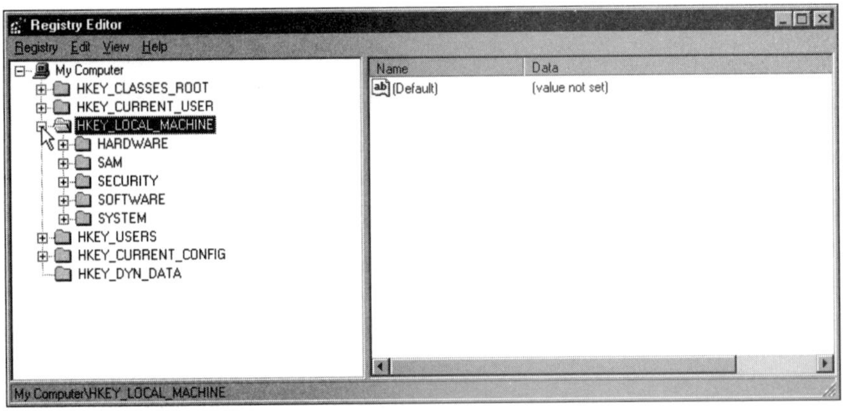

Figure 15-13: There are fewer first-level subkeys under HKEY_LOCAL_MACHINE in a Windows NT 4 computer.

The HARDWARE Subkey

In Windows NT 4, this key contains information about the hardware installed in the computer. It includes information about device drivers, resources (such as IRQ assignments), and other data regarding hardware (see Figure 15-14).

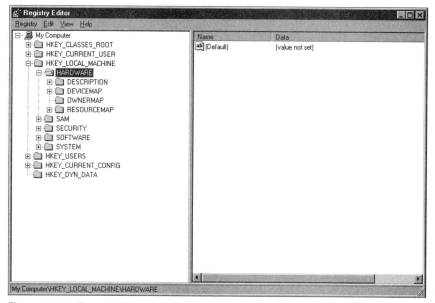

Figure 15-14: The subkeys under Hardware contain all the information Windows NT needs about the computer's hardware.

All the information contained in the Hardware subkey is volatile: it's built during each startup of the operating system and then deleted at shutdown. This is not a part of the registry you change, so use this subkey only for viewing information. Incidentally, a great deal of information appears in binary format in this key, so changing it isn't exactly a cakewalk, anyway. If you want a more readable list of the hardware devices and their current states, open Windows NT Diagnostics (on the Start menu, under Programs → Administrative Tools). Move to the Services tab and choose Devices. The information that appears (see Figure 15-15) is obtained from the registry.

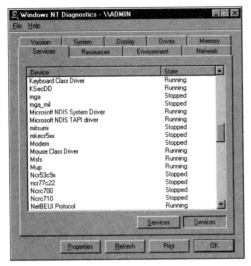

Figure 15-15: Registry information from
`HKEY_LOCAL_MACHINE\HARDWARE` is in a more
user-friendly form in the NT Diagnostics window.

The subkeys under `HKEY_LOCAL_MACHINE\HARDWARE` play very specific roles, and we'll look at them next.

\HARDWARE\DESCRIPTION SUBKEY

During startup of the operating system, NTDETECT.COM (the Windows NT Hardware Recognizer) and NTOSKERNEL.EXE find and build a database of hardware. The information about that hardware, usually determined by reading the firmware, appears in the `DESCRIPTION` subkeys (see Figure 15-16).

The way the database is built, as described here, is true for Intel or compatible-based PC computers only. RISC-based computers use the ARC database supplied by the firmware and other non-PC-compatible machines have similar hardware recognizer programs that are specific to the machine type.

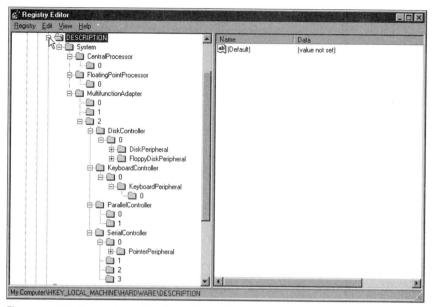

Figure 15-16: The hardware identified during the operating system startup is described and displayed in the registry.

The hardware that is detected and displayed in the `\HARDWARE\DESCRIPTION` registry subkey includes:

◆ Bus/adapter types

TIP The specific subkey for a bus/adapter type changes its name depending on the adapter. PCI and ISA buses are called `MultifunctionAdapter`, EISA buses use `EisaAdapter`, and TurboChannel buses bear the name `TcAdapter`.

◆ Video adapter

◆ Keyboard

◆ Mouse

◆ SCSI controllers

◆ Floating-point coprocessor

◆ Serial ports

♦ Parallel ports

♦ Floppy drives

 Note the lack of a network adapter in the preceding list. NICs are not automatically detected during system startup (although they are during the
installation of the operating system) and are not displayed in the
\Hardware subkey.

\HARDWARE\DEVICEMAP SUBKEY

This subkey holds values that specify locations in the registry for specific information the operating system needs about hardware components (see Figure 15-17).

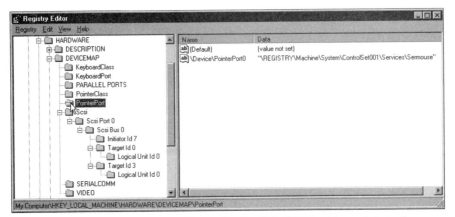

Figure 15-17: The PointerPort subkey under the DEVICEMAP subkey points to the
Sermouse service entry in the registry.

Each data entry, which is a registry subkey, can be followed, and when you
arrive at the destination you'll find a driver controlling the port or service
displayed in the DEVICEMAP subkey.

\HARDWARE\OWNERMAP SUBKEY

Don't panic if you don't see this subkey in your registry — it exists only for PCI
devices and if you don't have any of those, you won't have this key. The purpose of
this subkey is to associate PCI drivers with PCI devices. By the way, if you've used
Windows NT 3.51 and were comfortable with its registry setup, this subkey will be
unfamiliar. It never existed before Windows NT 4.

\HARDWARE\RESOURCEMAP SUBKEY

This subkey is well-named because it maps drivers to the resources those drivers use (see Figure 15-18). Each subkey has data obtained from the applicable device driver (during operating system startup) about the resources it's using, such as IRQ, I/O, and/or DMA resources.

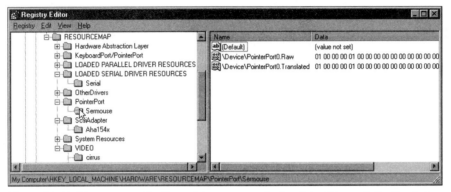

Figure 15-18: The resources for the serial mouse are displayed, but I haven't the foggiest idea what the data says.

For a more user-friendly view of the information, open Windows NT Diagnostics. From the Start menu, choose Programs → Administrative Tools and go to the Resources tab. Choose Devices, select the Device you want information about and choose Properties (see Figure 15-19).

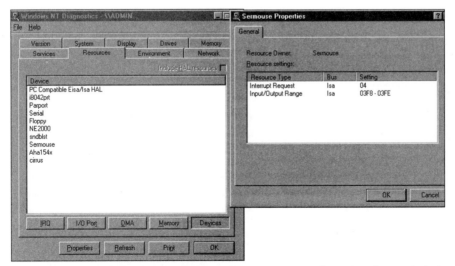

Figure 15-19: The Windows NT Diagnostics program turns the information about a device's use of resources into something most of us can read and understand.

The SAM Subkey

SAM stands for Security Account Manager, and this key holds the user and group account information (see Figure 15-20). The information in the subkeys under SAM is maintained in User Manager; don't play around with these entries in the registry (well, you probably couldn't if you wanted to — all the data is binary).

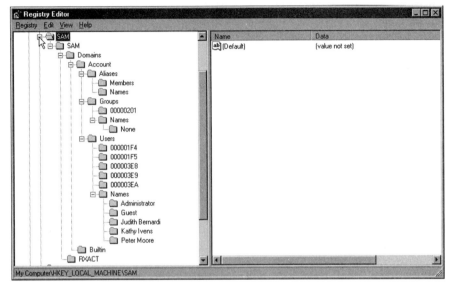

Figure 15-20: User information is maintained in HKEY_LOCAL_MACHINE\SAM.

The information in SAM and its subkeys is also mapped to HKEY_LOCAL_MACHINE\ SECURITY\SAM, and when you make changes in User Manager, both registry locations are updated.

The SECURITY Subkey

The SECURITY subkey has all the security information for the computer, such as password policy, user rights and permissions, and who belongs to which groups (see Figure 15-21). All this information is configured with User Manager and should not be altered in the registry.

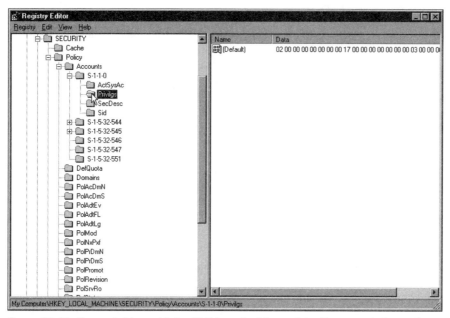

Figure 15-21: You probably couldn't edit this part of the registry if you wanted to — the account name subkeys aren't English, and the data is binary.

The SOFTWARE Subkey

For the most part, the software information in this key (see Figure 15-22) is the same as you'll find in Windows 95 and 98 (discussed earlier in this chapter). However, a few subkeys in the Windows NT 4 SOFTWARE key are unique to this operating system, so I'll discuss them here.

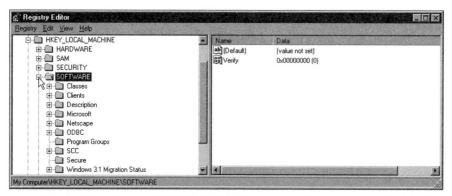

Figure 15-22: HKEY_LOCAL_MACHINE\SOFTWARE has some subkeys specific to Windows NT 4.

\SOFTWARE\PROGRAM GROUPS SUBKEY

In NT 3.5x, the Program Groups subkey held a list of program groups that users of the computer could access. Windows NT 4 has changed the use of this subkey (there aren't really any program groups now), and it is now used to specify whether the program groups from the previous version of Windows (if NT 4 was an upgrade from a previous version of Windows NT) have been converted to the new Explorer structure. The data in this subkey is easy to read if it exists:

- ◆ The existence of a data value entry named ConvertedToLinks means program groups were converted.

- ◆ Data indicating the completion of the conversion is Boolean — a data value of 1 (0x1) means yes, a data value of 0 (0x0) means no.

\SOFTWARE\SECURE SUBKEY

Microsoft provided this subkey for applications that need security and protection for configuration changes. If an application registers the fact that its configuration can be changed only by an administrator, a subkey for that application is created under the \SOFTWARE\Secure subkey. This is an unusual circumstance, and the odds are that this subkey is empty in your system.

If you develop applications and want to ensure that configuration changes can be made only by an administrator, make sure you reference this key with the appropriate information when you design the registry import portion of your installation routine.

\SOFTWARE\WINDOWS 3.1 MIGRATION STATUS SUBKEY

This subkey exists for users who installed Windows NT 4 as an upgrade from Windows 3.x. There are two subkeys under this one: IniFiles and REG.DAT. For each of those subkeys (which are file types in Windows 3.x), there appears an indication of the successful migration of the files to the Windows NT 4.0 format.

Because it is rare to have moved directly from Windows 3.x to Windows NT 4, this subkey and its expanded subkeys are probably empty on your system. And, it's logical to think you could probably erase them safely. Don't! If the subkey isn't found during system startup, Windows NT 4 performs a whole migration process that searches for the files in an effort to migrate them. Operating system startup takes enough time without adding that process to it!

The SYSTEM Subkey

This subkey holds data needed for system startup that is stored rather than computed during the operating system startup. The subkey is organized into other subkeys, including control sets that contain data about devices and parameters (see Figure 15-23).

Figure 15-23: The structure of the HKEY_LOCAL_MACHINE\SYSTEM subkey is designed to provide startup information to the operating system.

\SYSTEM\CLONE SUBKEY

This subkey holds the control set used last during system startup. If the startup was good, the contents of this subkey become the LastKnownGood control set (which you can choose by pressing the space bar during startup if you're having a startup failure).

\SYSTEM\CONTROLSET*NNN* SUBKEY

The numbered ControlSet subkeys are backups for the ControlSet used to start the operating system, the same way many of us saved old copies of CONFIG.SYS when we made changes. If the changes caused a problem with the boot process, we could go back to the last version to ensure a good bootup. Or, we had multiple copies of CONFIG.SYS representing different device configurations (and we even wrote batch files to change one of those versions to the right filename, when we wanted to reboot using the configuration available in that backup version). The difference is that we don't have to write the ControlSets to a file when we make changes; Windows NT takes care of it automatically. The numbered ControlSets are also available to choose from when you press the space bar during startup.

\SYSTEM\CURRENTCONTROLSET SUBKEY

This subkey is really a pointer to the ControlSet that is being used for system startup. The pointer target is found in the Select subkey (discussed next).

ControlSet Subkeys

Each ControlSet key has the same four subkeys: Control, Enum, Hardware Profiles, and Services.

Control contains data used as controls by the system, such as the computer's name and the subsystems that need to be started.

Enum has hardware configuration information for devices and drivers that the operating system loads.

Hardware Profiles holds information specific to existing hardware profiles if multiple hardware profiles are configured.

Services contains data about the drivers, file system, and other services that are loaded by the operating system. This subkey also indicates the order of loading.

\SYSTEM\SELECT SUBKEY

This subkey has four value entries that determine how the operating system uses the control sets (see Figure 15-24):

◆ Current indicates the number of the control set that was used for system startup for the current session.

◆ Default indicates the number of the control set that the operating system will use when it next starts. The user can interrupt this (in case of boot failure) with the space bar.

◆ Failed indicates the control set that was replaced if LastKnownGood was invoked by the user during system startup for the current session.

◆ LastKnownGood displays the number of the control set that is a clean copy of the last control set that produced a good system start.

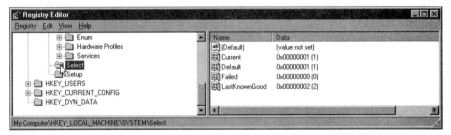

Figure 15-24: The Select subkey controls the way the operating system uses control sets.

\SYSTEM\SETUP SUBKEY

This subkey is used only by the Windows NT 4.0 setup program, and there is no reason to change any of the values.

Summary

This chapter described both HKEY_LOCAL_MACHINE — which keeps the configuration data for your computer — and the different subkeys under HKEY_LOCAL_MACHINE. The next chapter covers the HKEY_USERS key.

Chapter 16

HKEY_USERS

HKEY_USERS IS ONE of the two "real" keys in the registry (the other is HKEY_LOCAL_MACHINE). All the other registry keys are aliases (subsets) of these two keys. The primary alias for HKEY_USERS is HKEY_CURRENT_USER (which is always the registry information for the currently logged-on user).

Both the Windows software and application software write information to both HKEY_LOCAL_MACHINE and HKEY_USERS. In many cases, the information is identical — it just gets stored in more than one place.

As you change configuration options or make changes directly to the registry, the information that started out as identical data values may become different.

When that happens, the registry uses a pecking order to resolve the problem. Any configuration data kept in HKEY_USERS has precedence over data stored in HKEY_LOCAL_MACHINE. This ensures that specific configuration options set by users are met when that user logs on.

HKEY_USERS holds user configuration information for a computer. Although Windows 95, Windows 98, and Windows NT 4 approach HKEY_USERS with the same general principles, there is some difference in the execution. They all install a subkey named Default, whose settings are the default settings for all new users who log on to the machine. They also include a subkey for the currently logged-on user. Both the Default and current user subkeys have additional subkeys representing configuration information; however, some of those subkeys differ between operating systems.

In the following sections, the discussion and illustrations are for the current user rather than the Default subkeys.

HKEY_USERS in Windows 95 and 98

In a Windows 95 or 98 computer, the subkeys are for the default user and the current user (see Figure 16-1).

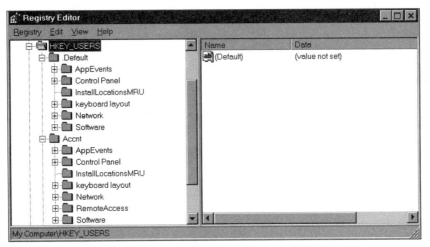

Figure 16-1: It's easy to identify the current user when you look at the Windows 95 or 98 registry.

The subkeys you can expect to find for a Windows 95 or 98 user are:

◆ AppEvents

◆ Control Panel

◆ InstallLocationsMRU

◆ keyboard layout

◆ Network

◆ RemoteAccess (not for Default — it appears after a remote access connection has been configured by a user)

◆ Software

AppEvents Subkey

AppEvents are the associations between events and the sounds produced when those events occur. The events can be generated by the operating system and by software applications. When you expand the AppEvents subkey, two subkeys appear: EventLabels and Schemes.

These keys represent the configuration of the computer for sounds, displaying both the installed sound schemes and the sounds chosen for specific events by users. You can make changes to the AppEvents in the registry, but it's far easier to configure sound associations with the Sounds applet in the Windows 95 or 98 Control Panel (see Figure 16-2).

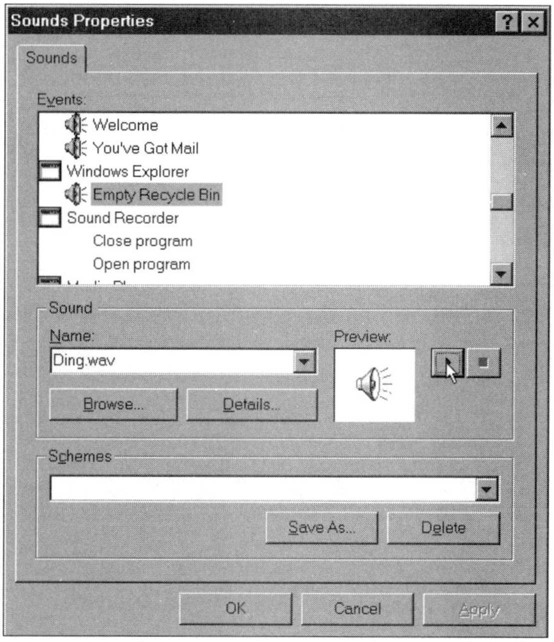

Figure 16-2: It's easier to use the Sounds applet because you don't have to know the path and filename of the sound you want to assign to an event.

EVENTLABELS

The subkeys displayed when you expand EventLabels represent sound events (see Figure 16-3). The current user's list of subkeys is the same as the Default user's subkeys, and also includes EventLabels for any application software added by the current user. The EventLabels subkeys contain the default values for events. The value entries are the titles, or names, of the sounds associated with the events.

SCHEMES

Expanding the Schemes subkey produces a display of two subkeys: Apps and Names.

Schemes\Apps, when expanded, has a subkey for every sound event, just like the EventLabels subkey. However, the Schemes\Apps subkeys contain the actual sounds, not just the default values set by the operating system.

Drilling down into a Schemes\Apps subkey displays additional subkeys. The Schemes\Apps\.Default subkey holds subkeys similar to those under EventLabels, but you can expand each subkey further to show subkeys for the current sound (.Current), the default sound (.Default), and for each sound scheme (sometimes called "theme") installed in the computer. Notice that a period appears in front of the names of the current and default subkeys that are part of the basic operating system installation (see Figure 16-4).

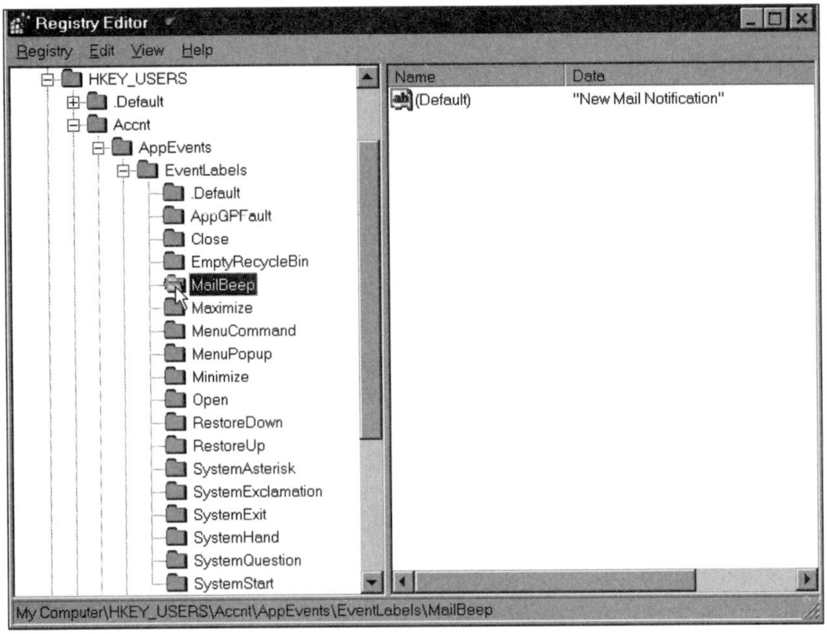

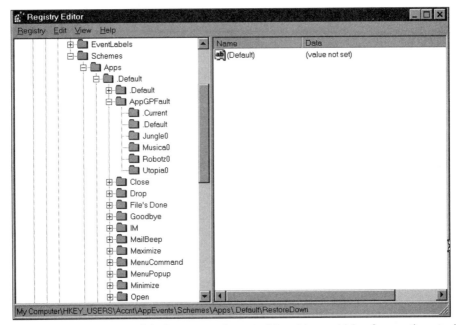

Figure 16-3: This user has added a mail beep sound for mail notification; the rest of the subkeys match those for the Default user.

Figure 16-4: Expand one of the keys to see the rest of its subkeys, which reference the actual sound files.

The data in the subkeys consists of *path\filename* references to the sound file, instead of a name or title for the sound event. For example, the `EventLabel` subkey named `\EmptyRecycleBin` has a data value of "Empty Recycle Bin", while the `Scheme\App\.Default` data value for emptying the Recycle Bin is `c:\%systemroot%\media\ding.wav`.

`\Schemes\Names`, when expanded, lists the names of all the schemes installed in the computer (Figure 16-5).

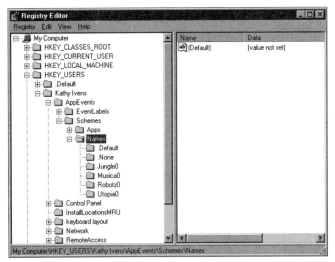

Figure 16-5: This user hasn't added any third-party sound schemes.

Control Panel Subkey

The `\Username\Control Panel` subkey holds subkeys containing configurable settings that are manipulated in the Control Panel (Figure 16-6).

ACCESSIBILITY
The `Accessibility` subkey holds data for settings that are configurable through the Accessibilities applet in the Control Panel (Figure 16-7). In fact, if you want to make changes, it's far easier (and safer) to make the changes through the Control Panel.

The data values in the `\Control Panel\Accessibility` subkey indicate whether special settings have been turned on by user configuration. It's Boolean, so a "1" indicates that the user selected one or more accessibility settings.

In the subkeys under `Accessibility`, the data values show the current value, which means that values exist in the subkeys even if `Accessibility` options haven't been configured (Figure 16-8).

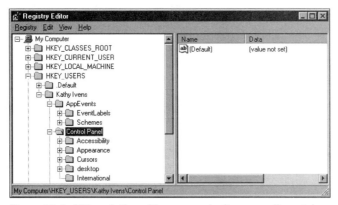

Figure 16-6: Although the subkey names don't necessarily match
Control Panel applets, the subject matter is recognizable.

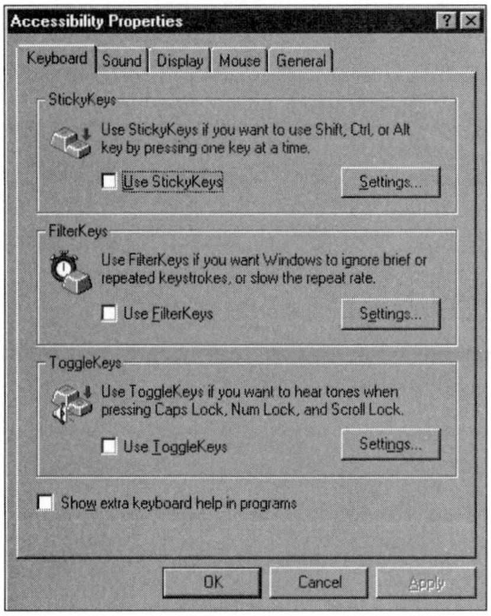

Figure 16-7: You can change the way the
keyboard, mouse, and other elements of your
system behave with the Accessibility Properties
dialog box.

APPEARANCE

The \Control Panel\Appearance subkey contains the name of the color scheme
the user selected (see Figure 16-9). The subkey \ControlPanel\Appearance\
Schemes displays every available scheme found in the Display applet in the Control
Panel (which you can also reach by right-clicking a blank spot on the desktop and
choosing Properties). Although the data is hex, you can change the value of the
Appearance subkey by entering the scheme name (don't forget the quote marks).
It's probably safer, though, to use the Display Properties dialog box to make
changes – for one thing, you can see a preview of the scheme.

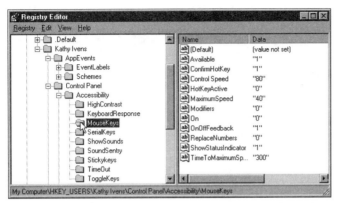

Figure 16-8: The MouseKeys settings, as shown in the data values, reflect the fact that special accessibility settings haven't been turned on.

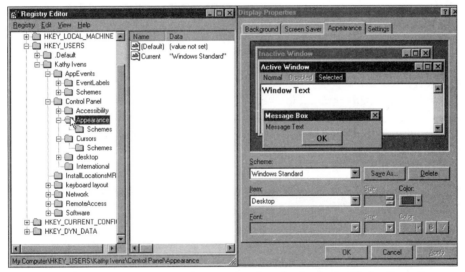

Figure 16-9: The value of the subkey data matches the selection in the Display Properties dialog box.

CURSORS

The \Control Panel\Cursors subkey contains a data value that specifies the cursor scheme selected by the user. If the default cursor scheme (None) wasn't changed, the value of the data is "default".

Expand this subkey to explore \Control Panel\Cursors\Schemes; the contents of this subkey match the available schemes in the Mouse Properties dialog box, which you can open from the Control Panel (see Figure 16-10).

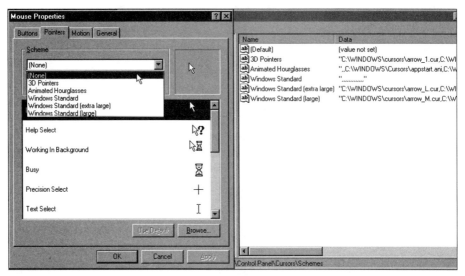

Figure 16-10: If you want to change the appearance of your pointers, you can choose a different scheme.

DESKTOP

This subkey contains information about the interface the user has established. The subkey \Control Panel\Desktop\WindowMetrics specifies the fonts (using hex data values) and the mathematics for the fonts, borders, icons, and other elements of the desktop (see Figure 16-11).

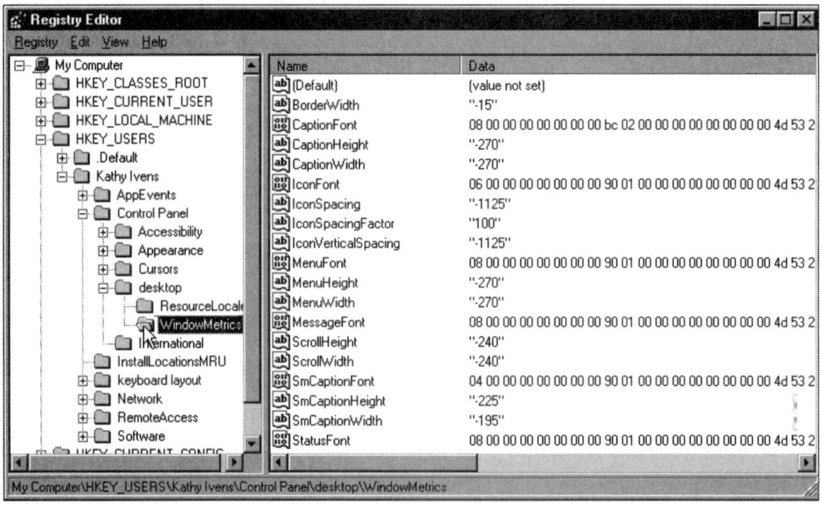

Figure 16-11: This is how your desktop gets to look the way it does.

INTERNATIONAL

The \Control Panel\International subkey holds the data value for the keyboard language selection. The standard United States English keyboard is "00000409".

InstallLocationsMRU Subkey

This key exists only in Windows 95 and 98, and it's a history of your recent application installation activities (see Figure 16-12).

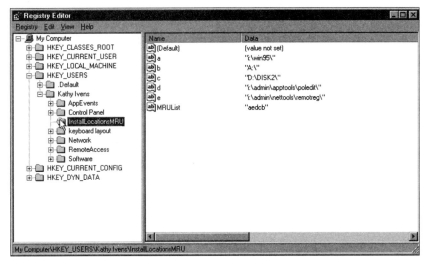

Figure 16-12: Windows 95 and 98 keep a history of your Most Recently Used sources of software installation.

Keyboard Layout Subkey

This key contains the data needed to determine the right keyboard layout. If you have changed the configuration of your keyboard, either to another language or a specific keyboard type, pointers to any necessary associated files (such as .DLL's) are placed in these subkeys.

This key and its associated subkeys contain layout information only; other configuration settings, such as repeat rates, are not found here.

Network Subkey

Windows 95 and Windows 98 use this subkey and its branches to store information about the network connections made by the computer.

Two subkeys exist under the Network subkey: Persistent and Recent. The Persistent subkey displays a subkey for each current persistent connection, and the Recent subkey stores information about nonpersistent connections that the user made.

PERSISTENT

Windows 95 and Windows 98 define a *persistent* connection as a connection that is mapped to a drive letter. When such a connection is made, the drive letter becomes a subkey (see Figure 16-13).

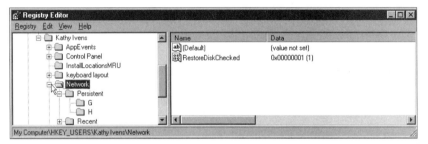

Figure 16-13: The subkeys represent currently mapped connected drives, while the data value of 1 in the Network subkey indicates that the option to reconnect at logon was enabled when the connection was mapped.

The data in the specific persistent connections includes the following values (see Figure 16-14):

♦ ProviderName, which is the network provider. The data is obtained from HKEY_LOCAL_MACHINE\System\CurrentControlSet\Services.

♦ RemotePath, which is the UNC for the shared resource that is mapped for this persistent connection.

♦ UserName, which is the name of the user who created this mapping.

RECENT

Windows 95 and Windows 98 keep the same data information for each connection that isn't mapped, under the \Network\Recent subkey. It names each subkey for the UNC of the shared resource (see Figure 16-15).

When you look at this figure, you probably think that something just doesn't look right — and you're correct. The slashes are leaning in the wrong direction. You cannot use a backslash in a registry key, so forward slashes are substituted and a period appears at the beginning of each UNC. This format (a period and forward slashes) is translated as backslashes.

RemoteAccess Subkey

The RemoteAccess subkey holds information about any Remote Access Service installed. The subkey exists only if the user has established a Dial-Up Networking connection. The data values in this subkey and its branches specify some of the connection configuration settings (see Figure 16-16).

Software Subkey

Although this subkey is organized much like the Software subkey in HKEY_LOCAL_MACHINE, it contains the specific software settings the user has established (see Figure 16-17).

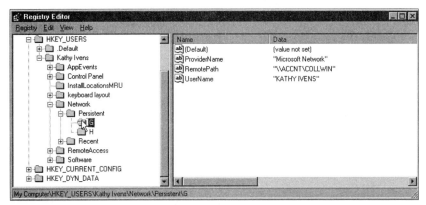

Figure 16-14: Each subkey that represents a mapped connection contains the specific information for that connection.

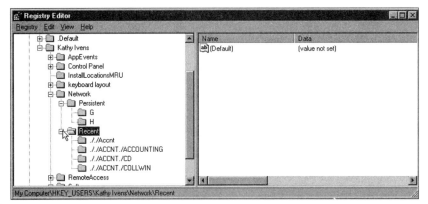

Figure 16-15: The recently accessed connected shares are tracked — the data for each subkey is the same as found in the Persistent subkeys.

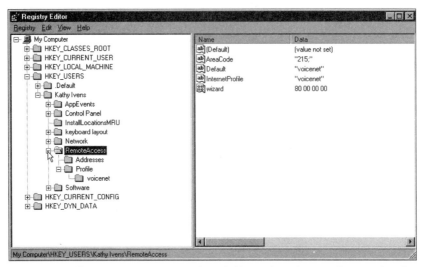

Figure 16-16: The RemoteAccess section of this user's registry entries contains the default dialing and connection properties.

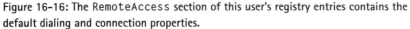

Figure 16-17: Expand any of the software subkeys to see the configuration for the user whose registry entry you're examining.

HKEY_USERS in Windows NT 4

Windows NT 4 uses a slightly different approach to get to the same place regarding HKEY_USERS. The subkeys for this key are the same as for Windows 95 and 98: a .Default key with default settings that can be applied to any new user, and the current user's subkey. As you can see in Figure 16-18, however, the latter is named with the SID (security I.D. string).

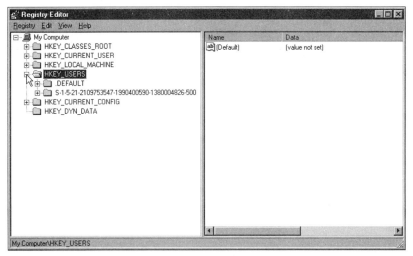

Figure 16-18: Windows NT 4 uses an SID instead of a user name for the currently logged-on user settings.

When you expand the current user, the following subkeys appear:

◆ AppEvents

◆ Console

◆ Control Panel

◆ Environment

◆ Keyboard Layout

◆ Network

◆ Printers (if a printer has been installed)

◆ Remote Access (if a Dial-Up Networking connection is established)

◆ Software

- ◆ UNICODE Program Groups

- ◆ Windows 3.1 Migration Status (if NT 4 was installed as an upgrade over Windows 3.1*x*).

AppEvents Subkey

The AppEvents key in Windows NT 4 works much like the same key in Windows 95 and 98. Expanding the key displays two subkeys: EventLabels and Schemes.

EVENTLABELS

The subkeys you see when you expand EventLabels are events (see Figure 16-19). The current user's list of subkeys is the same as the Default user's subkeys, and also includes EventLabels for any application software added by the current user. The data in all the EventLabels subkeys are the titles, or names, of the sounds associated with the events.

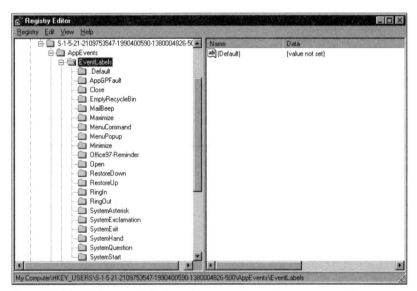

Figure 16-19: All the events that can have sound associations appear when you expand the EventLabels subkey.

SCHEMES

\AppEvents\Schemes can be expanded to the next level of subkeys: Apps and Names. If you expand \AppEvents\Schemes\Apps you'll find additional subkeys representing system and application events. Each of these subkeys has at least the two subkeys .Current and .Default, and there may be other subkeys (for example, Open and Close to indicate separate events). Figure 16-20 shows the expanded registry of a typical Windows NT 4 computer.

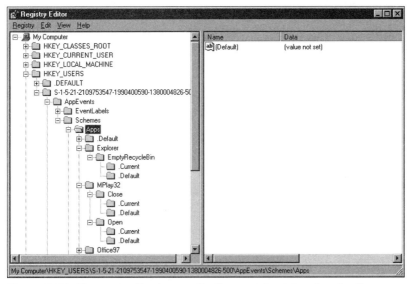

Figure 16-20: The events of various applications and the data values for them are easy to locate in the registry.

The .Current subkey contains the name or title of the sound associated with the event, and the .Default subkey contains the path and filename.

\AppEvents\Schemes\Names contains subkeys for sound schemes already installed on the computer.

Console Subkey

Console is unique to Windows NT 4, and its data values represent the screen settings for character-based work (see Figure 16-21). Information about the size of the window, fonts, colors, and so forth is maintained.

The techy jargon for the interface for character-based applications is Character User Interface, which is usually spelled out as CHUI and pronounced "chewy."

Control Panel Subkey

This Windows NT 4 subkey is much larger than its counterpart in Windows 95 and 98 (see Figure 16-22).

Without going into every single subkey and its associated data, it might be interesting to examine some of the Windows NT `Control Panel` registry entries:

◆ Every time a screen saver is accessed (used), it becomes a registry entry. If it has special attributes, those values are indicated in the data. If it flies, soars, makes noises, or otherwise requires timing or sound effects, for example, those values are tracked. For instance, the screen saver named Mystify (the haunted house with cats that walk across the front lawn and lights that mysteriously go on and off) has a number of settings kept as data values (see Figure 16-23).

◆ When color values are tracked, they are in RGB format (see Figure 16-24).

◆ There are keyboard and mouse subkeys that contain data values representing speed, repeat rates, and so on.

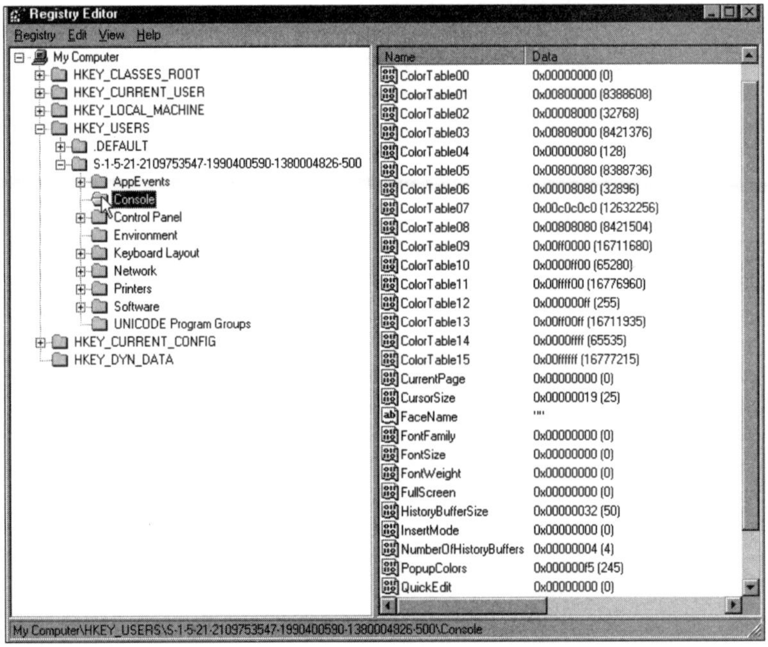

Figure 16-21: The information in the `Console` subkey determines what your environment looks like when you run character-based applications in a Console window.

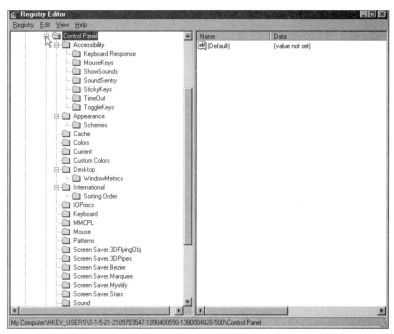

Figure 16-22: The configuration options kept in the registry extend far beyond those contained in the Windows 95 and 98 registries.

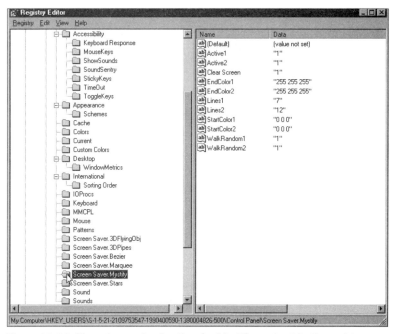

Figure 16-23: The colors and animation for Mystify are kept in the registry.

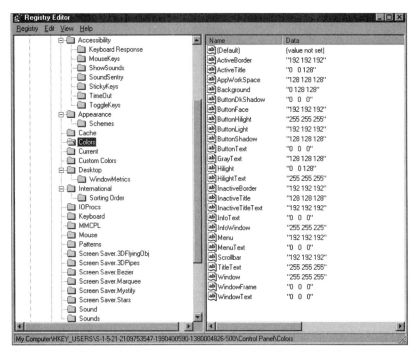

Figure 16-24: Almost all references to data about color values display the
Red–Green–Blue values.

Perhaps the best way to get an idea of the range of information kept in the
Windows NT 4 registry, regarding the `Control Panel` subkey, is to examine the
registry data for a typical computer. In the following registry dump, it's easy to see
the type of configuration information that is kept in the registry, and it's also easy
to figure out how to change it with Control Panel applets.

As you read through the information, notice the hierarchical structure. If you
don't understand the hierarchy and you want to make changes or add subkeys,
you'll probably put data in the wrong place.

The structure creates one level for each item controlled by the Control Panel (such
as Accessibility or Appearance). For most of those entries, you'll find additional
items, one level down. Those items are usually the subkeys that contain the data.

```
[HKEY_USERS\S-1-5-21-2109753547-1990400590-1380004826-500\Control
  Panel]

[HKEY_USERS\S-1-5-21-2109753547-1990400590-1380004826-500\Control
  Panel\Accessibility]

[HKEY_USERS\S-1-5-21-2109753547-1990400590-1380004826-500\Control
  Panel\Accessibility\Keyboard Response]
"AutoRepeatDelay"="1000"
```

```
"AutoRepeatRate"="500"
"BounceTime"="0"
"DelayBeforeAcceptance"="1000"
"Flags"="82"

[HKEY_USERS\S-1-5-21-2109753547-1990400590-1380004826-500\Control
 Panel\Accessibility\MouseKeys]
"Flags"="18"
"MaximumSpeed"="80"
"TimeToMaximumSpeed"="3000"

[HKEY_USERS\S-1-5-21-2109753547-1990400590-1380004826-500\Control
 Panel\Accessibility\ShowSounds]
"On"="0"

[HKEY_USERS\S-1-5-21-2109753547-1990400590-1380004826-500\Control
 Panel\Accessibility\SoundSentry]
"Flags"="2"
"FSTextEffect"="0"
"WindowsEffect"="0"

[HKEY_USERS\S-1-5-21-2109753547-1990400590-1380004826-500\Control
 Panel\Accessibility\StickyKeys]
"Flags"="466"

[HKEY_USERS\S-1-5-21-2109753547-1990400590-1380004826-500\Control
 Panel\Accessibility\TimeOut]
"Flags"="2"
"TimeToWait"="300000"

[HKEY_USERS\S-1-5-21-2109753547-1990400590-1380004826-500\Control
 Panel\Accessibility\ToggleKeys]
"Flags"="18"

[HKEY_USERS\S-1-5-21-2109753547-1990400590-1380004826-500\Control
 Panel\Appearance]

[HKEY_USERS\S-1-5-21-2109753547-1990400590-1380004826-500\Control
 Panel\Appearance\Schemes]
"Brick"=hex: (HEX DATA NOT SHOWN TO SAVE SPACE)
"Maple"=hex: (HEX DATA NOT SHOWN TO SAVE SPACE)
"Spruce"=hex: (HEX DATA NOT SHOWN TO SAVE SPACE)
"Teal (VGA)"=hex: (HEX DATA NOT SHOWN TO SAVE SPACE)
"Red, White, and Blue (VGA)"=hex: (HEX DATA NOT SHOWN TO SAVE SPACE)
"Wheat"=hex: (HEX DATA NOT SHOWN TO SAVE SPACE)
"Pumpkin (large)"=hex: (HEX DATA NOT SHOWN TO SAVE SPACE)
"Eggplant"=hex: (HEX DATA NOT SHOWN TO SAVE SPACE)
"Rainy Day"=hex: (HEX DATA NOT SHOWN TO SAVE SPACE)
"Desert"=hex: (HEX DATA NOT SHOWN TO SAVE SPACE)
"Marine (high color)"=hex: (HEX DATA NOT SHOWN TO SAVE SPACE)
"Windows Standard (extra large)"=hex: (HEX DATA NOT SHOWN TO SAVE
 SPACE)
"Storm (VGA)"=hex: (HEX DATA NOT SHOWN TO SAVE SPACE)
"Windows Standard"=hex: (HEX DATA NOT SHOWN TO SAVE SPACE)
```

```
"Windows Standard (large)"=hex: (HEX DATA NOT SHOWN TO SAVE SPACE)
"Rose"=hex: (HEX DATA NOT SHOWN TO SAVE SPACE)
"High Contrast Black (large)"=hex: (HEX DATA NOT SHOWN TO SAVE
  SPACE)
"High Contrast Black (extra large)"=hex: (HEX DATA NOT SHOWN TO SAVE
  SPACE)
"High Contrast White (large)"=hex: (HEX DATA NOT SHOWN TO SAVE
  SPACE)
"High Contrast White (extra large)"=hex: (HEX DATA NOT SHOWN TO SAVE
  SPACE)
"Rose (large)"=hex: (HEX DATA NOT SHOWN TO SAVE SPACE)
"Lilac"=hex: (HEX DATA NOT SHOWN TO SAVE SPACE)
"Slate"=hex: (HEX DATA NOT SHOWN TO SAVE SPACE)
"Plum (high color)"=hex: (HEX DATA NOT SHOWN TO SAVE SPACE)
"High Contrast Black"=hex: (HEX DATA NOT SHOWN TO SAVE SPACE)
"High Contrast White"=hex: (HEX DATA NOT SHOWN TO SAVE SPACE)

[HKEY_USERS\S-1-5-21-2109753547-1990400590-1380004826-500\Control
  Panel\Cache]

[HKEY_USERS\S-1-5-21-2109753547-1990400590-1380004826-500\Control
  Panel\Colors]
"Background"="0 128 128"
"AppWorkSpace"="128 128 128"
"Window"="255 255 255"
"WindowText"="0   0   0"
"Menu"="192 192 192"
"MenuText"="0   0   0"
"ActiveTitle"="0   0 128"
"InactiveTitle"="128 128 128"
"TitleText"="255 255 255"
"ActiveBorder"="192 192 192"
"InactiveBorder"="192 192 192"
"WindowFrame"="0   0   0"
"Scrollbar"="192 192 192"
"ButtonFace"="192 192 192"
"ButtonShadow"="128 128 128"
"ButtonText"="0   0   0"
"GrayText"="128 128 128"
"Hilight"="0   0 128"
"HilightText"="255 255 255"
"InactiveTitleText"="192 192 192"
"ButtonHilight"="255 255 255"
"InfoText"="0   0   0"
"InfoWindow"="255 255 225"
"ButtonLight"="192 192 192"
"ButtonDkShadow"="0   0   0"

[HKEY_USERS\S-1-5-21-2109753547-1990400590-1380004826-500\Control
  Panel\Current]
"Color Schemes"="Windows Default"
```

```
[HKEY_USERS\S-1-5-21-2109753547-1990400590-1380004826-500\Control
 Panel\Custom Colors]
"ColorA"="FFFFFF"
"ColorB"="FFFFFF"
"ColorC"="FFFFFF"
"ColorD"="FFFFFF"
"ColorE"="FFFFFF"
"ColorF"="FFFFFF"
"ColorG"="FFFFFF"
"ColorH"="FFFFFF"
"ColorI"="FFFFFF"
"ColorJ"="FFFFFF"
"ColorK"="FFFFFF"
"ColorL"="FFFFFF"
"ColorM"="FFFFFF"
"ColorN"="FFFFFF"
"ColorO"="FFFFFF"
"ColorP"="FFFFFF"

[HKEY_USERS\S-1-5-21-2109753547-1990400590-1380004826-500\Control
 Panel\Desktop]
"CoolSwitch"="1"
"CoolSwitchRows"="3"
"CoolSwitchColumns"="7"
"CursorBlinkRate"="530"
"ScreenSaveTimeOut"="900"
"ScreenSaveActive"="0"
"SCRNSAVE.EXE"="(NONE)"
"ScreenSaverIsSecure"="0"
"Pattern"="(None)"
"Wallpaper"="(None)"
"TileWallpaper"="0"
"GridGranularity"="0"
"IconSpacing"="75"
"IconTitleWrap"="1"
"IconTitleFaceName"="MS Sans Serif"
"IconTitleSize"="9"
"IconTitleStyle"="0"
"DragFullWindows"="1"
"HungAppTimeout"="5000"
"WaitToKillAppTimeout"="20000"
"AutoEndTasks"="0"
"FontSmoothing"="0"
"MenuShowDelay"="400"
"DragHeight"="2"
"DragWidth"="2"
"WheelScrollLines"="3"

[HKEY_USERS\S-1-5-21-2109753547-1990400590-1380004826-500\Control
 Panel\Desktop\WindowMetrics]
"BorderWidth"="1"
```

```
[HKEY_USERS\S-1-5-21-2109753547-1990400590-1380004826-500\Control
 Panel\International]
"Locale"="00000409"
"sLanguage"="ENU"
"sCountry"="United States"
"iCountry"="1"
"sList"=","
"iMeasure"="1"
"sDecimal"="."
"sThousand"=","
"iDigits"="2"
"iLZero"="1"
"sCurrency"="$"
"iCurrDigits"="2"
"iCurrency"="0"
"iNegCurr"="0"
"sDate"="/"
"sTime"=":"
"sShortDate"="M/d/yy"
"sLongDate"="dddd, MMMM dd, yyyy"
"iDate"="0"
"iTime"="0"
"iTLZero"="0"
"s1159"="AM"
"s2359"="PM"

[HKEY_USERS\S-1-5-21-2109753547-1990400590-1380004826-500\Control
 Panel\International\Sorting Order]

[HKEY_USERS\S-1-5-21-2109753547-1990400590-1380004826-500\Control
 Panel\IOProcs]
"MVB"="mvfs32.dll"

[HKEY_USERS\S-1-5-21-2109753547-1990400590-1380004826-500\Control
 Panel\Keyboard]
"KeyboardSpeed"="31"
"KeyboardDelay"="1"
"InitialKeyboardIndicators"="2"

[HKEY_USERS\S-1-5-21-2109753547-1990400590-1380004826-500\Control
 Panel\MMCPL]

[HKEY_USERS\S-1-5-21-2109753547-1990400590-1380004826-500\Control
 Panel\Mouse]
"SwapMouseButtons"="0"
"DoubleClickSpeed"="500"
"DoubleClickHeight"="4"
"DoubleClickWidth"="4"
"MouseThreshold1"="6"
"MouseThreshold2"="10"
"MouseSpeed"="1"
"SnapToDefaultButton"="0"
"ActiveWindowTracking"=dword:00000000
```

```
[HKEY_USERS\S-1-5-21-2109753547-1990400590-1380004826-500\Control
 Panel\Patterns]
"(None)"="(None)"
"Boxes"="127 65 65 65 65 65 127 0"
"Paisley"="2 7 7 2 32 80 80 32"
"Weave"="136 84 34 69 136 21 34 81"
"Waffle"="0 0 0 0 128 128 128 240"
"Tulip"="0 0 84 124 124 56 146 124"
"Spinner"="20 12 200 121 158 19 48 40"
"Scottie"="64 192 200 120 120 72 0 0"
"Critters"="0 80 114 32 0 5 39 2"
"50% Gray"="170 85 170 85 170 85 170 85"
"Quilt"="130 68 40 17 40 68 130 1"
"Diamonds"="32 80 136 80 32 0 0 0"
"Thatches"="248 116 34 71 143 23 34 113"
"Pattern"="224 128 142 136 234 10 14 0"

[HKEY_USERS\S-1-5-21-2109753547-1990400590-1380004826-500\Control
 Panel\Screen Saver.3DFlyingObj]

[HKEY_USERS\S-1-5-21-2109753547-1990400590-1380004826-500\Control
 Panel\Screen Saver.3DPipes]

[HKEY_USERS\S-1-5-21-2109753547-1990400590-1380004826-500\Control
 Panel\Screen Saver.Bezier]

[HKEY_USERS\S-1-5-21-2109753547-1990400590-1380004826-500\Control
 Panel\Screen Saver.Marquee]
"Font"="Times New Roman"
"Size"="24"
"Text"="Your text goes here."
"TextColor"="255 0 255"
"BackgroundColor"="0 0 128"
"Mode"="1"
"Speed"="14"
"CharSet"="0"

[HKEY_USERS\S-1-5-21-2109753547-1990400590-1380004826-500\Control
 Panel\Screen Saver.Mystify]
"Clear Screen"="1"
"Active1"="1"
"WalkRandom1"="1"
"Lines1"="7"
"StartColor1"="0 0 0"
"EndColor1"="255 255 255"
"Active2"="1"
"WalkRandom2"="1"
"Lines2"="12"
"StartColor2"="0 0 0"
"EndColor2"="255 255 255"

[HKEY_USERS\S-1-5-21-2109753547-1990400590-1380004826-500\Control
 Panel\Screen Saver.Stars]
```

```
"Density"="50"
"WarpSpeed"="10"

[HKEY_USERS\S-1-5-21-2109753547-1990400590-1380004826-500\Control
  Panel\Sound]
"Beep"="yes"
"ExtendedSounds"="yes"

[HKEY_USERS\S-1-5-21-2109753547-1990400590-1380004826-500\Control
  Panel\Sounds]
"SystemDefault"=","
```

Environment Subkey

This subkey also exists only in Windows NT 4. It contains the data that reflects system and user environment variables. You can configure certain environment variables in the System icon in the Control Panel (see Figure 16-25), and the data in this subkey reflects those settings.

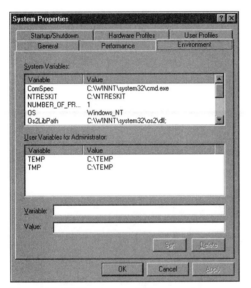

Figure 16-25: The user variables seen here are the data values for the Environment subkey.

Keyboard Layout Subkey

Just like the Windows 95 and 98 registry, this Windows NT 4 registry key holds information about the language used for the user's keyboard (usually "00000409", which is United States English).

Network Subkey

Windows NT 4 uses this subkey only for persistent (mapped) connections. A subkey exists for each persistent connection (see Figure 16-26), and the data values specify the following information:

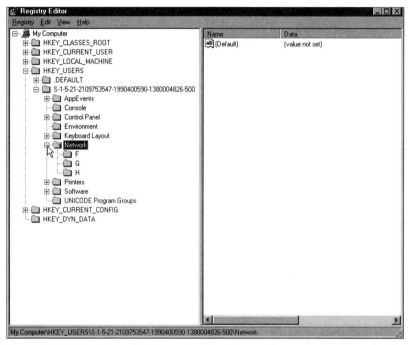

Figure 16-26: A subkey exists for each mapped connection under the Network subkey.

- ◆ ConnectionType
- ◆ ProviderName
- ◆ ProviderType
- ◆ RemotePath
- ◆ UserName

The most interesting thing about this subkey is that according to Microsoft it doesn't exist. In fact, the official Microsoft description of this key is that in older versions of the operating system, the key was used to track persistent connections, but it is no longer used. Of course, there it is—you're looking at it!

Microsoft goes on to say that because this subkey is no longer used, it stores information about persistent connections in HKEY_CURRENT_USER\Software\

`Microsoft\WindowsNT\CurrentVersion\Network\Persistent Connections`. (`HKEY_CURRENT_USER` is, of course, an alias for the current user we've been examining under `HKEY_USERS`).

If you go to the subkey referenced by Microsoft for persistent connections, you'll see something similar to Figure 16-27.

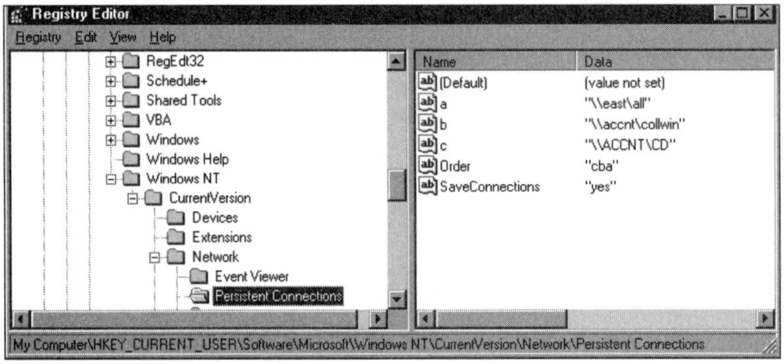

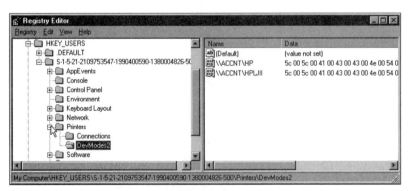

Figure 16-27: These *are* the persistent connections for this computer, but the drive letters aren't stored in the data.

I have no explanation, nor do I have any guesses.

Printers Subkey

User-specific settings for printers are stored in this subkey (no `Printers` subkey exists for the `HKEY_USERS\.Default` key). The information about the default printer is in the `Printers` subkey (the printer name, the spooler, and the port), and data for remote printers appears in subkeys below the `Printers` key (see Figure 16-28).

Figure 16-28: This user connects to two remote printers.

Incidentally, no hardware-specific information about printers is available in this part of the registry – that information is kept in HKEY_LOCAL_MACHINE\System\ CurrentControlSet\Control\Print.

Software Subkey

The Software subkey contains subkeys for system and application software, similar to the contents of HKEY_LOCAL_MACHINE\Software. However, the data values in this section of the registry reflect the user's configuration options.

The largest subkey under Software is almost always Microsoft, because it contains all the operating system features that are installed, along with any Microsoft application software that was also installed.

In fact, exploring this section of the registry reveals some surprising (to me) information about configuration options. For example, after I set up a number of categories in Microsoft Outlook 97 in order to track projects, I found them in the registry (see Figure 16-29).

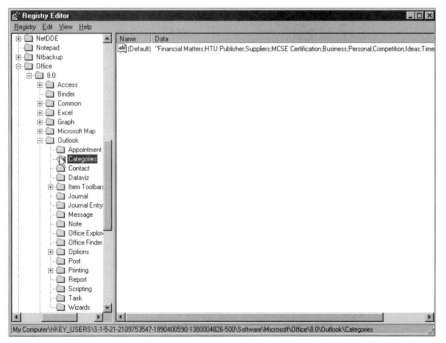

Figure 16-29: Information I thought would be kept only within application configuration files is actually stored in the registry.

UNICODE Program Groups Subkey

This subkey refers to application software that is written using a feature called UNICODE. The subkey exists for no particular reason in Windows NT 4; it is never referenced. If you upgraded to Windows NT 4 from a previous version of Windows NT, you may find some data relating to this subkey, but that's just some old references that were transferred (and the data is binary so you probably won't be able to tell where it's from).

UNICODE programming will be available and used under Windows NT 5, however, so this subkey will have data when you update your network to the next version of the operating system.

Windows 3.1 Migration Status Subkey

This subkey exists only if you upgraded to Windows NT 4 from Windows 3.x. If it does exist, the data specifies whether or not program group (.GRP) and .INI files were successfully converted. If the key exists, don't delete it, because Windows NT 4 will start the migration process during the next boot.

Summary

HKEY_USERS, which holds user configuration information for a computer, was the topic of this chapter. Next, we'll cover the HKEY_CURRENT_CONFIG key.

Chapter 17

HKEY_CURRENT_CONFIG

THIS REGISTRY KEY ISN'T REAL — it's an alias (subset) of HKEY_LOCAL_MACHINE. The specific key under HKEY_LOCAL_MACHINE that provides the alias differs between Windows 95/98 and Windows NT 4.

When you back up your registry, either with backup software or by exporting the registry, this key is not backed up because it's merely a duplicate of part of an existing key. In fact, only HKEY_LOCAL_MACHINE and HKEY_USERS are backed up or exported during a registry backup. All the other keys, including the one we're discussing here (HKEY_CURRENT_CONFIG) are created during system startup by duplicating the appropriate subset from the two major keys. If you change the registry in either the main key or the subset, the change is written to both keys.

HKEY_CURRENT_CONFIG in Windows 95 and 98

In Windows 95 and 98, this key is an alias for HKEY_LOCAL_MACHINE\Config \Profile# where the profile number is 0001, 0002, and so on (see Figure 17-1).

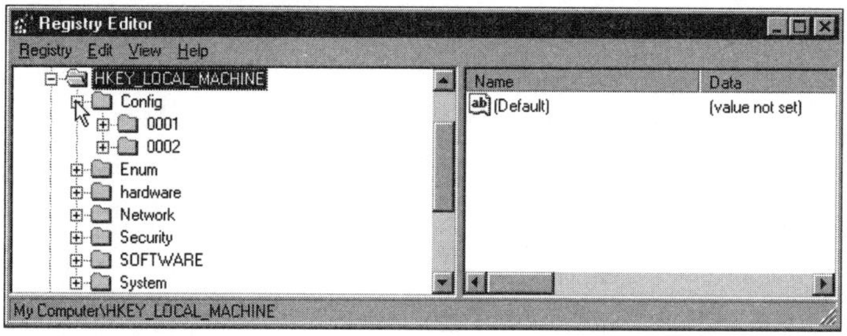

![Registry Editor window]

Figure 17-1: HKEY_LOCAL_MACHINE\Config\Currently selected profile is aliased as HKEY_CURRENT_CONFIG.

Profile refers to hardware profiles, not user profiles. If multiple hardware pro-files aren't enabled for the computer, the single existing profile is numbered 0001.

When you expand the registry key HKEY_CURRENT_CONFIG, you see two subkeys: Display and System. Under these keys are the configuration data values for the current hardware configuration of the computer.

Display Subkey

Expand the Display subkey to see its two subkeys: Fonts and Settings. These subkeys hold data values that regulate the display of operating system elements.

FONTS
The \Display\Fonts subkey specifies the fonts currently being used by the operating system (as opposed to application software). These are system screen fonts, not TrueType fonts (see Figure 17-2).

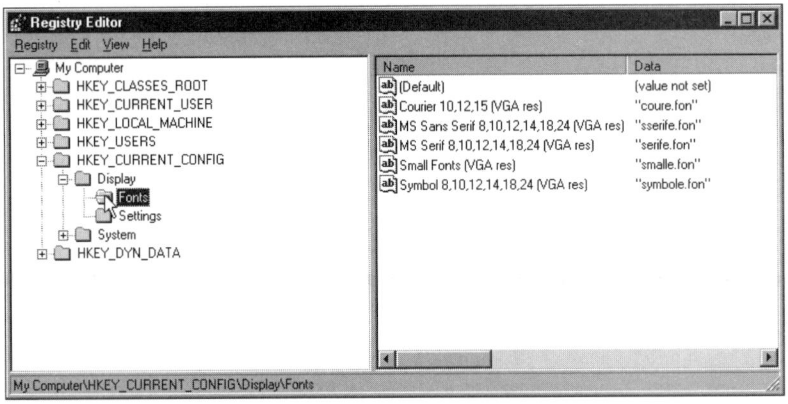

Figure 17-2: The fonts available to the operating system are kept in this subkey.

You can make font changes directly in the registry if you know the exact names of the fonts you want to use, but it's far easier and safer to use the Display Properties dialog box to make changes (see Figure 17-3). You can open the Display icon in the Control Panel, or right-click on a blank spot on the desktop and choose Properties.

Figure 17-3: You can change the fonts the system
uses with the Display Properties dialog box.

To change fonts, move to the Appearance tab and select a system element that
involves fonts from the Item text box (you'll know if the element has a font option
because the Font text box becomes accessible). Then, move to the Font text box
and change the font. When you click OK, the change is made and takes effect
immediately. In fact, the registry uses these system icons (see Figure 17-4).

Figure 17-4: This is the same registry section as shown in Figure 17-2, but I obviously
made a stupid font change because I can't read the data — hold on a minute
while I change it back.

The data values in this subkey are strings, so you could make changes directly into the registry – except you can't figure out which font goes with which item, so you're really not sure what you're changing. This data listing doesn't assign fonts to specific elements in Windows, it just lists the available fonts. For instance, the font change I made to produce the unreadable data panel was for Icon fonts (so the registry data must be considered an icon title).

SETTINGS

The data in `\Display\Settings` shows the Window metrics for the operating system (again, not for application software). This data specifies size, color, and resolution (see Figure 17-5).

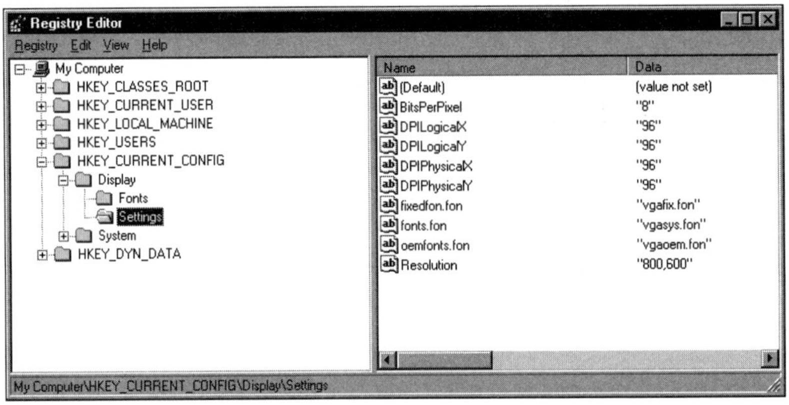

Figure 17-5: The look of your system windows is controlled by this data.

The data is interpreted as follows:

- ◆ BitsPerPixel is a symbol that stands for color depth (in this case "8", which means 256-color).

- ◆ DPILogicalX is the number of horizontal dots per inch for the font display.

- ◆ DPILogicalY is the number of vertical dots per inch for the font display.

- ◆ DPIPhysicalX is the actual number of dots per inch displayed horizontally on your monitor.

- ◆ DPIPhysicalY is the actual number of dots per inch displayed vertically on your monitor.

- ◆ Fixedfon.fon is the name of the screen font.

- ◆ Fonts.fon is the filename for the screen font.

◆ Oemfonts.fon is the filename for the oem fonts.

◆ Resolution is the selected screen resolution (which always refers to pixels).

All these data items are strings, which means you could make changes directly to the registry – but it's not a good idea to make changes this way. Instead, use the Settings tab of the Display Properties dialog box (see Figure 17-6).

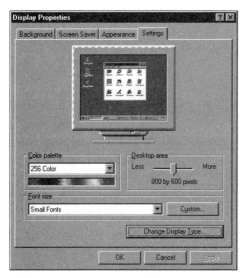

Figure 17-6: It's safer to change the settings for the display of operating system windows with the Display Properties dialog box.

The two items in this registry key that refer to the actual number of dots per inch displayed on your monitor are a function of the monitor – and how Windows 95 and 98 believe the monitor behaves. You can change the monitor setting by choosing Change Display Type on the Settings tab of the Display Properties dialog box. When the Change Display Type dialog box opens, the current settings appear (see Figure 17-7).

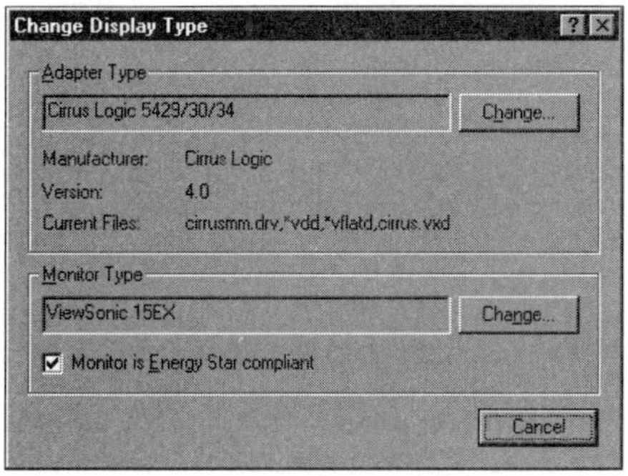

Figure 17-7: You can change the current adapter, drivers, and monitor type – but move carefully, because you could end up with an unreadable display.

To change the actual display, you need to choose Change in the Monitor Type section of the dialog box, and then select a monitor type that will accommodate the changes you want to make (and the new monitor type has to be acceptable to your physical monitor). Before doing this, however, you should speak to the manufacturer.

System Subkey

I find this subkey to be an interesting approach to registry information — and you can read the word *interesting* as if it had a question mark. The subkey expands to show a number of additional subkeys (see Figure 17-8); there's not much logic to this tree because most of the data panels really don't contain any information.

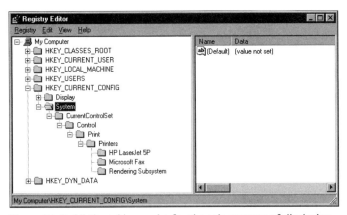

Figure 17-8: All the subkeys exist for the sole purpose of displaying the names of printers.

The subkey Printers has the name of the default printer in its data panel. At the bottom of the tree, subkeys appear for each printer installed on this computer, but none of those subkeys contain any data. Additionally, you'll find a subkey named Rendering Subsystem, which probably refers to the printer drivers — but there's no way to tell, because that subkey doesn't contain any data either.

Makes you wonder why Microsoft called this subkey System instead of Printers.

HKEY_CURRENT_CONFIG in Windows NT 4

This registry key is new to Windows NT (with Windows NT 4), and it represents the currently used hardware profile. It is an alias to HKEY_LOCAL_MACHINE\System\ CurrentControlSet\Hardware Profiles\Current (see Figure 17-9).

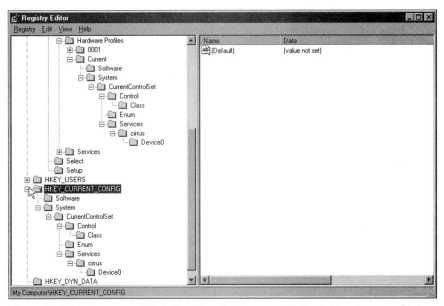

Figure 17-9: Hardware-specific information for the currently loaded hardware profile is stored in HKEY_CURRENT_CONFIG.

This key was added to Windows NT 4 to make the operating system compatible with the same key in Windows 95 and 98. That way, programs that use data in the subtree HKEY_CURRENT_CONFIG can function on all three operating systems.

 Do not take the compatibility rationale to mean that compatibility exists between the registries in Windows 95/98 and Windows NT 4. It doesn't! This compatibility is in structure only and is a service to programmers.

If you program for Windows NT 4 and need to insert data in the Class and Enum subkeys of HKEY_CURRENT_CONFIG, you still have to use the Device Installer API (or the Config Manager API). If you refer to the subtree by path, the application won't run on Windows 95 or 98.

In Windows NT 4, when a configuration change for a specific profile is made to a value entry in the Software or System subkeys in HKEY_LOCAL_MACHINE, the original value entry doesn't change. The change is made only to the appropriate section that is the duplicate for HKEY_CURRENT_CONFIG.

When you expand HKEY_CURRENT_CONFIG, you see two subkeys: Software and System. The System subkey expands to show the other subkeys shown in Figure 17-9.

If you haven't created additional profiles nor made hardware changes to the default settings, the subkeys in HKEY_CURRENT_CONFIG are devoid of data except for the display settings in HKEY_CURRENT_CONFIG\System\CurrentControlSet\ Services\X\DeviceY, where X is the name of your video adapter and Y is the number of the particular device (starting with 0). Information about video settings appears in the data panel (see Figure 17-10).

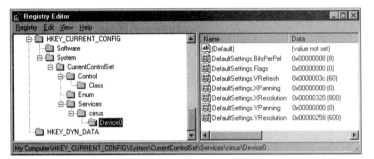

Figure 17-10: The video settings for the current profile appear in the device subkey.

Summary

In this chapter, you learned about HKEY_CURRENT_CONFIG, which is an alias of HKEY_LOCAL_MACHINE. We also covered the different subkeys that can be found under HKEY_CURRENT_CONFIG.

Appendix A

About the CD-ROM

THE CD THAT ACCOMPANIES this book has some very handy utilities, and I'm sure you'll learn to love and depend on many of them. You'll find several types of programs on the CD-ROM, including utilities that help you edit and work with the registry, and utilities that help you configure your system for easier use.

Following is some information about the programs on the CD, along with the URL in case you want more information, have questions, or want to register online. For installation information for each program, turn to the CD-ROM Installation Instructions at the back of the book.

 Remember how shareware works: you're honor-bound to register and pay for the software if you plan to use it.

Registry Utilities

The following utilities can help you configure, edit, and manage the registry.

ConfigSafe 95 and NT

If you're tired of diagnosing system problems by trying to figure out exactly what a user has done to modify his or her system, then ConfigSafe is for you. ConfigSafe monitors your system for all changes made to critical files, folders, the registry, and your network settings.

Reports that you can generate with ConfigSafe include registry reports, system file reports, drivers, directory structures, network connections, and more. Additionally, ConfigSafe actually restores your system to a previous configuration that was working before the problems occurred.

Go to http://www.imagine-lan.com/ for more information.

DumpReg v1.1

This Windows NT and Windows 95 program from Somarsoft dumps the registry, making it easy to find keys and values matching a string. The Windows NT version enables you to sort dumped entries by reverse order of last modified time, making it easy to see changes made by recently installed software. The shareware version on the CD-ROM is fully functional except for printing.

Go to http://www.somarsoft.com for more information.

NTRegmon — Registry Monitor v3.2

If you want to keep an eye on what's happening in the registry while you work in NT, install NTRegmon. This device driver/GUI combination monitors and displays many of NT's internal operations. Its powerful search and filtering features enable it to track down system or application configuration problems.

Go to http://www.ntinternals.com/ntutil.htm for more information.

RegEdit v2.0

RegEdit 2.0 from Somarsoft can be used with Visual Basic to view or modify user registry profiles. For example, according to Somarsoft, "a 10 line VBA for Excel program can change the mail server path in the registry profiles of all users at once." This is a useful tool for Windows NT system administrators who can program in Visual Basic. The shareware version on the CD-ROM is fully functional except for registration message boxes. You may need to install vb40032.dll (inside the RegEdit directory).

Go to http://www.somarsoft.com for more information.

Registry Editor Extensions (RegEditX)

This freeware utility enhances the ease and speed of using the Windows Registry Editor by adding a combo box that holds a listing of all the keys visited. Each time you wish to return to a particular key, you simply open the drop-down list and select the desired key. The history list is even retained from session to session.

Go to http://www.dcsoft.com/prod01.htm for more information.

Registry Saver v1.2

Backup is one of the most important operations a computer user can perform. This is especially true with the Windows registry. With Registry Saver, you can automatically create a registry backup every time you start your computer. Then, by running a Registry Saver batch file, you can quickly and easily use the backup file to restore a corrupted registry.

To uninstall Registry Saver or to change the frequency with which it runs, you need to run the Registry Saver Options.exe file.

Go to http://computing.net/software97/registrysaver.html for more information.

Regmon — Windows 95 Registry Monitor v3.2

Regmon is the Windows 95 version of NTRegmon. It monitors the Windows 95 registry for all activity, and creates a log that can be saved to a text file for viewing or printing. Regmon provides both menus and toolbar buttons for accessing its main features. You can turn monitoring on and off, disable event capturing, control listview scrolling, and create the text file log with a click of the mouse.

Go to `http://www.ntinternals.com/95util.htm` for more information.

WinHacker 95 v2.0

WinHacker 95 enables you to access many of your Windows settings that are usually available only through the registry. You can change startup settings, Windows Explorer settings, and even rename your Start menu if you want. If you occasionally forget to use the Add/Remove Programs feature to uninstall an application, you end up with a nonexistent but unremovable program name on the list. WinHacker 95 enables you to go into the list and edit it. You can add a cascading list of Control Panel items to your Start menu, or change your task manager time-out values, if you wish. You can even disable your CD AutoInsert notification without going into the device manager. WinHacker 95 offers a wealth of options for customizing Windows 95 painlessly and effortlessly.

Go to `http://www.winhacker.com/` for more information.

System Configuration Utilities

The following programs make it easier — and sometimes, more fun — to work with Windows 95 and Windows NT.

AssistBar 98 v2.1

AssistBar 98 from Visual Z is a fully customizable toolbar utility that enables you to access programs, folders, files, shortcuts, and even special folders such as My Computer and Control Panel, with a single click. The AssistBar initially appears as a small icon in the top right corner of your screen. Click it once and it expands to the width of your screen. Click the red double arrow icon to change to edit mode. You can then quickly add and move items on the toolbar simply by dragging and dropping. Right-click anywhere on the AssistBar and it disappears. You can move it so it slides over the top of the Taskbar, or place it on the screen vertically. This is a handy addition to the Taskbar that offers quick access to your most frequently used items.

Go to `http://www.visualz.pair.com/index.htm` for more information.

Diskeeper Lite for Windows NT

Disk defragmentation is necessary to keep your system running at its optimum speed. Diskeeper Lite is a fast, manual defragmenter that is designed exclusively for Windows NT 4.0 (build 1381 or higher). Restoring and maintaining system performance is a snap with Diskeeper Lite.

Go to `http://www.executive.com/` for more information.

GoldWave v3.24

GoldWave, a digital audio editor for Windows, also includes a sound player, recorder, and converter. Not only does it support a large number of audio formats including .wav, .voc. afc, .au, and binary data, it also features real-time amplitude, spectrum, and spectrogram oscilloscopes, intelligent large file editing, and a variety of effects. You can create new and unusual sounds with Doppler, distortion, echo, flange, and transpose effects.

Go to `http://www.goldwave.com/` for more information.

Instant Drive Access v1.46

Instant Drive Access, which resides in your system tray, adds a pop-up menu that includes all your available drives (including network drives), as well as several Windows features, such as the Control Panel and Settings. Regardless of where you are, you can access your drives without opening My Computer or the Windows Explorer. You can also add programs and shortcuts to the menu in submenus.

Magic Folders

If you have any information that's "for your eyes only," you need Magic Folders. This handy utility hides folders you choose, and all the files contained in those folders, from everyone but you. Sensitive, financial, business, and personal information will no longer be available to prying eyes when you step away from your computer. This also eliminates the possibility that someone could accidentally delete important files. Magic Folders is especially useful for those who share a computer, whether at home in or the office.

Go to `http://www.PC-Magic.com` for more information.

"Makes Files Invisible" (MFI)

MFI, from the same folks who bring you Magic Folders, enables you to hide individual files without hiding the entire folder. In fact, you can't hide a folder — just files within the folder. Files that you hide become invisible, and do not appear on any listings including application find/open dialog boxes (nor can they be run, modified, or deleted).

Go to `http://www.PC-Magic.com` for more information.

OuttaSight v2.0

If you want to hide entire applications from view, rather than just files or folders, OuttaSight is the utility you need. Residing on the system tray, OuttaSight can be locked to prevent users from unhiding applications. Additionally, you can view system windows and drag and drop between views.

Go to `http://rosa.simplenet.com/oos/` for more information.

Ping Thingy v2.53

When it comes to diagnosing network problems, you should start by verifying your connections, by pinging each machine on the network. Ping Thingy dispatches ICMP Echo requests to a remote host, and displays the results for each Echo reply.

Go to `http://indigo.ie/~zippy/download.htm` for more information.

Remind Me

Memory going? Not to worry, Remind Me can help you remember those important events in your life, without the hassle of a full-blown PIM or some other unwieldy software application. It's a simple reminder utility whose only purpose in life is to keep you out of trouble, by letting you know in advance that important events are approaching. It even lets you use plain English when entering dates. You can enter terms such as "Every Thursday," "14 days from today," "the last Saturday in June," and so on.

Go to `http://www.PC-Magic.com/` for more information.

Start Menu Cleaner v1.3

If you've been using Windows for any length of time, your Start menu is probably getting a little cluttered. When you install an application, this creates folders and shortcuts that are left behind when you uninstall. Of course, you always intend to go back and clean them up, but how often do you actually do it? Now, you don't have to think about it. With Start Menu Cleaner, you can scan your system for empty folders and for shortcuts with nowhere to go, and remove them automatically.

Go to `http://www.mithril.d.se/` for more information.

SumDir32 v1.10

SumDir32 is a handy little utility that checks your system and reports the number of files in any selected drive or folder. It tells you how many files are there, the number of total bytes, the number of hidden files and their total size, and the number of system files and archive files. It also has a Free Space feature, which scans all your drives (those that contain media) and displays the volume label, available space, used space, used space as a percentage of total disk space, and cluster size.

Go to `http://www.dvnc.net/jandk/SumDir32/` for more information.

VueIcons v5.1f

With VueIcons, you can use the Windows 95/NT Explorer to display images as icons. VueIcons supports GIF, JPEG, TIFF, BMP, TGA, and PCX formats. Images within zip files or encoded files are not accessible to VueIcons unless extracted or unencoded.

Go to `http://www.hamrick.com/upg.html` for more information.

WinZip v6.3

WinZip is the most popular file compression utility available for Windows. The Windows 95 version supports long filenames and drag-and-drop compression within Windows Explorer. Ideal for use with files from the Internet, WinZip supports a variety of file formats including TAR, gzip, Unix compress, UUEncode, XXencode, BinHex, MIME, ARJ, LZH, and ARC. It is also fully compatible with PKZIP and enables spanning for multi-floppy disk ZIP files.

Go to `http://www.winzip.com/` for more information.

Index

(continued)

(continued)

IDG BOOKS WORLDWIDE, INC.
END-USER LICENSE AGREEMENT

READ THIS. You should carefully read these terms and conditions before opening the software packet(s) included with this book ("Book"). This is a license agreement ("Agreement") between you and IDG Books Worldwide, Inc. ("IDGB"). By opening the accompanying software packet(s), you acknowledge that you have read and accept the following terms and conditions. If you do not agree and do not want to be bound by such terms and conditions, promptly return the Book and the unopened software packet(s) to the place you obtained them for a full refund.

1. **License Grant.** IDGB grants to you (either an individual or entity) a nonexclusive license to use one copy of the enclosed software program(s) (collectively, the "Software") solely for your own personal or business purposes on a single computer (whether a standard computer or a workstation component of a multiuser network). The Software is in use on a computer when it is loaded into temporary memory (RAM) or installed into permanent memory (hard disk, CD-ROM, or other storage device). IDGB reserves all rights not expressly granted herein.

2. **Ownership.** IDGB is the owner of all right, title, and interest, including copyright, in and to the compilation of the Software recorded on the disk(s) or CD-ROM ("Software Media"). Copyright to the individual programs recorded on the Software Media is owned by the author or other authorized copyright owner of each program. Ownership of the Software and all proprietary rights relating thereto remain with IDGB and its licensers.

3. **Restrictions on Use and Transfer.**

   (a) You may only (i) make one copy of the Software for backup or archival purposes, or (ii) transfer the Software to a single hard disk, provided that you keep the original for backup or archival purposes. You may not (i) rent or lease the Software, (ii) copy or reproduce the Software through a LAN or other network system or through any computer subscriber system or bulletin-board system, or (iii) modify, adapt, or create derivative works based on the Software.

   (b) You may not reverse engineer, decompile, or disassemble the Software. You may transfer the Software and user documentation on a permanent basis, provided that the transferee agrees to accept the terms and conditions of this Agreement and you retain no copies. If the Software is an update or has been updated, any transfer must include the most recent update and all prior versions.

4. **Restrictions on Use of Individual Programs.** You must follow the individual requirements and restrictions detailed for each individual program in Appendix A of this Book. These limitations are also contained in the individual license agreements recorded on the Software Media. These limitations may include a requirement that after using the program for a specified period of time, the user must pay a registration fee or discontinue use. By opening the Software packet(s), you will be agreeing to abide by the licenses and restrictions for these individual programs that are detailed in Appendix A and on the Software Media. None of the material on this Software Media or listed in this Book may ever be redistributed, in original or modified form, for commercial purposes.

5. **Limited Warranty.**

   (a) IDGB warrants that the Software and Software Media are free from defects in materials and workmanship under normal use for a period of sixty (60) days from the date of purchase of this Book. If IDGB receives notification within the warranty period of defects in materials or workmanship, IDGB will replace the defective Software Media.

   (b) IDGB AND THE AUTHOR OF THE BOOK DISCLAIM ALL OTHER WARRANTIES, EXPRESS OR IMPLIED, INCLUDING WITHOUT LIMITATION IMPLIED WARRANTIES OF MERCHANTABILITY AND FITNESS FOR A PARTICULAR PURPOSE, WITH RESPECT TO THE SOFTWARE, THE PROGRAMS, THE SOURCE CODE CONTAINED THEREIN, AND/OR THE TECHNIQUES DESCRIBED IN THIS BOOK. IDGB DOES NOT WARRANT THAT THE FUNCTIONS CONTAINED IN THE SOFTWARE WILL MEET YOUR REQUIREMENTS OR THAT THE OPERATION OF THE SOFTWARE WILL BE ERROR FREE.

   (c) This limited warranty gives you specific legal rights, and you may have other rights that vary from jurisdiction to jurisdiction.

6. **Remedies.**

   (a) IDGB's entire liability and your exclusive remedy for defects in materials and workmanship shall be limited to replacement of the Software Media, which may be returned to IDGB with a copy of your receipt at the following address: Software Media Fulfillment Department, Attn.: *Optimizing the Windows Registry*, IDG Books Worldwide, Inc., 7260 Shadeland Station, Ste. 100, Indianapolis, IN 46256, or call 1-800-762-2974. Please allow three to four weeks for delivery. This Limited Warranty is void if failure of the Software Media has resulted from accident, abuse, or misapplication. Any replacement Software Media will be warranted for the remainder of the original warranty period or thirty (30) days, whichever is longer.

(b) In no event shall IDGB or the author be liable for any damages whatsoever (including without limitation damages for loss of business profits, business interruption, loss of business information, or any other pecuniary loss) arising from the use of or inability to use the Book or the Software, even if IDGB has been advised of the possibility of such damages.

(c) Because some jurisdictions do not allow the exclusion or limitation of liability for consequential or incidental damages, the above limitation or exclusion may not apply to you.

7. **U.S. Government Restricted Rights.** Use, duplication, or disclosure of the Software by the U.S. Government is subject to restrictions stated in paragraph (c)(1)(ii) of the Rights in Technical Data and Computer Software clause of DFARS 252.227-7013, and in subparagraphs (a) through (d) of the Commercial Computer–Restricted Rights clause at FAR 52.227-19, and in similar clauses in the NASA FAR supplement, when applicable.

8. **General.** This Agreement constitutes the entire understanding of the parties and revokes and supersedes all prior agreements, oral or written, between them and may not be modified or amended except in a writing signed by both parties hereto that specifically refers to this Agreement. This Agreement shall take precedence over any other documents that may be in conflict herewith. If any one or more provisions contained in this Agreement are held by any court or tribunal to be invalid, illegal, or otherwise unenforceable, each and every other provision shall remain in full force and effect.

my2cents.idgbooks.com

CD-ROM Installation Instructions

THE FOLLOWING TABLE provides instructions for installing software included on the CD-ROM. The instructions assume you're viewing the files from Windows Explorer. The programs for which the Action is "double-click" have a setup or installation program. The programs for which the Action is "Copy to a new folder on your hard drive" have an executable file you can double-click after you've transferred the folder.

Program	CD–ROM Folder	File(s)	Action
AssistBar 98	\AssistBar98\Runtime 2.0	Setup.exe	Double-click
Runtime files must be installed before installing AssistBar	\AssistBar98\AssistBar98 v.2.01	Setup.exe	Double-click
ConfigSafe 95	\ConfigSafe 95	Install.exe	Double-click
ConfigSafe NT	\ConfigSafe NT	Install.exe	Double-click
Diskeeper Lite	\Alpha	Setup.exe	Double-click
	\Pentium x86	Setup.exe	Double-click
	\PowerPC	Setup.exe	Double-click
DumpReg	\DumpReg	DumpReg.exe	Double-click
GoldWave v3.24	\GoldWave v.3.24	All	Copy to a new folder on your hard drive
Instant Drive Access	\Instant Drive Access v.1.46	All	Copy to a new folder on your hard drive
Magic Folders	\Magic Folders	Magic.exe	Double-click
Make Files Invisible	\Make Files Invisible	Install.exe	Double-click
OuttaSight v2.0	\OuttaSight v.2.0	Setup.exe	Double-click
NTRegmon	\NTRegmon\Alpha	All	Copy to a new folder on your hard drive
	\NTRegmon\x86		
Ping Thingy v2.53	\Ping Thingy v.2.53	ping32.exe	Double-click
RegEdit	\RegEdit	All	Copy to a new folder on your hard drive
Registry Editor Extensions	\Registry Editor Extensions	Setup.exe	Double-click
Registry Saver v.1.2	\Registry Saver v.1.2	All	Copy to a new folder on your hard drive
Regmon 95	\Regmon 95	All	Copy to a new folder on your hard drive
Remind Me	\Remind Me	All	Copy to a new folder on your hard drive
Start Menu Cleaner	\Start Menu Cleaner v.1.3	All	Copy to a new folder on your hard drive

continued

Program	CD-ROM Folder	File(s)	Action
SumDir 32 v.1.10	\SumDir 32 v.1.10\disk 1	Setup.exe	Double-click
VueIcons v.5.1f	\VueIcons v.5.1f	vueico51.exe	Double-click
WinHacker v.2.0	\Winhacker v.2.0	wh95v202.exe	Double-click
WinZip v.6.3	\WinZip v.6.3	Setup.exe	Double-click